TRIATHLON
ACHIEVING YOUR PERSONAL BEST

TRIATHLON
ACHIEVING YOUR
PERSONAL BEST

Compiled by Rod Cedaro
Foreword by Greg Welch

With contributions from
Dr. Louise Burke PhD
Rodney Cedaro MApp Sc
Gayelene Clews BA
Dr. Peter Larkins MBBS, BMed Sc, FACSP, FASMF
Dr. Brian McLean PhD
Dr. Bruce Mason PhD

Facts On File

Dedication

In loving memory of Anne Elizabeth Cedaro (1969–1992)
who died tragically while training for her first triathlon.
The memory of her and her love will endure in those
who were fortunate enough to know her.

Triathlon: Achieving Your Personal Best
Copyright © 1993 by Rod Cedaro

Facts On File, Inc.
460 Park Avenue South
New York, NY 10016

Published in Australia by Murray Child & Company Pty Ltd.

Library of Congress Cataloging-in-Publication Data
Triathlon: achieving your personal best/compiled by Rod Cedaro: foreword by Greg Welch: with contributions from Luise Burke . . . [et al.].
    p.   cm
Reprint. Previously published: Triathlon: into the nineties.—
Sydney: Murray Child.
    Includes Index.
        ISBN 0-8160-2948-2
        1. Triathlon—Training.   I. Cedaro. Rod.
GV1060.73.T75   1993
796. 42—dc20   93–4007

Runnning injury diagrams are from "Common Running Injuries," *Patient Management*, March 1989, Adis Press International Pty Ltd. The table of first aid care (48 hrs) "PRICEM" and "HARM" is from "Better Management of Common Sports Injuries," *Modern Medicine*, April 1991
Edited by Carolyn Child
Designed by Emma Seymour
Exercise drawings by Kristy Bruce

Facts On File books are available at special discounts when purchased in bulk quantities for businesses, associations, institutions, or sales promotions. Please contact our Special Sales Department in New York at 212/683-2244 or 800/322-8755.

Manufactured by R.R. Donnelley & Sons
Printed in the United States of America

10 9 8 7 6 5 4 3 2 1

This book is printed on acid-free paper.

Foreword

Triathlon is a unique, gruelling and challenging sport and, as such, occupies a position of great importance in the field of athletics. It 'stands tall' as a new and vital athletic activity as do the successful participants.

During the past fifteen years or so Triathlon has been put on the map by such famous races as the Hawaiian Ironman, the Nice Triathlon and, since becoming official, the World Championships. These and other body-torturing events have produced great athletes whose physical endurance is legend in the sporting world: Dave Scott, known as 'the Man'; Mark Allen, 'the Grip'; Scott Molina, 'the Terminator' and Scott Tinley, 'the Tinman'. All of these guys from California really started something big and are known as the 'Big Four'.

Since 1990 Australia has been the strongest triathlon country in the world and has produced such great names as Stephen Foster, Marc Dragon, Gayelene Clews, Louise Bonham, Michelle Jones, Greg Stewart, Brad Bevan, Greg Welch, Tim Ahern and Nick Croft. All of these people have won either world or national titles.

However, one name I have left out, for a very good reason, is Rod Cedaro. In the competitive world of Triathlon, Rod stands out from the crowd. His name is synonymous with the sport and he is probably the most recognised endurance triathlete in Australia. His competitive and intelligent approach to the sport is undoubtedly inspired by his academic background. He has a wide knowledge of all aspects of the sport and his friendliness to others of all levels is widely known.

In compiling this book Rod has enlisted the aid of Australia's leading triathlon and sports experts, and it is obvious that there are no other books available which are as complete as this one. I will certainly be using this book myself because I know it will assist me with my training program and will help me to better understand nutrition and physiology.

Rod, you are a champion athlete and a champion guy!

Greg Welch
9 December 1992

Acknowledgments

The principal author would like to take this opportunity to thank the following people for their invaluable contributions to *Triathlon: Into the Nineties.*

The contributing authors, Gayelene, Peter, Brian, Bruce and Louise. Thanks for putting up with my demands and meeting your deadlines.

Mary Jane Dwyer and John Meredith of *EXCEED SPORTS NUTRITIONALS* and Chris Black of *SUNRICE AUSTRALIA* for their financial assistance in funding the photographs supplied by Rod Cedaro, Gayelene Clews, Phillip Clews and family, Wayde Clews and Alan Mitchell, and the diagrams in Appendix B supplied by Kirsty Bruce.

Murray, Carolyn and Emma of the publishers, Murray Child & Company, for their enthusiasm and dedication in undertaking and completing such a huge task.

Greg Welch for his contribution of the foreword, as well as all the athletes who gave their time and energy in the photographic sessions.

Simon Spaulding of *ROSEBANK HELMETS,* Fred Falzon of *FRED FALZON ENDURANCE SPORTS* and Colin Pepper of *CONSULTRANS,* Rob de Castella of *DIADORA,* Helen and Mary Phillipou of *GUN IT SWEATS,* Evan Arnott of *ARNOTTS AUSTRALIA* and Guy Thompson and Mark Waldon of *LOOK* are to be thanked for their contributions of quality product used throughout the publication.

Finally to all the triathletes worldwide who make our sport the greatest possible test of human sporting endeavor. I sincerely hope that this book puts back even a small fraction into a sport that has given me immense personal satisfaction.

Rod Cedaro

Contents

About the Triathlon Federation U.S.A.

In a short time span, triathlon has evolved from a "fad" sport for gonzo ultra-endurance athletes to a mainstay athletic adventure for everyone.

Hundreds of thousands of triathletes around the world compete in thousands of events on every continent.

What was the "Sport of the 80s" has entered a new decade of existence and acceptance. The sport of triathlon, barely a decade old, has already appeared in the 1991 Commonwealth Games. The sport has been placed on the 1994 Goodwill Games program and is now part of the 1995 Pan American Games.

Internationally, more than 80 countries participate in the sport of triathlon and are members of the International Triathlon Union, the International Olympic Committee-recognized international federation for the sport.

With so much success on the international scene, inclusion in the Olympic Games is the next logical step. Triathlon is on the verge of gaining that much-coveted Olympic recognition.

Founded in 1982 as the United States Triathlon Federation, Triathlon Federation is the governing body for the sport of triathlon in the United States. Over 24,000 annual members participate in more than 400 sanctioned events across the country.

Tri-Fed's membership is as diverse and dynamic as the sport itself; from the novice triathlete who sees the finish line as an intense, personal victory, to the serious age group athlete who has devoted his or her life to high-level fitness, to the elite career triathlete who races 20 times a year and views the sport as a legitimate career.

By becoming an annual member of Tri-Fed/USA, one has access not only to the over 400 sanctioned events nationwide, but also to a plethora of other benefits. Membership benefits include an annual subscription to *Triathlon Times,* the official magazine of the Federation; a competition guide containing the rules of the sport and other Tri-Fed program information; exclusive use of the Tri-Fed Travel Desk, which provides free bike passes and other discounts on selected airlines; and the opportunity to be included in the National Rankings System.

Tri-Fed/USA encourages you to become an annual member. Not only will you be able to take advantage of some fantastic benefits, you will have the opportunity to voice your opinions and shape the focus of the sport. For membership information please call 1-800-TRI-1USA.

Introduction

It seems that anyone who has ever successfully combined the three disciplines of swimming, cycling and running into the single entity known as 'triathlon' has written a book of their exploits, advising how to prepare for the rigors of triathlon competition. So what makes this book any different? Some of the co-authors have successfully competed in triathlons both in Australia and throughout the world, others are yet to experience the sense of personal achievement that accompanies the successful completion of the 'sport of the 90s' as triathlon has often been termed.

The major difference with this book is that each of the contributing authors is an expert in his or her particular field of scientific endeavor. Consequently, in the ensuing pages you will read the latest scientific research compiled by specialists in an easy to follow format. This information is 'state of the art' and represents the latest developments in the sport of triathlon. Whether you're already an elite competitor, a 'middle of the packer' or the coach of a squad of triathletes, if the scientific principles contained within are applied, your (or your charges') triathletic pursuits can't help but benefit.

PART ONE
THE BASICS

Chapter One

General Training Physiology

Rod Cedaro

When the average person picks up a training related article written by a sports science specialist they are often bewildered by the use of the jargon contained within. In fairness to sports scientists, often there is really only one way to say something and as a consequence technical terms must be utilized. With this in mind the first part of this chapter will attempt to address this problem by providing brief explanations and definitions of some of the more commonly used terms. This is by no means an exhaustive list but should provide a sound basis to help understand some of the more technical terms that you may come across in this and some of your other readings. In this manner when these terms arise your understanding of the principles and concepts being discussed should be improved.

Acclimatization. Physiological changes that occur within the body in response to environmental stress, e.g. the improvement that occurs in the sweating mechanism over time due to training in hotter climates.

Adaptation. This is a general term referring to the body's ability to adjust to various demands placed upon it over a period of time. An example of positive adaptation is the improvement in performance that transpires in response to a sensibly constructed training regimen. On the other hand, overuse injuries due to chronic overtraining are examples of negative adaptation. The human body is an extremely adaptable mechanism and can adjust to a host of physical, as well as psychological stresses, provided that these stresses are applied slowly and progressively.

Adipose tissue. Storage site of fat cells known as 'adipocytes'. During prolonged exercise it is these cells that release free fatty acids (FFA) into the bloodstream to provide a fuel for exercise. The mobilization of this fuel is termed 'lipolysis'.

Aerobic metabolism. Aerobic literally means 'with oxygen'. It refers to one of the two metabolic pathways which produce adenosine triphosphate

(ATP) for muscular contraction. This is generally associated with endurance exercise.

Amino acids. These are the building blocks of protein which is the major constituent of the human muscular system. There are some twenty-two amino acids, eight (nine in children and stressed older adults) of which cannot be produced within the body and are termed the 'essential' amino acids and must be attained via dietary intake. Protein breakdown during prolonged exercise has been shown to contribute 10–15% of the substrate energy needs. Recently there has been much controversy in relation to the use of 'free form' amino acids as ergogenic (performance enhancing) aids; this issue will be addressed in chapter eight.

Anabolic steroids. Strictly speaking the correct name for these synthetic derivatives of the male sex hormone testosterone, is 'androgenic-anabolic steroids' (AAS), which promote male characteristics and protein synthesis (muscle building). These substances are used by athletes primarily in an attempt to increase muscular strength and decrease recovery time between exercise bouts so that a greater quantity/intensity of exercise can be completed. There are a host of negative side effects associated with the use of these substances, ranging from liver disorders to coronary heart disease. Furthermore, these synthetic hormones appear on the International Olympic Committee's (IOC's) list of banned substances and if detected their use results in disqualification from competition.

Anemia. This is a condition of decreased red blood cell (RBC) concentration which results in decreased endurance exercise performance, due to a diminished oxygen-carrying capacity.

Anaerobic metabolism. Anaerobic literally means 'without oxygen'. It refers to one of two metabolic pathways which produce ATP for muscular contraction. Generally this is associated with short duration, high intensity exercise. There are two types of anaerobic pathways (i) *Alactic:* ATP stored within muscle produces immediately available energy for approximately 10–15 seconds and (ii) *Lactic:* ATP is produced via the breakdown of glucose, in the absence of oxygen, which results in the accumulation of lactic acid, eventually requiring the athlete to slow down in order to dissipate this waste product.

Anaerobic threshold. This is the point where the exercise intensity increases to such a level that the body's energy requirements can no longer be met completely by the aerobic energy pathway. At this point the anaerobic energy system now contributes some of the energy needed for muscular contraction, and as a consequence lactic acid is produced at a faster rate than it can be cleared from the body. Eventually the athlete must slow down in order to remove this waste product.

Blood doping. A practice which has been outlawed by the IOC. It requires the removal of 500–1000 ml (17–34 fl oz) of an athlete's blood some six weeks prior to competition. The water component (plasma) of the blood is removed and the remaining 'packed cells', or concentrated RBC, are frozen. One week prior to competition these cells are resuspended and infused back into the body in an attempt to augment the body's oxygen-carrying capacity and so improve endurance performance. Research is divided as to its ergogenic benefits. Additionally, there are numerous detrimental side effects such as heart failure and high blood pressure.

Cardiovascular fitness. Literally meaning heart and circulatory system fitness. There are two aspects to cardiovascular fitness (i) *Peripheral:* Referring to the blood supply to working muscles via an enhanced capillary system, increased storage of muscle glycogen, a greater concentration of 'energy houses' (mitochondria) within the muscle cells and the removal of the waste products of exercise, e.g. carbon dioxide and lactic acid. (ii) *Central:* This is generally associated with improving the athlete's anaerobic threshold. Here the focus of training becomes high intensity exercise.

Cooldown. Low intensity exercise that follows a hard workout. The theory behind such activity is that by continuing to exercise gently following high intensity exercise the body is given the opportunity to remove waste products and return blood to the heart from the working musculature.

Dehydration. Excessive water loss. *Note:* A decrease in body weight of 2% due to fluid loss impairs performance. Losses of 8–10% in body weight can actually be fatal.

Electrolytes. Ions, primarily sodium, potassium and chloride. Involved in water balance amongst other functions.

Endurance. Can be looked at from two perspectives: cardiovascular, which has already been discussed, and local muscular which refers to a muscle or muscle group's ability to continue to contract submaximally for an extended period of time.

Ergogenic aids. Any substance, naturally occurring or synthetically produced, or phenomena (e.g. hypnosis) that are work enhancing aids. These practices are undertaken in the belief that they will improve performance beyond levels that could normally be anticipated by conventional training methods only.

Evaporation. The transfer of a fluid to a vapor with the resultant cooling of the object that previously held the fluid.

Fartlek training. A Swedish term literally meaning 'speed play'. Here the athlete exercises (in the strict sense of this term it refers to running over natural terrain but the concept can be equally applied to biking or swimming) at his/her discretion, working hard at certain times during the exercise bout and easier at other times.

Fatty acids. Used as a fuel source for aerobic metabolism.

Glycogen. The storage form of glucose, a fuel source. If free fatty acids are considered 'standard petrol' then glycogen can be viewed as 'super'. It is the storage fuel that is drawn upon when the intensity of exercise is so great that the energy requirements can no longer be met by fat. Glycogen is found stored within musculature as well as the liver. That stored within the muscles is utilized directly by those muscles only during physical exertion. That stored within the liver is utilized to maintain blood glucose levels.

Glycolysis. The anaerobic process whereby glycogen is broken down to lactic acid and in doing so produces ATP for muscular contraction.

Heart rate monitoring. This is the practice of measuring the number of beats the heart is producing—either manually by palpating one of the various pulses of the body, or mechanically with the use of a telemetry unit which measures the electrical charges of the heart and displays this on a watch-type unit—as an indication of the intensity of exercise.

Hypoxia. Low oxygen content. This term is often misused by coaches— particularly coaches of swimmers. When an athlete practices breath-holding techniques while exercising there is an appreciable increase in the desire to breathe, and this is often incorrectly seen to be the result of hypoxia; in actual fact this stimulus is due to an increasing concentration of carbon dioxide within the blood (hypercapnia) which has an excitatory effect upon the smooth muscle reponsible for the breathing reflex.

Hypoglycemia. Low blood glucose concentration.

IFDIMF principle. An acronym for the various constituent aspects of aerobic exercise conditioning: IF=initial fitness, D=duration, I=intensity, M=mode, F=frequency.

Interval training. The practice of taking a mode of exercise which is normally completed over a certain duration at a certain speed and breaking it up into smaller portions and completing those portions at a greater speed/intensity than can normally be maintained for the usual duration of this exercise mode. The intensity may be fixed by maintaining a constant heart rate, velocity/time and the rest duration is generally fixed by having the athlete commence the next repeat of the interval at a certain time, e.g. swim 8 x 50 metres (55 yards) 'on the minute' means that the athlete swims 50 metres (55 yards) eight times, commencing each subsequent 50 metre (55 yards) repeat one minute after starting the previous one.

Lactic acid. A waste product produced during the anaerobic glycolysis of glycogen. It is this substance that produces the 'burning' sensation within the working musculature during intense exercise.

Long slow distance (LSD) training. Here the athlete exercises at a relatively low intensity, i.e. 60–70% of maximal capacity, for a prolonged period, generally in excess of the duration of time that the exercise is to be completed during competition.

Maximal heart rate. This is the maximum number of beats that an athlete's heart can produce in a one-minute period. This will vary depending upon age and exercise modality. For a man this is predicted to be 220 minus his age; for a woman, 205 minus half her age. However, these formulae are only predictions and will vary from athlete to athlete and exercise modality to exercise modality, so they should be established on an individual basis.

Minerals. Inorganic compounds that regulate a variety of physiological functions, such as oxygen transport, neural excitability, energy metabolism and acid-base status.

Oxygen debt. This is a term that has been utilized to define excessive post-exercise oxygen consumption, i.e. the body is repaying a 'debt' incurred during the exercise period. See figure 1.1.

Oxygen deficit. When exercising intensely the body is unable to meet all of its energy requirements from the aerobic energy system; as a result the energy requirements must be met via anaerobic metabolism. This shortfall between the energy requirements and what can be supplied via the aerobic energy system is termed the oxygen deficit and is depicted in figure1.1.

Periodization. This is the process of breaking up a training period into a host of discernible phases which are designed to produce a particular training effect. For example, during the early aspects of an endurance training program the emphasis of the program may be upon improving peripheral cardiovascular fitness by incorporating longer distance

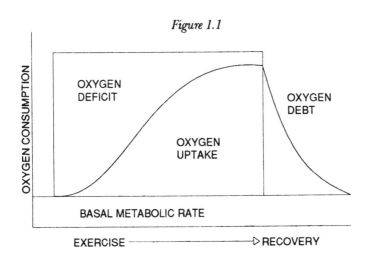

Figure 1.1

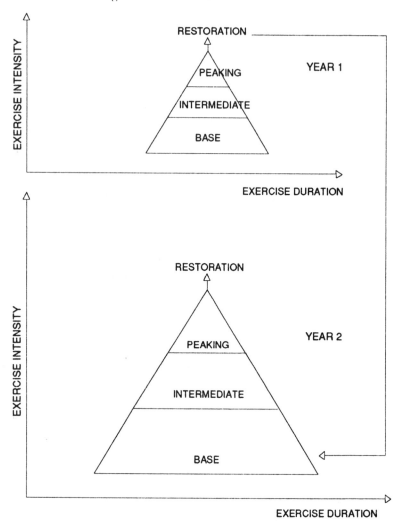

Figure 1.2

training at a lower intensity; as the athlete gets closer to competition the onus will begin to shift towards higher intensity exercise over a shorter duration with more rest. Finally, the athlete moves into the competition phase in which he/she races, recovers and races again. What has been exemplified here is the concept of 'periodization' whereby all the distinct phases of training interrelate in a planned integrated manner over a period of time in order to enhance the overall performance at a specific time. See figure 1.2.

Resistance training. Most people relate this to weight training; while this does form an aspect of this type of training it is certainly not the only type. Any training modality which forces the body to work against a load which is greater than that to which it is normally subjected meets this criteria, e.g. swimming with hand paddles, cycling uphill in hard gearing, running in heavy training shoes through the hills.

Sprint training. The practice of subjecting the body to extremely high intensity workloads for a short time, followed by a complete recovery period. The rationale behind such training is to force adaptation and subsequent improvement in the specific muscles' ATP–PC system, so as to develop a 'finishing kick' or the ability to surge in order to break away from an opponent. It is essential with such training that it be completed at maximum intensity over a short period (up to 20 seconds) and complete recovery must be allowed between efforts (2–5 minutes depending upon the athlete's level of conditioning). One further note on this type of work is that it should only be used after a sound aerobic base has been firmly established and then only sparingly as it places a huge stress on the body's skeletal–muscular system and can promote injury.

Strength. The ability of a muscle to exert force against a resistance.

Target training zone. When an endurance athlete trains to improve performance, research has shown that the intensity of exercise must be within the range of 60–85% of the athlete's maximal heart rate to effect an improvement in aerobic function. Those athletes that are more highly conditioned should be endeavoring to attain the upper range of this zone, while novices and beginners will obtain aerobic benefit from the lower limits. This training zone concept is depicted in figure 1.3.

Training phases. This term relates back to the previously defined concept of 'periodization' where we discussed the need to structure an athlete's training schedule to ensure optimal performance at the appropriate time. These training phases are the backbone of periodization, they define the mix of duration and intensity of, and recovery from, exercise to bring about the desired adaptations. Broadly speaking there are four training phases:
Base phase or preparation: Here the exercise is of a low intensity, long duration and non-specific nature. The athlete simply tries to maintain

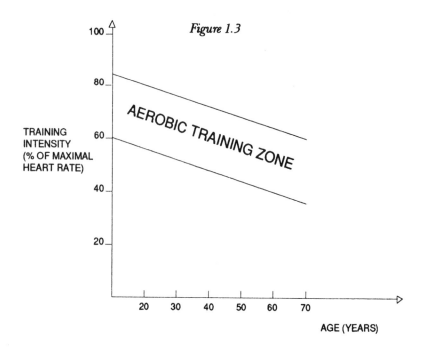

general fitness and improve peripheral cardiovascular function.

Intermediate phase or pre-season: Within this phase the onus is shifted away from the duration of exercise and a greater emphasis is placed upon the intensity of exercise. The type of activity that the athlete should now engage in is specific to activity that will be encountered in competition. Intervals are introduced for the first time and the athlete now tries to gain central cardiovascular fitness while still maintaining peripheral function.

Peak phase or competition: All emphasis is placed on high quality exercise and recovery. The athlete trains intensely or races, then allows a period of recovery, which may incorporate complete rest, low intensity exercise, massage etc—and then stresses the body once more with a bout of high intensity exercise. Here the athlete is attempting to optimize central cardiovascular function and push the anaerobic threshold back further.

Restoration phase or off-season: After a competitive phase all athletes should have a period away from their primary activity in order to allow their bodies time to repair. When we race, the stress of exercise is such that we may create micro-tears, slight muscular strains and the like, that if ignored and trained through will develop into major debilitating injuries. Additionally, from a psychological perspective an athlete must be given a break from a hectic training schedule in order to 'freshen up' mentally before having to face the rigors of another base phase.

The above discussion is depicted diagramatically in figure 1.2.

Vitamins. These are essential elements of our nutrition that regulate various physiological processes.

VO_2 max. An abbreviation for 'maximal oxygen uptake'. It is simply a measure of the maximum amount of oxygen that can be consumed per minute during maximal exercise.

Warm up. Prior to any rigorous exercise it is important to elevate the body's core temperature and prepare the musculature that is about to be engaged. The warm up should have the effect of increasing blood flow to the active musculature, stretching tendons, muscles and ligaments and preparing the athlete psychologically for the upcoming exercise/competition. Additionally, research suggests that warm up prior to rigorous physical activity may actually safeguard the athlete against injury.

LIMITATIONS TO PHYSICAL PERFORMANCE

All too often athletes, particularly young ones, equate improvements in performance solely with hard physical training. While this may be true to some extent, it is really only part of the picture. There is a wide variety of influences that affect an athlete's performance and unless all of these are addressed optimal physical perfomance can not be attained. The four categories of influences affecting optimal performance are depicted in figure 1.4. You will notice that all aspects of this formula must be in balance in order to obtain full potential; if one aspect is neglected or another over-emphasized performance will suffer accordingly. Let's look at each separate aspect and see how they integrate to form the whole and as such promote optimal performance. If you get nothing else from reading this book, at least realize that there is a host of factors that influence physical performance, so don't always equate improvement with hard physical training. In fact, this may actually be detrimental to your performance at certain times.

Genetic predisposition. This can be defined as 'choosing one's parents'. In other words if your parents are Scott Molina and Erin Baker you stand a much better chance of being an elite level performer than if they are couch potatoes. Not only will having the right 'gene pool' stand you in good stead from a physiological perspective (high percentage of slow twitch muscle fibres, innate high maximal oxygen uptake capacity) but also the experiences that you receive early in life will help influence your desire to become and remain involved with sport. If this initial involvement is a fulfilling and positive experience, the chances are that you will continue to seek such experiences by remaining involved. In other words, if your parents and other significant people within your life provide positive feedback, and you continue to enjoy your involvement and find it rewarding, this sets up a perpetual cycle which promotes its own continuance.

Training/rest/recovery. All too often only one aspect of this category is attended to: training. Athletes and their coaches will at sometime or another see their performances diminish or stagnate. Their initial reaction to rectify this situation is to train harder. However, they may have neglected to recognize the fact that over the last couple of weeks other stresses have started to increase—relationship problems, exams, illness and the like. Training, like many other influences on an athlete, is simply another form of stress. The human body is an extremely adaptable mechanism and if a stress is applied slowly and progressively over a prolonged period the body will adapt and strengthen so as to cope with such loads. However, often we are simply unable to control outside influences that we may interpret as being stressful. As a consequence the athlete doesn't sleep as soundly at night and doesn't feel particularly hungry after training so doesn't eat as much carbohydrate as usual. The result is a subtle, and in the early stages even an inappreciable decline in performance. If this cycle continues and the athlete keeps training hard while ignoring the influence of these other factors, then performance will continue to decline.

Athletes and coaches alike must be mature enough to stand back from their training and performances and ask objective questions. If there is a possibility that performance is suffering because of an outside influence beyond the athlete's control, then this must be taken into account when setting the training program. Depending upon the severity of this stress, the athlete's training load should be decreased and in severe cases terminated until the extraneous influence is removed or at least brought under control.

In order for training to be effective it must be well structured, directional, progressive and flexible. As has been outlined in the previous section, training should be broken up into a series of phases that are all brought together under the collective notion of periodization. This will be elaborated on later in the specific chapters relating to each of the separate disciplines, as well as chapter eleven, 'Putting it all Together'. Suffice to say at this point that training is not 'the be all and end all' of physical performance. Athletes need to 'train smart', in other words know when to train hard and when to back off. The hard/easy notion of training is of central importance to all training regimens. Athletes must stress their bodies then allow ample recovery time for regeneration before applying stress once more. An excellent rule of thumb is: 'you can't train a tired body'. If you continue to apply stress, in the form of training, to an already tired body 'maladaptation' will occur. Initially this maladaptation will show up as impaired performance, however, if training is pursued the consequences of such action may be far more devastating—debilitating overuse injuries and psychological burnout due to the frustration of continued hard training with a lack of return for the effort invested. Effectively, the athlete will end up losing more valuable training time as a result of injury or frustration, all of which could be avoided by simply allowing sufficient recovery time.

As has already been mentioned, rest and recovery must be considered jointly with training so as to optimize the mix of stress and regeneration which will allow the triathlete to progress to a higher level of conditioning. Rest refers to the period of time between training sessions. Triathletes shouldn't simply see this as 'time off' as they wait for the next training session. In fact, rest periods should be planned and used constructively so as to optimize recovery before the subsequent training; in this manner the body will be able to fully reap the benefits of the next session. While each triathlete will recover at different rates, depending upon their individual level of conditioning, prior training history and the intensity of previous training session etc., there is a series of practices that will speed recovery in all triathletes:

1. Warm up and stretch thoroughly prior to the main body of the training session.
2. During training sessions don't allow the body to become dehydrated. During shorter training sessions consume 150–250 ml (5–8 fl oz) of water every 15–20 minutes. If a training session extends beyond an hour to an hour and a half, consume the same

quantity of fluid and add some carbohydrate and electrolytes to help maintain performance. As you will be using such preparations in competition, training is the ideal forum to practice these strategies. There are numerous commercially available powders that are scientifically formulated to meet these requirements.

3. Cooldown and stretch following the main body of the training session.
4. Replace fluid and carbohydrate as soon after the termination of exercise as is possible. From a practical perspective, one of the commercially available liquid meals meets these requirements quickly and conveniently. See chapter eight for an elaboration on this point.
5. After a heavy/intense training session or race, subsequent session(s) should consist of 'active recovery'. In other words, the triathlete should exercise gently in order to help speed the removal of waste products from the musculature and provide fresh oxygenated blood and nutrients.
6. There are a host of other practices which will help to speed the rate of recovery between training/racing sessions. These include: massage, flotation tanks, spa baths/whirlpools, stretching, a high carbohydrate diet and adequate hydration, and mental relaxation techniques such as meditation.
7. As a general rule, check the resting morning heart rate. If this is elevated by more than 5–10 beats per minute above normal, have an easier session to ensure adequate recovery. Remember, you can't train a tired body!

Psychological considerations. Over the last decade 'sports psychology' has become a widely practiced and valuable tool in the athlete's preparation for competitions. Some successful practitioners or 'sports psychologists' are making a lucrative income from advising elite athletes how to improve their performances with mental preparation. However, successful athletes have been practicing psychological skills for years, long before it was formally termed 'sports psychology', and many already have their own methods of preparing mentally for both competition and training. While this point will be discussed at length in chapter nine, what is important to recognize here is that if the triathlete isn't psychologically prepared for the upcoming task, performance will be below par as a result.

Nutritional concerns. As with the previous section, this subject is simply too involved to be discussed in a couple of short paragraphs, so a complete chapter (eight) has been dedicated to this specific topic. For the time being, however, the following analogy may be useful. If we view the human body as an automobile and the food that we ingest as fuel, it is obvious that if we try to run that car on standard fuel when it has been tuned for super, performance will be less than ideal. The human body must replace its carbohydrate stores from one exercise bout to the next, otherwise performance will be adversely affected. Recent research has shown that heavily training endurance athletes need to ingest 525–650 g (18–23 oz) of carbohydrate per day in order to adequately replenish muscle and liver glycogen stores (Costill,1988). If heavily training athletes don't consume at least 60% of their total energy intake in the form of carbohydrate, then they will find it extremely difficult to restore the body's glycogen stores to an adequate level for subsequent training sessions.

GETTING THE MIX RIGHT
Having realized that there is more to optimizing performance than simply training hard and long, what must next be considered is how to get this mix of contributing ingredients correct. From a practical perspective, unless you are considering dabbling in genetic engineering, your genetic potential is already fixed and established. However,

Figure 1.4

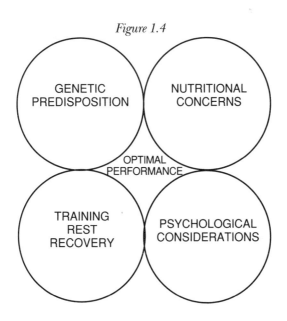

what we can do by attending to those other aspects (training/rest/ recovery, nutritional concerns and psychological considerations) is reach our full triathletic potential as defined by our genetic make-up. How do we know when to back off the training, when to consume more carbohydrate or when to get a massage to soothe those aching muscles? Firstly, let me say that there simply isn't one formula that can be applied equally to all triathletes, as each triathlete will differ from another in a wide variety of ways. That is why it is ludicrous for coaches to have all their triathletes completing the same training and recovery schedules. In order for triathletes to reach their potential, programs must be 'individualized', i.e. tailored to the specific requirements and circumstances of the individual triathlete. Each of the concerns that have already been discussed at length must be addressed and a conditioning schedule formulated accordingly.

Rather than providing a set formula or program by which to attain your ideal performances, this book, if used correctly, will provide you with the tools and knowledge with which to construct your own training schedule, based upon scientific principles and taking into account the influences of your own unique situation. In effect, after reading this book you should be able to construct your own scientifically designed training regimen, choose and set up the correct equipment to suit your requirements, and consume a diet that meets all your training, competition and recovery requirements, etc. In other words, you should be well on the way to being the best triathlete that you have the potential to be.

Reference

Costill, D., 1988, 'Carbohydrate for exercise: dietary demands for optimal performance', *International Journal of Sports Medicine* 9, pp. 1–18.

PART TWO
LET'S GET WET

Chapter Two

The Biomechanics of Swimming

Dr. Bruce R. Mason

The speed of a swimmer is determined by the resultant force acting on the swimmer's body in the direction of the forward movement. When swimming in still water the two pertinent forces are the propulsive force which occurs as a consequence of the swimmer's propulsive actions and the opposing resistive force which is caused by the swimmer attempting to move through the water. To increase swimming speed, the swimmer must increase the propulsive force or decrease the resistive force or do both. The technique or style of the swimmer is able to affect both the propulsive and the resistive forces. This chapter will first look at the ways in which a good technique may be used to increase propulsive force and reduce the resistive force. Mention will also be made of some common inefficiencies which occur within the front crawl stroke.

The commencement of the front crawl stroke is hand entry. Entry should occur in line with the shoulder and sufficiently forward in front of the swimmer's body to permit a short forward underwater glide and then an outwards and downwards pressing movement of the hand after the hand enters the water. Hand entry should occur with the thumb down and the palm of the hand facing outwards and downwards at an angle of about 45° to the surface of the water. The hand should enter

Figure 2.1: Position of the swimmer immediately after hand entry. Note the extension of the arm.

the water with the finger tips pointing forward and downward. The swimmer should attempt to make the wrist and elbow enter the water through the hole made by the hand. An entry in this fashion keeps the resistive force to a minimum. The forward underwater glide serves to rid the hand of surrounding air. The sign of a good entry is minimum splash. Common inefficiencies which occur during entry are: entering with the palm of the hand facing directly down, dropping the hand into the water rather than sliding it in, having hand entry occur too close to the body, entering the hand across the line of the body rather than in a forward direction, and elbow dropping into the water preceding or at the same time as the hand entry. In short, many of these problems occur as a consequence of poor arm recovery. The main problem associated with a flat hand entry is that air gets trapped under the hand. Dropping the hand in the water is generally an indication of the swimmer attempting to reach too far forward before entry and this usually results in a splashing action. Under reaching of the hand on entry is commonly indicated by a movement of the hand toward the surface of the water, following entry. Entry of the hand across the line of the body is generally an indication that the preceding arm recovery action occurred too far outside the line of the body. The action of hand entry across the line of the body serves to increase the resistive forces. An early drop in the elbow is generally associated with flat hand entry and is a direct consequence of a poor arm recovery action and an indication of muscle fatigue. Usually a good hand entry will serve to reduce the resistive force and prepare the hand and arm to increase the propulsive force later in the stroke.

The short forward and sideways pressing movement of the hand, which occurs following hand entry and the forward glide, is referred to as the 'catch' and results in an extension of the arm. A good catch or

Figure 2.2: Position of the swimmer immediately after the catch. Note the cocking of the wrist prior to the commencement of downsweep.

'press' serves to rid the underneath surface of the hand of air bubbles. At the completion of the catch the hand is slightly outside the line of the swimmer's body. The catch is an important part of the stroke as it may be regarded as setting the hand in the water in preparation for the propulsive arm actions. A good catch occurs in an outward and downward direction rather than in just a downward direction. The advantage of the sideways press rather than a downwards press is that the path of the following hand action has a greater possible distance over which it may travel to obtain propulsion during the remainder of the stroke. Elite swimmers have been observed to bend their thumb inwards at the distal joint during the catch and following downsweep. This is done to assist the swimmer in gaining a feel for the water. At the completion of the press the arm should have the shape of an arch with the elbow high in the water and the wrist cocked downwards. This position of the arm allows the force derived during the early stage of the following propulsive actions to be directed backwards rather than downwards. The main objective of the catch is to obtain a feel for the water, to position the hand ready for maximizing propulsion and to reduce air trapped around the hand.

The downsweep follows the catch. During the downsweep it is important for the elbow to remain high. This is done by developing a large arch in the arm—keeping the elbow high until the hand is aligned in the same vertical plane as the elbow and shoulder. Male sprint swimmers exhibit a long lever from the shoulder to the hand at the completion of the downsweep which leaves the hand deep in the water. Distance swimmers do not generally have as long a lever. A shorter lever arm is obtained by having a greater bend at the elbow. Having a longer lever would have an advantage in developing propulsive force but there would be a corresponding increased force placed on the

Figure 2.3: Position of the swimmer during the early phases of the downsweep. Note the long lever with the elbow rising to produce an arch in the arm.

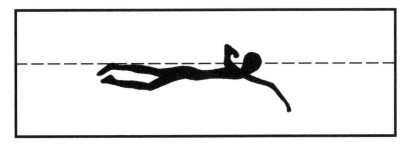

Figure 2.4: Position of the swimmer during the downsweep phase. Note the long arch in the arm produced by bending at the elbow and wrist.

muscles of the shoulder. A common fault in front crawl swimming is to try and maintain too long a lever and this causes the elbow to drop and release the water pressure on the hand and arm. To remedy this problem the swimmer in the short term should decrease the lever length of the hand from the shoulder by increasing the bend at the elbow. Sufficient strength must be developed around the shoulder and elbow joint before the length of the lever arm is again increased. A long lever must not be maintained at the expense of dropping the elbow.

Following the downsweep the hand changes its direction toward the midline of the body. There should not be an abrupt change of direction but rather a smooth flowing movement from a downwards backward direction to an inward direction. This part of the stroke is referred to as the insweep and the hand moves from outside the line of the body in an inward and slightly upward direction toward the midline of the body. It is at this point in the stroke that the elbow changes its alignment and moves toward the body. Care should be taken not to allow the elbow to drop prematurely during the previous downsweep phase so as to release the water pressure during the backward and

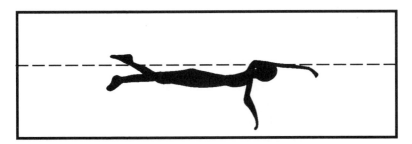

Figure 2.5: Position of the swimmer at the commencement of the insweep. Note the change in the bend of the elbow. A long lever is maintained at this phase of the stroke.

downward motion of the hand. Probably the greatest problem associated with the insweep is that some swimmers reduce the action of the insweep movement because they believe very little propulsion can result from the action. This fault manifests itself as a single backward movement of the arm which extends from the catch to the commencement of arm recovery. Such a technique problem resolves itself into a narrow hand path with little lateral movement. Generally also associated with this technique problem is a downward acting catch. The fault probably occurs because the swimmer falsely believes that forward propulsion cannot occur as a consequence of a sideways movement of the hand.

Figure 2.6: Position of the swimmer during the backsweep. The forearm is kept in a position so as to provide an effective push (as in drag-oriented propulsion) against the water.

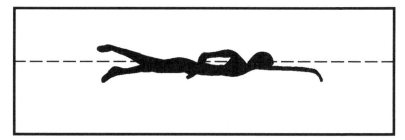

Figure 2.7: Position of the swimmer toward the end of the backsweep. Note that the hand is used effectively for propulsion as the hand moves beyond the hip.

Following the insweep, the hand changes direction in a smooth flowing manner so that it moves backward and upward toward the thigh. Pressure on the water should be maintained all the way to the thigh and not released prematurely. The greatest problem associated with the backsweep phase is that the hand begins recovery prematurely as it passes the waist so that the water pressure is released at this point and the hand is lifted from the water prior to the full propulsive potential of the backsweep being achieved.

Arm recovery is an important aspect of the stroke as problems during this phase may greatly reduce the propulsive potential as well as increase resistance. Many swimmers have a round-arm recovery rather than a high-elbow recovery. A high-elbow recovery is believed to be far superior to the round-arm recovery. The high elbow allows the elbow to be bent so that the hand stays closer to the centre line of the body. This has the effect of reducing the moment of inertia of the swinging arm which in the high-elbow recovery case is around the transverse horizontal axis. The moment of inertia of the limb may be regarded as

Figure 2.8: Position of the swimmer at the commencement of arm recovery. Note that the hand continues with the propulsive action beyond the hip prior to arm recovery commencing.

Figure 2.9: Position of the swimmer at the end of the arm recovery phase. Note that the arm moves comfortably forward through the air prior to hand entry.

representing the amount of the effort required to rotate the limb around the shoulder joint. A high moment of inertia for the arm requires more effort to rotate the limb than a low moment of inertia. The moment of inertia of the limb is determined by the mass of the limb segments and the distance the segments are from the joint about which they are rotating. As an example, an extended arm would have a greater moment of inertia than an arm bent at the elbow. In a simple rotational movement, the limb moves in a single plane. In practice, however, body movements are generally a little more complex than this. The axis of rotation may be regarded as the line passing through the joint at right angles to the plane of movement. Three main axes are generally used when dealing with human motion. These are the longitudinal axis, the transverse axis and a front/back axis. The longitudinal axis runs lengthwise down the body, the transverse axis runs from left to right across the body and in the case of swimming the front–back axis is a vertical axis which passes from the chest to the back of the body. These axes will be used to describe rotational motion in swimming.

The round-arm recovery, as opposed to high-elbow recovery, has an increased moment of inertia around the vertical axis. The greater the moment of inertia is of the swinging arm, the more the body must adjust to prevent a compensating 'fish-tailing' of the swimmer's trunk. This is particularly true if the moment of inertia is about the vertical axis as is the case with the round-arm recovery. The round-arm recovery also often results in the hand entering the water across as well as forward of the body, producing splash which increases resistance. In the round-arm recovery the hand is much more likely to enter the water in a flat position resulting in the hand taking air bubbles into the propulsive phase. A high-elbow recovery on the other hand orients the hand so that it enters the water on its side, as described previously, with the thumb closest to the water. This allows a natural hand entry with the fingers entering first, thumb down, and the palm of the hand at an angle of 45° to the water surface. The movement is such that the hand travels forward in the high-elbow recovery rather than across and in front of the body as commonly occurs in the round-arm recovery. As a consequence of the hand entry in front of the shoulder, the high bent-elbow recovery better prepares the hand for an outwards catch following hand entry.

Many questions are asked as to the propulsive nature of the kicking action. We do know that the legs serve to stabilize the upper body during such actions as arm recovery. They do this by moving away from the midline of the body. In this way the moment of inertia of the trailing section of the body around the longitudinal axis may be increased. This allows the rotational movements which occur around the front of the body to be compensated by the actions of the legs. A body in water experiences two natural forces—gravity and buoyancy. The gravitational force acts through the centre of mass while the buoyancy acts through the centre of volume. As a consequence of air in the lungs, the location of the centre of volume is closer to the head than the centre of mass. Because the buoyancy force acts in an upward direction as opposed to gravity which acts downwards, the feet of a swimmer have a tendency to sink. If a swimmer were to swim with the feet below the level of the trunk this would increase resistance. Another important function of the legs and feet is to keep the feet at a level in the water behind the trunk so as not to increase resistance as the body moves through the water. Not only is resistance a function of frontal surface area but it is also a function of body shape. Over the years as cars have become capable of higher speeds there has been the need to reduce air resistance. Car manufacturers have developed later models so that they present a smaller cross-sectional frontal area as well as having much more of a streamlined shape. Another feature of some cars is the introduction of spoilers which assist in reducing resistance. The legs and feet of a swimmer can be used in a similar fashion as the spoilers on cars to decrease the resistance of the swimmer travelling through water. This can probably be achieved more effectively with a six-beat rather than a two-beat kicking action.

The legs and feet of swimmers, as indicated previously, can be used successfully to reduce resistance. The feet may also be used successfully in propulsion. This can be illustrated with the use of a flotation device to hold the arms in front of the body and the feet can be used solely as a means of propulsion. Individuals vary considerably as to the effectiveness of their kicking action. Some swimmers abandon the six-beat kicking action in preference for the two-beat kick without really trying to improve the effectiveness of their six-beat kick. Swimmers should concentrate more on the development of a successful propulsive kicking action rather than relegating the feet to just resistance reduction. Probably one of the greatest faults in the kicking action is when the swimmer kicks more from the knees rather than from the hips.

Another important aspect of good technique is ample shoulder roll. Many swimmers reduce the extent of their shoulder roll around the longitudinal axis of the body. This may be considered a technique fault. Shoulder roll is used to enable the arms to recover effectively as well as to permit an easy breathing pattern. If shoulder roll is reduced, the body is forced to make unusual unsymmetrical jerky movements to permit the actions of arm recovery and breathing. A symmetrical breathing pattern has proved useful in competitive swimming. Many competitive swimmers have adopted a breathing pattern which occurs every one and a half strokes and results in the swimmer breathing on both sides of the body. An important aspect of shoulder roll and breathing is that the head should rotate around the long axis of the body rather than be lifted out of the water.

Swimming speed is the product of stroke length and stroke frequency. Stroke length is the distance the swimmer travels from right-hand entry to the next right-hand entry. Stroke frequency is the number of the previously defined stroke lengths completed in a minute. For each swimmer an optimum combination of both stroke length and stroke frequency exists for a particular distance swim in order to maximize swimming speed, given that the swimmer is physically prepared for the swim. The problem is to work toward identifying that combination. Naturally enough, the swimmer is able to effectively improve either stroke length or stroke frequency, disregarding the other. The secret is to optimize one and then try to improve the other without unduly affecting the first. This can best be done in a pool where distances are clearly marked out. The swimmer should attempt to maximize stroke length. Increasing stroke length can best be achieved by applying the principles of good technique covered earlier in this chapter. It is important to optimize all the phases of the stroke through the full range of the stroke to do this. During this activity the coach should record the number of strokes taken per pool length to swim the desired distance. This exercise will provide data about stroke length and stroke frequency if the time per pool length is also recorded. The next stage involves swimming the same distance again in a quicker time per pool length and once again recording both the number of strokes and the time per pool length. The aim here is to increase stroke frequency while at the same time retain the stroke length. An examination of both stroke length and stroke frequency will indicate the effect of the increased stroke frequency on a possible reduction of stroke length. If this exercise is pursued over a series of training sessions, concentrating on improving one while keeping the other constant, an optimum stroke length/stroke frequency combination may be identified. During training sessions which involve distance swims, the coach should periodically check to see that the optimum stroke length is not reduced. The swimmer and coach must remember that calculations made from swimming in a pool reduce the actual number of strokes per 50 metre (55 yard) length because of the distance travelled during turns. An allowance should be made for this during longer-course swims. An important aspect in optimizing stroke length is to gain maximum propulsion out of every aspect of the arm action as well as reducing resistance. This infers an optimization of arm and body movements as indicated in previous paragraphs. It should be remembered that it is more economical to get maximum distance out of each stroke length than to compromise and increase stroke frequency.

Swimmers should be conscious of unwanted changes which may creep into their technique. As a generality, swimmers are reasonably unaware of propulsive movements which they make in the water. This is possibly a consequence of performing their actions in a medium which is alien to humans. Because the swimming action is very repetitive small inefficiencies of technique may creep into a swimmer's style and unless rectified quickly may become entrenched into the technique and become very difficult to eradicate. Such inefficiencies are most likely to occur during a series of hard workouts when the swimmer becomes tired. The most successful method to monitor technique in swimming is to periodically film the swimmer on video. This may be done either using an underwater viewing window or a specially made housing for the video camera. There is also now available a 'coach scope' which permits the underwater filming to be performed on pool deck when the camera is mounted onto equipment. The coach scope behaves as a submarine periscope in reverse. Above-water video footage taken from the pool deck is not nearly as beneficial for technique analysis as is footage taken below the water. Several passes of the swimmer should be shot from each side as well as from in front. All the filming should be done as the swimmer performs at full effort. Faults that are apparent at full effort are not always observable when swimming at a slower pace. The video footage enables the swimmer and the coach to view the swimming style both in slow motion and in freeze frame with nothing more than a domestic recorder and television monitor. As well as detecting the movements of the swimmer, the video may also be used as a timing device to calculate such things as stroke frequency. This is possible because video frames can occur between twenty-five times and thirty times per second. Before filming ensure that the water clarity is good and there is plenty of light. This is probably best achieved in an outdoor pool on a sunny day. Video filming and stroke correction procedures should become a regular practice within the training schedule.

Only at the initial stages of learning a sport do we consider there is a single right way to perform an activity. Once an athlete reaches an intermediate or elite level in the sport they develop their own distinctive style based upon their previous learning history and on the physical attributes they have inherited. For this reason there is no right nor wrong way to perform an activity; however, all athletes have inefficiencies of style. It is important for the swimmer and coach not to interfere with a stroke technique unless they can identify these inefficiencies. Technique change is not warranted purely because the actions of the swimmer under consideration do not resemble those of other elite performers. Change on this basis may in fact result in a poorer performance rather than an improved performance. Unless an inefficiency is clearly identified in the swimmer's stroke, modification should not take place. Using information obtained from video or film, together with knowledge about the basics of good stroke technique and an understanding of the biomechanical principles involved, the coach and swimmer should identify technique inefficiencies and go about making modifications to eradicate those inefficiencies.

It is important for a swimmer and coach to not only understand correct or efficient technique, they should also know and understand the principles of biomechanics which govern their sport. Actions which occur or actions which they may consider introducing that are not covered in books can be evaluated by the coach and swimmer if they have an understanding of the biomechanical principles which affect the actions under consideration. In the next few paragraphs an explanation of the biomechanics principles associated with resistance and with propulsion in swimming will be examined.

Resistive forces are considerable in swimming and occur as a consequence of movement through water. Similar resistive forces are experienced in air but the resistive forces in water are higher at slower velocities as a consequence of the higher density of water. Resistance does not just increase proportionally with velocity but it is a function of velocity squared. It is for this reason that it is most economical to swim at a constant velocity rather than varying the velocity by speeding up and slowing down within the race. Similar to movement in air there would be a corresponding reduction in resistance as a consequence of 'slip streaming' or 'drafting' behind another swimmer. We are unaware of any studies which have actually quantified the effect of slip streaming in swimming-related activities. Information about the benefits of slip streaming at various distances behind the lead swimmer are unknown, however the author would suggest that more than

2 metres (2.2 yards) would result in very little assistance. There are other concerns about swimming behind another swimmer which should also be considered, such as being hit in the face by a foot and working with inconsistent water conditions.

Resistive forces in swimming are a direct consequence of drag, which can be classified as three types: *form, surface* and *wave.* Form drag is related to the cross-sectional area of the body exposed to the oncoming flow, the shape of the body and the relative velocity of the flow. Surface drag is related to the extent of the body's surface area, the smoothness of the body's surface and the relative velocity of the oncoming flow. A swimmer operates at the interface between two fluids—air and water. Some of the kinetic energy of the swimmer is transformed into waves and this process of transformation acts to reduce motion. This is termed wave drag and is the third form of drag which may act upon a swimmer. A swimmer is, however, able to affect the magnitude of each of the above three forms of drag. Probably the greatest resistive force in swimming comes about as a result of form drag. Wave drag accounts for the next greatest resistive force followed by surface drag which accounts for the least.

Form drag may be decreased by having a good streamlining of the hand during hand entry into the water and streamlining of the swimmer's body generally as it glides through the water. This is particularly true in maintaining the head alignment with the horizontal axis of the body as well as utilizing a good shoulder roll. The feet and legs may be used effectively like spoilers on a car to reduce form drag. The result of the kicking action to raise the level of the legs and body so that they are in alignment with the shoulders may further reduce form drag by reducing the cross-sectional area exposed to the oncoming water. Appliances such as wetsuits often trap air and their buoyancy may assist in the elevation of the body in the water resulting in less cross-sectional area of the head and shoulders exposed to the oncoming water. Care should be taken in the selection of a wetsuit in that a heavy suit as well as restricting the swimmer's movements can considerably increase cross-sectional area to the oncoming flow, which in itself may increase form drag. Air in the wetsuit may also assist in elevating the trunk and legs to the alignment of the shoulders which once again reduces the frontal surface area. Any relatively fast forward movement by parts of the body, such as the hands and arms during recovery, should be performed as much in the air as possible.

Surface drag is affected by the material in the swimsuit that is worn by the swimmer. It is better to wear friction-reduced swimwear or friction-reduced wetsuits as this reduces the surface drag on the body. Similarly, shaving down exposed sections of the skin and wearing swim caps will also reduce surface drag.

The action of raising and lowering the head in exaggerated breathing movements as well as crashing the arms down into the water following arm recovery produces splashing and waves and this results in unnecessary added resistance as a consequence of wave drag. The stroke technique employed should avoid these inefficiencies. As an example of the effect of wave drag, in the 1956 Olympic Games the Japanese breaststroke swimmers swam the entire first lap under water. In doing so they were able to reduce the wave drag to which the surface competitors were subjected and gained an advantage over the other swimmers. In a swimming stroke where the hand recovery occurs completely under the water there is a definite advantage, if the rules permit, in keeping the entire body under the water to avoid the resistance caused by wave drag. When hand recovery can occur over the water in a stroke such as the front crawl, the advantage of keeping the entire body under the water is lost because of the added resistance required to recover the hands through the water.

Prior to the 1970s, propulsive forces in swimming were thought to be due entirely to action–reaction forces. The swimmer was thought to exert a backward action against the water which propelled the swimmer forward. This type of propulsion is termed drag propulsion because it relies on the large surface area of the hand to push backward on the water. Lateral and vertical movements of the hands were explained in terms of looking for stationary water which had not been previously accelerated by the hand. The horizontal and vertical movements of the hand were also thought to occur as a result of shoulder roll.

In the 1970s, swim coaches began to realize the importance of lift propulsion to the swimmer. This was predominantly due to the biomechanical research performed by 'Doc' James Counsilman of Indiana and the publications which followed. As lift propulsion is probably more misunderstood than any other aspect in the biomechanics of swimming, an emphasis will be placed upon explaining this concept. The term 'lift' gives a false impression that the force is always directed upward. This is generally not the case. The lift force is, however, always directed at right angles to the direction of movement or of fluid flow, which itself can occur in any direction. Lift force is best explained by an airplane wing or airfoil. When the airfoil moves forward a layer of air has to separate with some particles of air travelling under and some over the wing. Due to the shape of the airfoil the path over is longer than the path under the wing. As two particles of the air, separated by the movement of the airfoil, must come together after they pass over and under it, the air which passes above the wing must travel at a faster speed than the air which passes underneath. Bernoulli's Principle in fluid dynamics states that in a non-viscous, steady flowing fluid, regions of high velocity have a lower pressure than regions of low velocity. Air and water are non-viscous fluids to which Bernoulli's Principle applies. Consequently there is a region of low pressure above the wing and a region of high pressure beneath. This pressure differential results in a lift force which is inversely proportional to the difference in relative flow velocity of the air above and below the wing.

It should be noted at this time that because the wing is moving forward it experiences a resistive force or drag which acts against the direction of movement. This drag force is always present and acts at right angles to the lift force. Some racing cars have airfoils which are designed in reverse to the airplane wing and which cause the lift force to be exerted in a downward direction. This is done to increase the load on the wheels which then produces a greater traction force between the road and wheels and it also serves to reduce the chance of the car becoming airborne.

The human hand can perform the action of the airfoil when held outside a moving car window. Altering the shape and inclination of the hand to the oncoming flow of air causes lift forces to be experienced. As water is much denser than air, similar forces can be experienced when the hand is moved through water at much slower speeds. These forces may also be produced if the hand is moved in a vertical alignment through the water causing a lift force to be experienced in a horizontal direction. This movement is best illustrated if the elbow is maintained in a position slightly beneath water level and the forearm is swung sideways through the water like a pendulum. By adjusting the alignment of the hand to the water through which it is slicing, horizontal lift forces will be felt.

Probably the most convincing practical evidence to support the existence of lift force in swimming occurs when an individual floats vertically in the water and sculls the hands horizontally to keep afloat. Apart from the buoyant force on the swimmer's body, this method of propulsion relies totally upon lift propulsion. The big advantage of lift propulsion over drag propulsion in this instance becomes obvious. During the horizontal sculling stroke both directions become propulsive by altering the alignment of the hand with each change of direction. Alternatively, if drag propulsive stroke was employed to keep the swimmer afloat half the stroke would be classified as recovery during which time propulsion could not be achieved.

During lift propulsion the angle to which the airfoil is inclined to the direction of fluid flow is termed the angle of attack (see figure 2.10). Gradually increasing the angle of attack will result in greater lift forces. Along with this increase in lift is a corresponding increase in drag which acts against the direction the airfoil is moving. The increase in lift, as a result of an increase in angle of attack, reaches a limit where lift forces are drastically reduced and drag forces remain high. This angle in an airplane wing relates to the airplane stalling. An optimum angle of attack in free-flight activities such as the javelin and discus throw of from 4°–15° is required to maximize the lift-to-drag ratio and hence maximize the distance of the throw. Generally the swimmer's hand will use an angle of attack from 30°–50° which is well beyond the optimum angle to maximize the lift-to-drag ratio. A swimmer is able to obtain the desired lift-to-drag ratio in each phase of the stroke, which utilizes lift propulsion, by developing a feel for the water. It is important to note that the particular drag force mentioned here does not act

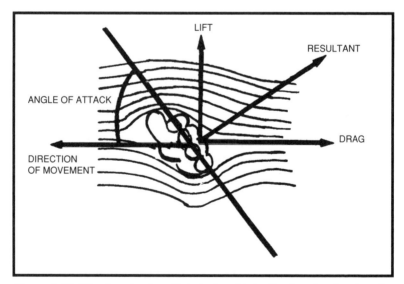

Figure 2.10: The direction in which the hand is inclined to the direction of water flow is termed the angle of attack.

against the direction of swimming but rather against the movement of the limb. The action of the lift forces on the hand is relayed to the body by way of the muscle stabilizers around the shoulder joint and to a lesser extent the elbow. As a consequence of this stabilization swimmers often develop an impression of pushing the water back as in drag-dominated propulsion.

The hand and arm actions in swimming cannot be totally classified as being solely lift propulsive or drag propulsive as generally both methods are evident at the same time. However, the arm stroke may be divided into phases in which one or the other may dominate, or where both methods of propulsion may contribute to a resultant propulsive force.

Differences occur in individual swimming styles as a result of training, strength and power, flexibility and anthropometric differences that exist between individual swimmers. These physical and learned abilities result in individuals developing their own distinctive style of stroke. The proportion of lift versus drag propulsion which occurs within the various phases of the stroke may vary considerably between one swimmer and the next. Probably the best way of assessing whether any particular phase of the stroke is more lift or drag oriented is to observe the direction of hand movement. When the hand moves more predominantly in the backward movement through the water the action is probably more drag oriented. If the hand movement pattern is more lateral or vertical in direction the action is probably more lift oriented.

In lift-dominated propulsion, the direction of the lift force can be assessed as being at right angles to the direction of hand movement. However, just because the hand moves vertically or laterally through the water does not mean that lift propulsion is successfully employed. Only when the hand is appropriately oriented in shape, pitch and angle of attack can lift propulsion be effectively achieved. In drag-dominated propulsion the hand must maintain an effective backward pressure on the water to be successfully employed. Although coaches should be tolerant of different stroking styles which result from individual differences between swimmers, they should always be prepared to modify the action of the limbs and change a swimmer's style if inefficiencies in the stroke technique are detected. This can only be successfully implemented if the coach fully understands the mechanics by which propulsion in swimming is achieved and he/she has access to video footage of the swimmer's actions.

Up until this point in the chapter the discussion about lift-propulsion hand movements has been over simplified for ease of explanation. In actual fact if purely laterally directed lift-oriented hand movements are utilized by the swimmer they would result in the production of an additional lateral force which would act upon the swimmer's body. This lateral force would be produced at the same time as the desired forward directed lift-propulsive force. The lateral force occurs as a consequence of drag on the limb which is always produced with, and at right angles to the lift force (see figure 2.11). The lateral force would probably result in a sideways body movement during arm stroke.

In order to counteract the effect of the lateral force, the swimmer modifies the hand movement pattern so that the horizontal lift force has a medial component which is opposite in direction to the drag force's lateral component. This is achieved by moving the hand in a backward medial direction rather than in purely a medial direction. This change in direction of hand motion modifies the drag force which is then directed forwards as well as laterally.

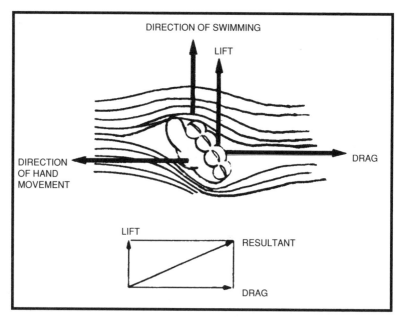

Figure 2.11: When the hand moves through water lateral forces occur because of drag. These always occur with, and at right angles to, the lift force. The resultant force is a vector sum of the lift and drag forces.

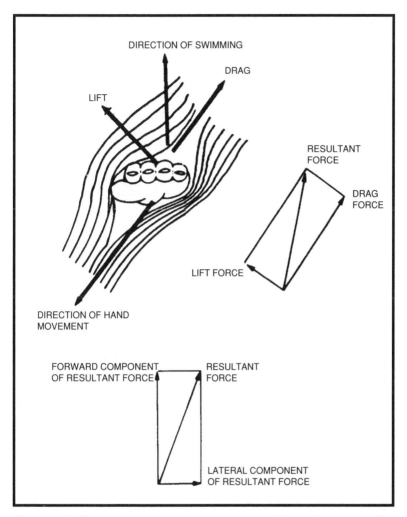

Figure 2.12: The resultant force is the vector sum of lift and drag forces. The propulsive force is the forward component of the resultant force.

The propulsive force which is actually used to propel the swimmer forward is the forward component of the resultant force. The resultant force is the vector sum of the lift and drag forces and is best illustrated by using a parallelogram of vector diagram (see figure 2.12). The forward propulsive force so obtained will be greater in magnitude than either the lift or drag forces comprising it. It is for this reason that the swimmer is willing to increase the drag force well beyond that which would be attained if a maximum lift-to-drag ratio was used. The medial component of the lift force does not totally overcome the lateral component of the drag force and so the net lateral force is never really reduced to zero. This force is, however, utilized by the swimmer to initiate shoulder roll, to enable arm recovery and breathing movements to occur. The rolling body motion results as a consequence of the net lateral force acting as an eccentric force on the swimmer. The force is applied to the hand and arm which behave as a lever that extends out from the long axis of the body to rotate the swimmer's body about the long axis.

Actual hand location and orientation with respect to the body, as well as the attack and pitch angles to the oncoming flow are able to be measured during swimming trials using modern biomechanics techniques and equipment. Optimum hand attack and pitch angles to the oncoming flow in the various phases of the stroke, for the location of the hands identified previously, can be calculated using biomechanical computer programs. To date, this information has only been used to highlight inefficiencies in the stroke but has not been used effectively to modify stroke technique to the hand positions prescribed by the computer program. Swimmers rely on a feel for the water to be able to move and angle their hands effectively for propulsion. A feel for the water is generally taught by swim coaches by using devices such as paddles and other equipment on the hands during swimming activities. If inefficiencies are detected by biomechanical methods then modifications are able to be made and biomechanical reassessment performed.

Air trapped in the hands reduces the effect of lift propulsion, very much like an airplane wing is affected by air turbulence. This is because the layers of fluid coming in contact with the hand are not uniform in nature. It is very important for this reason that air is effectively removed from around the hands during hand entry. Research studies to identify the best finger position to obtain maximum lift propulsion did not find large differences between the various positions. The important aspect was that the finger position remained natural and comfortable and the hand was slightly cupped. Even with the fingers slightly apart ample lift propulsion was achieved by such finger positioning. The author believes that the thumb is also used by many swimmers to monitor the flow characteristics of water around the hand.

More lift-oriented propulsive movements of the hand occur during the first half of the armstroke and more drag-oriented movements take place during the latter half of the stroke. That is, more lift-oriented propulsion occurs than drag-oriented propulsion prior to the hand moving behind the plane of the shoulders. Drag-oriented propulsion predominates after the hand moves behind the plane of the chest. It should also be noted that although the propulsion force is primarily derived from the hand, a similar action occurs with the forearm and the upper arm to a lesser extent so that propulsive forces are produced from the entire upper extremity.

Other theories about propulsion in swimming include vortex theory and undulation movement theory. Vortex theory believes that a change in direction of the limb results in the shedding of a vortex and the formation of a new flow pattern in the opposite direction around the limb to the shed vortex. Because the limb is continually changing direction throughout the arm movement vortices are continually being shed and new flow patterns created. The flow pattern of moving fluid around the limb results in the application of Bernoulli's Principle to produce force. The formulators of the vortex theory believe that because of the small distances which the hand and arm make between changes of direction that insufficient force can be generated by the lift theory to explain the propulsive force which is generated by swimmers. These people believe that sufficient forces can be generated by the vortex theory. The formulators of the undulating movement theory derive their theory from the observations of animals, such as snakes, fish and dolphins and their movements in water. It is believed that because of the continual formation of non-symmetrical bends in the body, that energy is transmitted in such waves or bends. Similar but not as extensive bends occur along the long axis of the body in humans during swimming. Once again this theory relies on the application of Bernoulli's Principle.

Biomechanical research into propulsive techniques in swimming have recently focused on the hand motions of elite swimmers. Information obtained from such investigations indicates the importance of hand acceleration throughout the arm stroke from catch to the beginning of recovery.

Mechanical efficiency is a physiological measure which defines how effectively the swimmer's body uses its energy. A very small percentage of the total body energy reserves is used effectively, and is in the order of up to 10%. Propelling efficiency provides information about the effectiveness of a swimmer's technique.

In summary, the power required to swim at a set velocity is directly related to the cross-sectional area of the swimmer exposed to the water ahead and the coefficient of the drag. Decreasing the cross-sectional area or decreasing the coefficient of the drag will decrease the power requirement which then may be utilized to enable the swimmer to swim at a higher velocity. Decreasing the cross-sectional area is obtained by utilizing good streamlining, good hand recovery and good shoulder roll. Decreasing the coefficient of drag is best achieved by using the feet effectively, shaving down and wearing a cap.

The power requirement increases as a function of velocity cubed. This implies it is beneficial to aim toward a uniform inter- and intra-stroke velocity for reduced energy output.

Propelling efficiency may be increased by using good stroke technique. In summary, good technique may be attained by: producing large forces in the correct propulsive direction, reducing resistive forces, avoiding excessive movements, obtaining harmony in the breathing actions and propulsive movements, achieving optimum combination of effort and relaxation of muscles, and attaining a good transfer of force from one part of the body to the next.

Chapter Three

Physiological Considerations in Swimming

Rod Cedaro

Of the three disciplines involved in triathlon, swimming is technically the most difficult. It is therefore imperative to master the mechanics of the freestyle stroke in order to maximize the returns from physiological conditioning. The triathlete may become extremely 'fit' from a physiological perspective, but if he is not putting his hand in the right place or applying force correctly against the water, actual performance will be sadly diminished. Having mastered the basic stroke mechanics of freestyle (see chapter two), the triathlete must then work at constructing an individualized training regimen to optimize aerobic and anaerobic potential. There isn't one magical program that will turn a 30 minute 1500 metre (1650 yard) swimmer into a world beater. However, if you apply the following basic principles to your swim training, improvements will follow.

Energy for muscular contraction can be produced by one of three mechanisms, two of which facilitate relatively fast energy production and don't require oxygen; these are termed 'anaerobic'. The third is comparably slower and occurs in the presence of oxygen, i.e. 'aerobic metabolism' (see figure 3.1). As the majority of the demands associated with

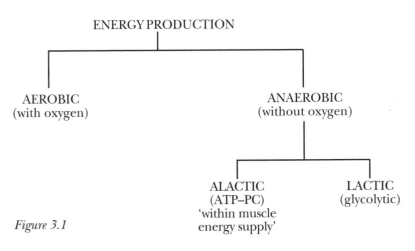

Figure 3.1

triathlon are of an aerobic nature, this is where the training emphasis must be concentrated. The training periods or phases known as 'macrocycles' should be broken up into three active and one restorative phase as depicted diagrammatically in figure 3.2. The duration of time spent in each macrocycle is dependent upon the following factors: (i) sporting background and initial fitness level and (ii) the length of the event being prepared for.

Figure 3.2

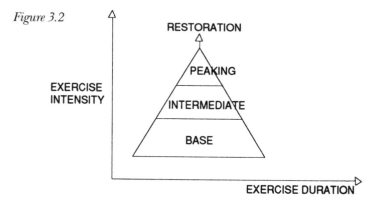

Initially let's consider the demands of each training cycle:

Base/off-season: Here the emphasis is on developing 'peripheral' cardio-vascular fitness. Training should be of low intensity (60–75% of maximal heart rate) and the duration of exercise greater than that which will be encountered during actual competition. Ideally the triathlete should be looking at spending as much time as possible, bearing in mind the constraints of competitive seasons, within this phase (15–25 weeks).

Intermediate/pre-season: This is also known as the 'preparatory phase'. The emphasis now shifts away from purely low intensity work and the triathlete starts to incorporate some 'quality' work (intervals) into the weekly regimen. The intensity of exercise increases while the duration is diminished. The transition from the base phase to the intermediate should be slow and progressive, the first month stressing a combination of volume and intensity, and the subsequent month focusing on 'sharpening' achieved by a greater intensity (75–85% of maximal heart rate) and decreased exercise duration. This phase should last from 1–2 months and is much more task specific than that which the triathlete was involved in during the previous phase.

Peaking/in-season: The emphasis of training is now placed upon the high intensity exercise to develop 'central' cardiovascular function by improving the triathlete's anaerobic threshold. Recovery sessions (both active and passive) need to be adequately interspersed between hard quality workouts so as to maintain peripheral fitness and avoid the excessive stress of continuous high intensity exercise. Prior to competition this phase lasts 2–3 weeks and then for the duration of the competitive phase, generally a total of 8–12 weeks.

Restoration: This cycle occurs at the completion of a racing season or after a major race that the triathlete may have been building up to for a period of time. The rigors of racing/hard training lead to 'kinks' or slight injuries and often psychological burnout from pushing the body through hard training/competition. The restoration phase requires the triathlete to ease off his/her training

Figure 3.3(a)

Type of Training	Levels	Heart Rate Intensity (% of Maximal)	Lactate [ ]
Compensatory	1	60–70	2
Aerobic endurance	2	75–80	2–3
Speed endurance	3	85–90	4–7
Simulation	4	Max.	Max.
Sprint	5	N/A	N/A

Figure 3.3(b)

Training Phase	Intensity of Exercise	Percentage of Total Training Time
Base	Compensatory	40–45
	Aerobic endurance	40–45
	Speed endurance/ simulation	10–20
Intermediate	Compensatory	25–35
	Aerobic endurance	35–40
	Speed endurance/ simulation	20–25
	Sprint	5–10
Peaking	Compensatory	20–30
	Aerobic endurance	40–50
	Speed endurance	10–15
	Simulation	10–15
	Sprint	up to 10

to allow ample time to regenerate/recuperate both physiologically as well as psychologically. During this phase the triathlete shouldn't really 'train', but rather 'exercise at leisure'. Activities should be largely unstructured and completed in a relaxed manner, e.g. if the triathlete feels like swimming, fine; if, on the other hand, a game of golf or tennis is more appealing during this phase, time would be better spent in these alternative activities. A minimum period of 2–4 weeks of 'down-time' is advisable with a period of up to six weeks of leisurely exercise, which is not uncommon for elite/professional triathletes who have been involved in long, arduous racing seasons.

Within (as it was known then) the German Democratic Republic, sports scientists devised a means of breaking training demands down into five progressively more intense/demanding categories or stages (see figure 3.3a). The emphasis within each of the macrocycles (base, intermediate and peaking) changes in relation to the type of work being accentuated. See examples in figures 3.3a and 3.3b on page 51.

Progressively the onus shifts away from the lower intensity exercise and is replaced by a lesser volume of training, more rest/active recovery and higher quality efforts. As a normal rule of thumb, the triathlete should never back up two quality sessions. Often training is emphasized at the expense of recovery/regeneration. If this continues the quality of performances will be severely hampered as the triathlete becomes progressively overtrained (figure 3.4). Rest/regeneration allows the body to 'supercompensate' for the stresses that are placed upon it by training, adapt and then progress to a higher level of

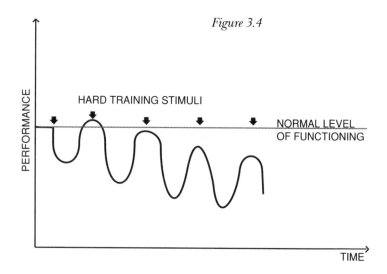

Figure 3.4

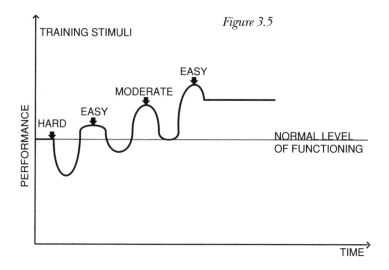

Figure 3.5

functioning (figure 3.5). The obvious question that then follows is, 'How do we know when enough is enough, too much or too little?'. This is largely an individual concern and will differ from athlete to athlete; however, there are a number rules:

1. If you came into a triathlon as a swimmer you will have already developed a firm training base. Therefore training volume can be increased by up to 10% per week—5% for an inexperienced swimmer.
2. Experienced swimmers need not spend so much time attending to stroke correction drills, while the majority of a novice's early training should focus on developing an effective stroke pattern.
3. Emphasize your weaknesses. This means if swimming is a weakness, but as a runner/cyclist you are quite competent, de-emphasize and maintain these latter two disciplines and focus on improving your swimming prowess.

THE SWIMMING PROGRAM

As has already been mentioned, the body can produce energy (ATP: adenosine triphosphate) in three distinct ways. (i) *Aerobically:* In the presence of oxygen. This tends to be a slower process in which the body oxidizes (burns) a combination of fat, carbohydrate and to a small extent protein, to fuel muscular contraction. (ii) *Anaerobically:* (a) Lactic Acid System: As the triathlete starts to increase the intensity of exercise there is a certain point—the so-called 'anaerobic threshold'—where the demands for energy can no longer be adequately met via aerobic metabolism. In order to keep pace with these increased energy requirements the triathlete starts to burn carbohydrate in the absence of oxygen. As a consequence the principal by-product of this form of metabolism (lactic acid) begins to accumulate within the triathlete's exercising muscles, subsequently passing out of the muscle into the bloodstream. In response the triathlete's breathing becomes labored and the exercising muscles experience a 'burning' sensation. The triathlete is then forced to decrease the exercise intensity (slow down) to dissipate this lactic acid. Well-conditioned athletes reach this anaerobic threshold point at a higher work output and are better able to tolerate this lactate accumulation than lesser-trained individuals. (b) Alactic (ATP–PC) System: Within muscles there is stored energy in the form of creatine phosphate (P-C); these high energy bonds can be used to power muscular contraction, at a high intensity, for between 10–20 seconds, e.g. swimming a 25–50 metre (27–55 yard) sprint (see figure 3.1).

These various energy systems do not operate independently of one another. Depending upon the event in question the contribution from each of these systems will vary accordingly. For this reason (i.e. the specificity of energy demands) triathletes' training programs need to be individualized as much as is practical. For example, if you have a squad of triathletes training for sprint and ultradistance events DON'T simply lump them in together, as the energy demands for these different events are poles apart. Generally speaking, the duration of most triathlons require that the majority of the energy contribution be derived aerobically. As a consequence, the majority of the training/preparation should reflect these demands. This can be achieved in a host of ways and by using a number of training modalities and regimens.

A. LONG SLOW DISTANCE

Theoretically, because triathlon is based primarily upon aerobic metabolism, we could suggest that the triathlete simply swim countless numbers of continuous laps at a low intensity (compensation-type work). In some instances, early in the base phase or following a race/hard training session, this would in fact be an appropriate form of training/recovery. However, research has frequently shown the need to work at higher intensities of exercise in order to force the body to adapt and improve.

B. LONG SLOW INTERVALS

With this type of training the set distance to be completed in competition is broken down into smaller segments and the triathlete completes these portions with measured recovery periods at an exercise intensity that is greater than that which could be maintained for the entire distance if it was tackled in its entirety. For example, if the triathlete can swim 1500 metres (1650 yards) in 24 minutes, then an appropriate long interval session may consist of 3 x 500 metres (550 yards) on 8:15. Here the triathlete would endeavor to complete the 500 metre (550 yard) repeat in less than 8 minutes, rest and commence the next repeat on 8:15. If this task is completed correctly, when the actual swimming time for the three 500s is tallied it should total less than the 24 minutes that the triathlete normally takes to complete the straight 1500 metre (1650 yard) swim.

C. Short Intervals

Here the emphasis is moved away from exercise duration and is placed upon intensity and speed. If we were to use the example of 1500 metres (1650 yards) in 24 minutes once more: When we divide the 1500 metres (1650 yards) by 15 we find that the triathlete is able to average 1 minute, 36 seconds per 100 metres (110 yards). Therefore a quality short interval session may call for the triathlete to complete 15 x 100 metres (110 yards) on 2:30 targeting less than 1:30 per 100 metres (110 yards). Once the triathlete finds it easy to complete these 15 x 100 metres (110 yards) on 2:30 in less than 1:30 per 100, then the intensity of exercise can be increased by decreasing the repeat interval to 2:20. Therefore the triathlete still targets 100 metres (110 yards) in less than 1:30, but the recovery after such an effort is cut by 10 seconds. Such a set teaches the triathlete to (a) swim at a greater velocity and (b) progressively adapt to shorter rest intervals by increasing lactate tolerance capacity. Eventually the triathlete is swimming the total distance (1500 metres [1650 yards]) at approximately 1:30 per 100 metres (110 yards) or in 22.30, an improvement of 1.5 minutes.

D. Fartlek

This is a Swedish term which when translated reads as 'speed play'. Generally it is used in association with running, however it can be equally applied to swimming or cycling. With this training modality the triathlete swims easy and surges as he/she sees fit. In other words, it is largely an unstructured training session with the triathlete determining subjectively when an 'effort' is applied. This type of training can be useful as a race simulation session. Often the triathlete will have to surge at a certain time (e.g. to break away from someone who is drafting); therefore this type of session provides a useful means by which to duplicate the rigors of actual competition.

Now that we've addressed the various macrocycles, or training phases, and training modalities (intensities, methods of achieving training goals), let's look a little more specifically at putting together an actual swim program for a triathlete, bearing in mind that this is strictly an example and should be modified according to each triathlete's unique situation and aspirations. What this routine will do, however, is provide an example of how to (a) structure a swim routine, (b) stress and rest the body and (c) progress through the various 'macrocycles' by 'microcycling' the training regimen.

Let us begin by using the example of a triathlete preparing for a race which incorporates a 1500 metre (1650 yard) swim. The demands of such a swim are primarily aerobic in nature; as a consequence training should reflect this. Research has shown time and time again that the most effective way to improve aerobic performance is by training at IAT, i.e. individual anaerobic threshold (Beck et al., 1986, Jacobs, 1986). If we refer back to our example cited previously (figure 3.2), you'll notice that much of the work should be between levels 2 and 3, i.e. heart rate 220–20 x .75–.85. During the base/pre-season phase a comprehensive endurance base must be established. If the triathlete has a background in swimming, as a primary sport or as a seasoned triathlon competitor, this phase should run 10–12 weeks, but longer if the triathlete is a novice swimmer or preparing for longer events. The greater emphasis should be on longer/lower intensity efforts. For example:

Monday
Comprehensive warm up/stretching.
4–6 x 400–600 metres (440–660 yards) at heart rate level 2.
Recover to heart rate 120 bpm.
2–4 x 300–500 metres (330–550 yards) at heart rate level 3.
Cooldown.
TOTAL 2200–5600 metres (2400–6125 yards).

Tuesday
Warm up and stretching as per Monday.
Fartlek session totalling 2000–3000 metres (2200–3300 yards). Vary heart rate between training levels 2 and 3 with occasional surges at level 4.
Cooldown.
TOTAL 2000–3000 metres (2200–3300 yards).

Wednesday
Rest.

Thursday

Warm up and stretching as usual.

Tolerance set: 4–6 x 300–500 metres (220–330 yards) at heart rate level 3 with a *short* rest interval.

1–3 x 400–600 metres (440–660 yards) at heart rate level 2 with a short rest.

Cooldown.

TOTAL 1600–3600 metres (1750–3940 yards).

Friday

Warm up and stretching as usual.

Speed session: 10–15 x 100–150 metres at heart rate level 4 (long rest/total recovery between efforts).

10–20 x 50 metres (as above).

5–10 x 25 at heart rate level 5 with long rest interval.

Cooldown.

TOTAL 2000–3000 metres (2200–3300 yards).

Saturday or Sunday

Warm up.

Threshold session: 2000–3000 metres (2200–3300 yards) at heart rate level 3.

Emphasis on stroke technique simulating race conditions (e.g. open water swimming/sighting, drafting etc.).

Cooldown.

TOTAL 2000–3000 metres (2200–3300 yards).

WEEKLY TOTAL 9425–15 700 metres (10 307–17 170 yards).

Now let's look at these sessions from the perspective of the energy systems they utilize:

Monday

Aerobic compensation/endurance session (low level of difficulty).

Tuesday

Speed/play session emphasizing aerobic component but stressing all energy systems (moderate difficulty).

Wednesday

Rest from specific swim training, allowing body to recover before subsequent session (recovery).

Thursday

Emphasis on teaching the body to tolerate lactic acid at threshold exercise intensities (approx. 4mM lactate). Followed by a recovery to dissipate lactate (moderate difficulty).

Friday
Quality session. Hard efforts working in excess of anaerobic threshold to build speed/power (difficult session).

Saturday or Sunday
Simulation swim at aerobic tolerance intensity to teach pacing, race strategy and skill development (open-water swimming/drafting).

While this program addresses all three energy systems, the emphasis is on lower intensity sessions and training volume rather than quality, even though there is a 'hint' of some harder quality training. In the early stages of this base phase the triathlete should be targeting the lower durations of these sessions. By applying the 5–10% rule the triathlete should endeavor to build these volumes to the upper limits that have been outlined. Therefore, by the end of the 8–12 weeks of the base phase the triathlete should be comfortably completing the longer duration workouts. Let us now consider how the triathlete should make the transition into the intermediate/pre-season training phase. Remember that this phase calls for increased intensity and decreased duration of exercise.

THE INTERMEDIATE PHASE
Again, depending upon the triathlete's training background and the event being prepared for, this phase generally lasts 4–6 weeks. The aim of training shifts from base/volume work, which is designed primarily to increase peripheral cardiovascular function, i.e. increased mitochondria concentrations within the muscles, improved glycogen storage capacity, greater capillarization of working muscles, increased oxidative enzyme concentration, etc. to improving the triathlete's anaerobic threshold or the central component of the cardiovascular equation. This involves maintaining the peripheral capacity, while at the same time teaching the body to operate at a greater intensity of exercise. There are a variety of training methods available to improve this capacity. The following program, which is an example that continues from the previous one, will address these various methods.

Monday
Warm up and stretch for 400–600 metres (440–660 yards).
4 x 200 metres (220 yards) descending 1–4 (i.e. heart rate increasing from exercise intensity 1 to 4. The first effort is easy, followed by a short rest, the second a little harder, the rest—on the same time interval—a little longer,

the third repeat almost maximal, the rest correspondingly longer, the final repeat a maximal effort).

For example: 4 x 200 metres (220 yards) on 3:00 minutes.

    1st repeat completed in 2:55 (5 second rest).

    2nd repeat completed in 2:50 (10 second rest).

    3rd repeat completed in 2:43 (17 second rest).

    4th repeat completed in 2:36 (N/A).

8–12 x 100–150 metres (110–165 yards) at heart rate level 3 (5 second rest between efforts).

Cooldown 400–600 metres (440–660 yards).

TOTAL 2000–3800 metres (2200–4156 yards) (moderate to high level of difficulty).

Tuesday

Rest (recovery day).

Wednesday

Warm up and stretch for 400–600 metres (440–660 yards).

Tolerance set: 10–20 x 50–75 metres (55–82 yards) at heart rate levels 3–4 (short rest interval).

10–20 x 25–50 metres (27–55 yards) at heart rate levels 3–4 (short rest interval).

Cooldown 400–600 metres (440–660 yards).

TOTAL 1550–2250 metres (1695–2460 yards) (moderate level of difficulty).

Thursday

Rest (recovery day).

Friday

Warm up and stretch.

Anaerobic endurance effort for 1750–2250 metres (1914–2460 yards) at heart rate level 3. Ideally an open-water swim to simulate race conditions.

Cooldown 400–600 metres (440–660 yards).

TOTAL 2550–3450 metres (2789–3773 yards) (high level of difficulty).

Saturday

Warm up and stretch.

Technique session of 3000–4000 metres (3300–4400 yards) at heart rate levels 1–2.

TOTAL 3800–5200 metres (4155–5686 yards) (low level of difficulty).

Sunday

Rest (recovery day).

WEEKLY TOTAL 9900–14 700 metres (10 825–16 975 yards).

Let's dissect each workout and discuss the reasoning behind each session:

Monday

This session is a combination of a 'peak set' and a 'threshold' or 'tolerance' set. *Peak set:* The triathlete is asked to swim progressively faster 200 metre repeats on the same interval. Therefore the work intensity increases and the corresponding recovery period also becomes longer. This set has a tendency to start off quite easy as the swimming is aerobic in nature and not too demanding; however, as the intensity increases and the triathlete accelerates in the later efforts, lactic acid begins to accumulate and the efforts become increasingly more difficult. This set attempts to teach triathletes (i) pacing, (ii) surging (useful for keeping up with a competitor who tries to break your draft), and (iii) lactic tolerance (accelerating/holding pace when marginally fatigued). *Threshold set:* Here the triathlete is required to elevate blood lactate concentrations to around anaerobic threshold levels and learn to tolerate this accumulation. Research reviewed by Jacobs (1986) has shown that by working at threshold levels—often suggested to correspond to blood lactate concentrations in the vicinity of 4 mM— endurance performance is enhanced. The moderate to high intensity of exercise forces lactate concentrations up to threshold levels. The short rest duration prior to commencing each subsequent effort isn't long enough to allow dissipation of the accumulating lactate, so the triathlete is forced to exercise with increased lactate concentrations, thus teaching his/her body to 'tolerate' this by-product of energy production.

Tuesday

Recovery day.

Wednesday

High intensity, short duration, short recovery set. The idea here is to establish the triathlete's ability to tolerate lactate and maintain high power outputs. For example, if the triathlete completed the first four 50 metre (55 yards) repeats in 42 seconds with an eight second recovery but the final six 50 metre (55 yards) repeats became progressively slower (e.g. 50 seconds to complete) this would be indicative of a poor lactate tolerance capacity. Ideally, the triathlete should be aiming at holding form and speed for the duration of the set. After completing a session such as this it is important to 'swimdown' in order to dissipate the lactate that has accumulated in the working muscle groups.

Thursday

Recovery day.

Friday

This session is something like a 'simulation swim'. It requires the triathlete to work at exercise intensities that approximate actual racing conditions. By 'time trialling' such a distance the triathlete is (a) teaching his/her body to work at anaerobic threshold so he/she learns how to pace him/herself and performances don't 'fall off' towards the end of the effort due to excessive lactate accumulation, (b) helping to force 'AT' back further, closer to maximal oxygen uptake, so that the triathlete can work at higher intensities for prolonged durations as will be required under race conditions. Effectively, this session works at improving central cardiovascular function.

Saturday

The emphasis during this session is upon active recovery. Following the Friday session the triathlete will have subjective feelings of 'heavy arms'. This session encourages recovery by delivering fresh, nutrient-rich, oxygenated blood to the muscle groups that have been taxed on the previous day and 'flushing' the muscle groups. The triathletes should be focusing on stroke technique during this session. Once more an open-water swim would be a useful option under these circumstances as it allows the triathlete to practice relevant skills (pack swimming, drafting, sighting, etc.). This swim is completed in a slower, continuous fashion at distances well in excess of that which will be experienced on race day. As a consequence—from a conditioning perspective—the aim is to maintain peripheral cardiovascular function.

Sunday

Recovery day in preparation for the following week's training.

Peaking Phase/In Season

During the peaking/in-season phase the onus is upon quality and recovery. The triathlete is stressed with high intensity exercise followed by either passive rest (complete rest day from swimming) or active recovery (low intensity work: compensation/aerobic endurance). During this phase competition can be used to replace quality training sessions. Generally the quality of exercise during competition is considerably higher than that which can be achieved during 'training sessions'. Athletes often claim that you 'can't train like you race'. It is therefore useful to schedule a host of 'training races' during this phase leading up to a major competition. This allows the triathlete to practice skills 'under pressure' which will help to prepare for the later competitions (often referred to as becoming 'race fit'). Here the triathlete focuses on central function with quality training; adequate recovery must be allowed prior to attempting again to work hard. In the case of swimming—providing the triathlete attends to post-exercise concerns such as fluid and energy replacement—which is a non-weight bearing exercise, the triathlete can generally recover more quickly from high intensity pool sessions than either cycling or more particularly running, which has a large 'eccentric' muscular contraction component. This class of muscular contractions has been shown to delay recovery and glycogen resynthesis (Costill and Hargreaves, 1990).

As far as pool training sessions are concerned, racing and quality training should be a more central focus; the other critical concern is to allow ample recovery/regeneration between quality workouts. This does not mean, however, that low intensity, longer sessions are completely neglected. In fact these 'aerobic sets' serve two important functions: they (a) help speed recovery by promoting blood supply to the working musculature that has been severely taxed by previous sessions, and (b) help maintain aerobic base fitness developed in the earlier phases. Once again a day to day example of such a phase could incorporate the following. (*Note:* Intensity is of central importance and duration is decreased.)

Monday
Warm up/stretching (400–600 metres [440–660 yards]) at level 1.
2000–3000 metre (2200–3300 yards) straight swim (with pull buoy if required) at level 1–2 intensity.
Cooldown 400 metres (440 yards) at level 1.
TOTAL 2800–4000 metres (3060 yards–4400 yards) (easy recovery session OR passive rest/massage).

Tuesday
Warm up/stretching (400–600 metres [440–660 yards]).
Fartlek session for 1½ to 2½ kilometres (1–1½ miles) with training intensity varying between levels 2–5.
Cooldown 400 metres (440 yards).
TOTAL 3000–3500 metres (3300–3830 yards) moderate difficulty session).

Wednesday
Rest day or technique session: 800–1000 metres (880–1100 yards) at level 1. Interchangeable with Thursday session.

Thursday
Warm up/stretching (400–600 metres [440–660 yards]).
8–15 x 100 metres (110 yards) at levels 3–4 (rest for 5–10 seconds).
400–600 metre (440–660 yard) recovery at level 2.
10–20 x 25–50 metres (27–55 yards) at level 5 (rest 30–45 seconds).
Cooldown level 1–2 for 400 metres (440 yards).

TOTAL 2250–4100 metres (2460–4480 yards) (moderate to high level of difficulty).

Friday

Warm up/stretching (400–600 metres [440–660 yards]).

5 x 200 metres (220 yards) at level 3 (10–15 second rest between efforts).

8–12 x 50–100 metres (55–110 yards) at level 4 (20–30 second rest between efforts).

4–6 x 25 metres (27 yards) at level 5 (20 second rest between efforts).

Cooldown levels 1–2 for 400 metres (440 yards).

TOTAL 2300–3350 metres (2515–3664 yards) (moderate level of difficulty).

Saturday

Rest or gentle level 1 swim for 400–600 metres (440–660 yards) (preferably open water at the race venue).

Sunday: Race 1500 metres (1650 yards) (hard session).

WEEKLY TOTAL 7550–17 650 METRES (8256–19 204 YARDS).

The justification for each of the above training sessions is as follows:

Monday

After having raced on the Sunday this session allows the body to recover gently in a non-weight bearing activity.

Tuesday

This session offers a blend of recovery work while still allowing the triathlete to incorporate some speed work into the session as he/she sees fit and subjectively 'feels' like pushing a little harder.

Wednesday or Thursday

These two sessions are interchangeable depending upon the importance of the Sunday race. If it is a more important race the triathlete should take the Thursday as a rest day. If the race isn't so much of a concern, rest Wednesday and train the Thursday session as indicated. The Wednesday/Thursday session incorporates anaerobic threshold work, which helps force back exercise intensity capacity and develops the triathlete's ability to hold a constant work output at threshold. The 10–20 x 25–50 metre (27–55 yard) efforts at exercise intensity 5 with a long rest interval is designed to develop explosive power and strength, which may be important when (a) surging to stay with a bunch, (b) attempting to break away from a bunch, or (c) sprinting for a turning buoy or finish line.

Friday

The Friday session is quite short but conducted at a reasonably brisk pace. It isn't as hard as the Wednesday/Thursday session—either intensity or volume wise—as the focus of this session is to help the triathlete develop tempo, pacing and rhythm for the Sunday race.

Saturday

Saturday should be largely a rest day with the triathlete doing next to nothing. If the course isn't familiar the triathlete may wish to swim out on the course for a couple of hundred metres, then turn around and look back towards the finish line so that the landmarks on shore can be identified and utilized the following day for navigational purposes.

Sunday

Race: The acid test. Puts the previous training on trial.

THE RESTORATION PHASE

The previous sections indicated how to 'cycle' the training regimen through the three 'active' phases; the fourth phase—restoration—is largely passive. Rather than following specified, structured, training sessions on a weekly basis the triathlete should 'exercise at leisure'; in other words, if you feel like going for a swim, do so, if not, don't. The duration of the restoration period should be directly proportional to the length of the build up period and racing season. Therefore, the longer the competitive season the longer the restoration phase. Typically a racing season will last for 2–3 months, and the restoration phase will therefore last 4–6 weeks before the triathlete again commences his/her subsequent base phase training. Figure 1.2 (see page 18) illustrates this concept diagrammatically

Restoration, however, does not mean that the triathlete does nothing. If this were the case much of the base aerobic fitness that has been established would diminish. Additionally, muscle tissue will atrophy and the body fat levels will tend to increase. Rather, the triathlete should remain active during this phase but avoid highly structured training regimens.

Heart rate monitoring—either manually (see figure 3.7) or with the use of a waterproof heart rate monitor (see figure 3.8)—can be an extremely useful training/coaching tool. With a little experience triathletes can establish what their maximal heart rates are and develop a 'feel' for the heart rate intensity at which anaerobic threshold occurs (based upon subjective feelings of labored breathing, burning sensations within the exercising muscle groups and the like). By doing this the triathlete can maximize training gains by exercising hard at appropriate times and recovering when necessary. For example, when a triathlete becomes excessively fatigued and then tries to complete an

Figure 3.7: With a little practice you can learn to monitor your heart manually.

Figure 3.8: Heart rate monitors are a valuable training tool.

'effort' that requires a significant elevation in heart rate, often the limbs are so fatigued that the heart rate can not be elevated to a sufficiently high enough level to be of cardiovascular benefit. In such a situation the triathlete would be better served by cutting the training session short and allowing for recovery.

Resistance training. Resistance training can be broken up into two distinct types (i) in-pool, which requires the use of 'swim aids' (hand paddles, pull buoys, drag suits, ankle bands, etc., see figure 3.9) or (ii) out-of-pool, which incorporates poolside resistance exercises (with latex surgical tubing) and weight room exercises. The latter category of exercises has been covered in detail in Appendix A. This chapter will focus on specific in-pool devices which can be used to increase muscular strength and endurance for swimming.

Paddles. As with any resistance work, the greater the load and the lower the number of repetitions the more the strength component of training is emphasized. Therefore, if the triathlete has a strength deficit in any phase of his/her swim stroke, paddles can be a useful adjunct to the training program to help rectify this shortcoming as they

 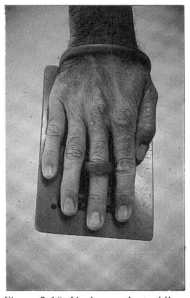

Figure 3.9: Some of the equipment that can be used to improve swimming performance.

Figure 3.10: Used correctly, paddles can improve both specific swimming strength and stroke mechanics.

increase the training load and help to promote upper body strength. Some coaches claim that paddles can also be useful by increasing the surface area of the hand and therefore helping to improve the triathlete's 'feel' for the water. On the downside, excessive use of hand paddles—particularly during the early phases of training or with novice swimmers—can actually promote overuse injuries of the shoulder region. As with any training the introduction of paddles needs to be accomplished slowly and progressively. First the triathlete should use smaller paddles over shorter distances, progressing to larger paddles over longer distances as the body adapts to this greater training stress.

The benefits associated with in-pool resistance training are probably best achieved through the base and intermediate macrocycles of the training regimen, as, once the triathlete is within the peaking phase, training should be as specific as possible. By putting large hand paddles on the hands the triathlete's pull patterns, arm cadence etc. are changed from what the triathlete will experience on race day. If, however, the triathlete still wishes to train with hand paddles during the peaking phase it is permissible providing a smaller paddle is utilized—no bigger than the size of the hand.

Drag suits. As is the case with hand paddles, drag suits increase the resistance that the triathlete must overcome in order to move through the water. If this particular swim aid is to be used the triathlete would be best served by limiting the use of this device to early on in the initial preparation (base and intermediate phases) and alternating it with explosive power/strength work (25–50 metre [27–55 yard] efforts) in which the technique isn't so critical.

Figure 3.11: Swimming with a drag suit creates additional resistance which stresses the swimming muscles in a highly specific manner.

Pull buoys. Only approximately 10–15% of forward momentum in swimming is derived from the legs. Generally it is agreed that the kicking motion of the legs is primarily used to stabilize and streamline the body. In triathlons, triathletes normally utilize a two-beat kick and often compete in wetsuits, which automatically improves the triathlete's body position in the water by placing the legs in a more streamlined position. In comparison to swimmers, triathletes stress their legs much more; consequently swim training is often completed with fatigued legs. Kicking in the pool can often augment this fatigue without contributing very much to race performance. For these reasons a pull buoy is beneficial from two perspectives: it (a) removes the need for the triathlete to kick to any great extent by allowing the legs to trail in a streamlined fashion—this allows some degree of recovery in the legs by de-emphasizing the kick—and (b) allows the triathlete to simulate the type of swimming that will likely be experienced during racing with a wetsuit on. Obviously triathletes shouldn't complete all their swim training with a pull buoy, particularly if upcoming competitions do not allow wetsuits. However, due to the specific nature of the training and the recovery that such an aid allows, a considerable

proportion of swim training should be conducted in this manner (40–70% depending upon the training phase and/or race specific considerations—fresh water, no wetsuits etc.).

Figure 3.12: The pull buoy helps to decrease frontal drag as well as simulate wetsuit swimming.

Figure 3.13: Ankle bands can place additional stress on the swimming muscles of the upper body by increasing frontal drag.

Fins. Those triathletes who don't have a swimming background often have poor plantar flexion through the ankle region (see figure 3.15 a/b) as a legacy of running and cycling, which de-emphasize movement in this plane and in actual fact are counterproductive to it. As a consequence, when such triathletes start to swim freestyle they are unable to achieve adequate plantar flexion to maintain a streamlined body position in the water. Consequently performance is decreased as the foot position creates additional drag (see figure 3.15b). By incorporating fins into the training regimen the triathlete is able to develop improved ankle flexibility faster—with the fin promoting tendon, ligament and muscle stretching through the front part of the lower leg and foot region. As with all other

Figure 3.14: Fins are useful for helping to improve ankle flexibility.

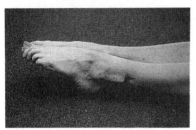

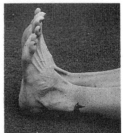

Figure 3.15(a): The ankle in a
plantar-flexed position.

Figure 3.15(b): The ankle in
a dorsi-flexed position.

training, the quantity of this type of training must be built up slowly and used sparingly as it fatigues the lower limbs quickly. If this is added to an already hectic cycling and running schedule this may have detrimental effects on training/performance in these two disciplines. Therefore any use of this adjunct to swim training must be limited, with its primary focus not so much as a 'training set' to improve cardiovascular fitness, but rather as flexibility training for the ankles.

REFERENCES:
1. Jacobs, 1986, 'Blood lactate implications for training and sports performance', *Sports Medicine* 3, pp. 10–25.
2. Beck, Mader, Muller & Hollman, 1986, 'Lactate threshold in the guidance of training', *Deutsche Zeitschrift fur Sport Medizin* Special Issue, pp. 10–15.
3. Costill, D., & Hargeaves, M., 1990, 'Carbohydrate, nutrition and fatigue', Proceeding of Fatigue Symposium. Footscray Institute of Technology, Victoria, Australia, pp. 56–61.

PART THREE
JUST ROLLIN' ALONG

Chapter Four

The Biomechanics of Cycling

Dr. Brian McLean

Cycling may appear to be a straightforward activity but the interaction between the body and the machine is a complex one, and the performance of the body–bicycle system can be influenced by many variables. One of the most fundamental factors affecting performance is the position of the body on the bike. Riding position influences the power that can be produced to move the bike, the physiological efficiency with which this power can be produced, and the resistance to motion caused by wind drag. Another important component contributing to bicycle performance is pedalling technique. The power required to move the bicycle is produced by applying force to the pedals, and the pedalling technique by which this force is applied can in many cases be improved. The choice of equipment will also affect the overall performance, as the aerodynamic characteristics and weight of the bicycle and rider influence the retarding forces which have to be overcome during cycling. In addition, the relative importance of weight and wind drag will vary according to the course and the conditions, and the most appropriate choice of equipment for one course may not be the same for another. By gaining an understanding of how these variables influence performance and by following a systematic approach to optimizing them you will get the best from your cycling effort.

RIDING POSITION

To a certain extent the bicycle is adjustable in that seat height, seat fore/aft position, handlebar stem length and handlebar height can all be altered. However, these parameters are adjustable only within certain limits, and the first step in being able to get the optimum riding position on the bicycle is getting a bicycle frame with the most appropriate dimensions. The dimensions describing the geometry of the bicycle are shown in figure 4.1. The most important measurement on a bicycle frame which customizes it to your particular body is the seat tube length, and this dimension can be determined from the measurement of lower limb length.

Top tube length is also important in customizing a frame, but this

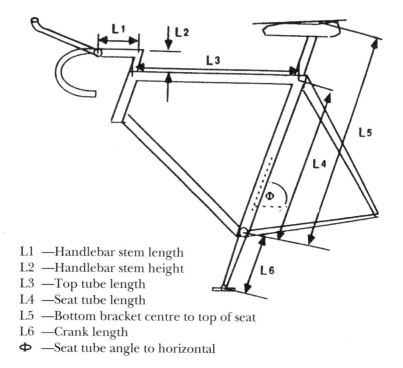

L1 —Handlebar stem length
L2 —Handlebar stem height
L3 —Top tube length
L4 —Seat tube length
L5 —Bottom bracket centre to top of seat
L6 —Crank length
Φ —Seat tube angle to horizontal

Figure 4.1 Dimensions describing the geometry of a bicycle

measurement is usually within 2 cm (¾ in) of the seat tube length even for those with custom built frames. Rather than top tube length alone, the relevant length for optimum upper body riding position is the top tube length plus handlebar stem length. Differences in top tube length can therefore be accounted for by selecting a suitable stem length. For road cyclists whose handlebar and stem are fairly standardized in their dimensions, this combined length can be prescribed within a small range of tolerance based on their upper body dimensions. For triathletes the many different systems of aerodynamic handlebars currently on the market, from those that allow adjustment to those that have no adjustment for position, make the prescription of a top tube and stem length difficult. The method used to overcome this problem is to observe the correct posture required to optimize riding position and aerodynamics and then select appropriately sized components that allow this posture to be achieved.

All the dimensions describing the optimum riding position can be prescribed from anthropometric measurements. To accurately determine these dimensions some basic anatomy is required and is included here since its knowledge is necessary in the prescription of riding position.

Greater trochanter. This is the large knob of bone just under the skin at the side of the upper thigh.

First thoracic vertebra. The vertebra beneath that which stands out most prominently beneath the skin at the base of the neck when the head is tilted forward.

Acromion process. The bony prominence beneath the skin at the side of the shoulder and the top of the arm.

Lateral epicondyle of the humerus. The large bony prominence on the outside of the elbow.

Head of the ulna. The bony prominence on the back of the wrist on the side opposite the thumb.

Lower Limb Length

Accurate measurement of the lower limb length is required to prescribe the seat tube length and the seat height. Lower limb length is defined as the height of the greater trochanter from the floor (trochanteric height). To determine the trochanteric height exactly, first find the bony surface just beneath the skin by pushing hard into the skin with the thumb. Then start moving upwards little by little until you can feel that you are pushing down on top of the bony knob. Mark this point on the skin. Measure from this point vertically down to the ground with feet slightly apart. This is the lower limb length. Figure 4.2 shows this trochanteric height

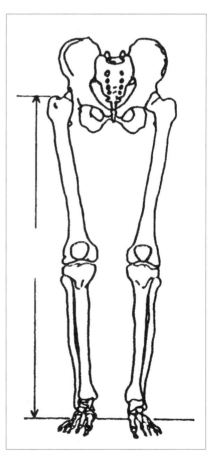

Figure 4.2: Trochanteric height measurement.

measurement and highlights the fact that the measurement must be to the top of the bone and not to the position where the bone is closest under the skin.

Choosing the Correct Frame Size
Having accurately determined this measurement seat tube length can be determined from figure 4.3.

TROCHANTERIC HEIGHT		SEAT TUBE LENGTH	
(cm)	(ins)	(cm)	(ins)
84.0	33.00	51.0	20.08
86.0	33.85	52.0	20.47
87.0	34.25	52.5	20.67
88.0	34.64	53.0	20.87
89.0	35.00	53.5/54.0	21.06/21.26
90.0	35.43	54.0/54.5	21.26/21.45
91.0	35.83	55.0	21.65
92.0	36.22	55.50	21.85
93.0	36.61	56.0	22.00
94.0	37.00	56.5	22.25
95.0	37.40	57.0	22.44
96.0	37.80	57.5/58.0	22.64/22.83
97.0	38.20	58.0/58.5	22.83/23.00
98.0	38.60	59.0	23.22
99.0	38.98	59.5	23.43
100.0	39.37	60.0	23.62
101.0	39.76	60.5	23.81
102.0	40.15	61.0	24.00
103.0	40.55	61.5/62.0	24.21/24.40
104.0	40.94	62.0/62.5	24.40/24.60
105.0	41.34	63.0	24.80

Figure 4.3: Bicycle seat tube length vs. lower limb length.

You don't want a bike any bigger than the size indicated in the table, but you may prefer to have a bike slightly smaller than this size as is the trend with many road racing cyclists. A smaller bike offers the advantage of being slightly lighter and stiffer. If you do choose this route a bicycle with a seat tube up to one centimetre smaller than shown in the table should be appropriate. However, if you choose a bicycle with seat tube length more than 1 cm (⅜ in) smaller than that prescribed in figure 4.3 you may have trouble getting a standard seat post long enough to achieve your optimum saddle height.

Determining Optimum Seat Height

It has long been known from laboratory studies that an optimum seat height exists both for minimizing oxygen cost and maximizing short-term power output. Our studies have shown that elite cyclists after many years of trial and error assessment of seat position arrive at a seat height which is very close to the optimum predicted from these laboratory studies. Consequently, we can be confident that the optimum predicted in the laboratory is also a realistic position that can withstand the practical realities of cycling, such as long hours in the saddle. Optimum saddle height is determined from lower limb length; however, we have also found that the type of shoe and the pedal system used will also have an influence on determining saddle height.

In the last few years there has been an explosion in the number of shoe pedal systems available for use by the cyclist. The traditional toe clip and strap with the slotted cleat under the shoe are rarely seen and now the 'ski type' binding of the LOOK and TIME pedal systems predominate. These newer systems offer the advantage of a more secure and comfortable attachment of the shoe to the pedals. In addition, there are many different shoes on the market and these come with different sole thickness.

The differing combinations of shoe and pedal systems can lead to differing thickness from the surface of the insole of the shoe, which makes contact with the foot, to the bottom surface of the cleat, which makes contact with the upper surface of the pedal. This thickness, which we call the sole/cleat thickness, effectively lengthens the lower limb and must be taken into consideration when determining the optimum seat height. In our laboratory we have measured sole/cleat thicknesses between 13 mm and 40 mm (½–1½ ins). Whenever a cyclist changes shoes or pedal system this thickness must be remeasured and appropriate changes made to the seat height. Further, many athletes now use orthotic devices in their cycling shoes. These are often only placed under the rear foot but if they are also under the forefoot then this thickness must be considered. The sole/cleat thickness should be determined with the orthotic in place.

Shoe sole/cleat thickness is measured from the upper surface of the shoe inner sole where the foot makes contact, to the bottom of the shoe cleat at the surface which makes contact with the pedal. In the case of traditional shoe cleats that are held by toe clips and straps this surface is at the base of the slot in the cleat. For Time pedals the sole of the shoe makes contact directly with the upper surface of the pedal and hence the thickness should be measured to the sole of the shoe only and not to the bottom of the cleat attachments. Knowing both lower limb length and sole/cleat thickness, the optimum seat height is prescribed by the formula:

Saddle Height = 0.98 (lower limb length + sole/cleat thickness).

This saddle height is defined on the bicycle in the following way: Bicycle saddle to crank axle distance is measured from the bottom of a straight edge placed between the rear and the tip of the bicycle seat, down to the centre of the crank axle, along the line of the bicycle seat tube. Saddle height is defined as saddle to crank axle distance plus crank length. (Saddle height = L5 + L6, see figure 4.1.)

Choosing a Crank Length
The relationship between crank length and lower limb length is not able to be so readily defined as the saddle height/lower limb length relationship. Unlike the relationship between seat height and lower limb length which shows an optimum relationship for both power output and oxygen uptake, as yet no optimum for crank length has been determined. However, we can get some indication of suitable crank length for different size legs by examining what elite cyclists are using.

We have found that many elite road cyclists are just as likely to choose one length as another. Only for cyclists with short or long limbs is the choice of crank length likely to be clear cut. Based on our study of internationally elite road cyclists, figure 4.4 indicates which crank length a cyclist with a lower limb length falling in any of the ranges shown would be most likely to use.

As the figure shows, for most lower limb length except the very short or very long there is a choice of two lengths. The fact that some cyclists with limbs from 91–95 cm (35¾–37½ ins) are likely to choose cranks of either length supports the fact that at present it is not clear which crank length is optimum for any athlete. Although a definitive crank length cannot at this time be confidently prescribed, this table may help you to make the decision as to which crank length you intend to use. Another factor worth considering in making your decision is that road time trial cyclists frequently use slightly longer cranks when time trialling than when riding road races.

TROCHANTERIC HEIGHT cm(in)	CRANK LENGTH USED mm
Less than 87.7 (34½)	170
87.7–90.7 (34½–35¾)	170 or 172.5
9 0.7–9 5.0 (35½–37½)	170 or 172.5 or 175
9 5.0–9 9.7 (37½–39¼)	172.5 or 175
longer than 99.7 (39¼)	175

Figure 4.4: Crank length vs. lower limb length.

Setting the Handlebars

Setting the correct position for the aerodynamic handlebars which are required to be competitive in triathlon requires optimizing the riding position to reduce aerodynamic drag and promote comfort and stability while riding. While standard road handlebars are necessary to provide handling stability and safety when road racing or training with a bunch, any triathlete or time trial cyclist who does not use aerodynamic handlebars when competing is disadvantaged compared to those who do. To understand how triathlon bars can provide an advantage we need to consider how wind resistance affects cycling speed, and this involves a little physics.

Wind resistance is not constant at all cycling speeds but increases with the square of the velocity. This means that as a cyclist doubles his speed from 20 to 40 km/hr (13–25 mph) wind resistance will increase four times. To overcome this wind resistance the power required is proportional to the wind resistance multiplied by the velocity. Thus the power required to overcome wind resistance is proportional to the cube of the velocity. The power needed to overcome wind resistance at 40 km/hr (25 mph) is consequently eight times that at 20 km/hr (13 mph). Rolling resistance on the other hand is constant at any velocity and consequently at velocities around 30 km/hr (19 mph) wind resistance makes up nearly 90% of the total resistance the bike rider has to overcome. At time trial velocities greater than 40 km/hr

(25 mph), wind resistance is close to 100% of the total.

Although velocity has the largest influence on wind resistance it is also dependent on the frontal surface area projected to the wind and the shape of the body moving through it. The larger the frontal surface area the greater the amount of oncoming air that strikes the body and the greater the force needed to move through it. Frontal surface area is influenced by your size and your position on the bicycle. Size is important as a bigger bike rider will have a bigger frontal surface area. Similarly, an upright position will project a larger surface area to the wind than a crouched position. Shape is also important, as the shape affects the amount of turbulence of the wind as it moves over a body. Some shapes cause more turbulence than others and even if they have the same frontal surface area the increased turbulence will increase the wind drag. In the case of the bike rider, shape is influenced by the posture and the positioning of the limbs and head.

It is the difference that triathlon bars make to position that underlies their effectiveness. Triathlon bars allow you to ride in a position that reduces your frontal surface area, and they reduce the turbulence created by the arms and back. These changes in position reduce the force of the wind drag and thus reduce the power required to ride at any speed. By setting up your position so that you present as small a surface as possible to the oncoming air and reduce turbulence you will minimize wind drag.

This is how the triathlon bars provide their advantage. A further advantage of the bars is that in long time trials, because the forearms are supported, the trunk does not have to be held up and the aerodynamic position can then be held comfortably for long periods. However, knowing how to set up a position for triathlon bars is not straightforward. The wide range of positions used by triathletes using these bars, and the experimental nature of many of these positions, has not allowed the emergence of consistent guidelines. The special needs of the triathlete in having to run immediately after stepping off the bike has prompted the search for a position that makes it easier on the legs when that transition occurs. Some triathletes feel that benefit may be gained from being well forward with respect to the bottom bracket; however, the suggestion that this position is more biomechanically efficient for pedalling has yet to be proven true or false.

Analysis of the time trial position of two world class athletes, one who uses a standard seat position and the other a forward seat position, provides insight into the similarities of the two methods of positioning.

Figure 4.5(a): Schematic diagram of the time trial position of Shane Cleveland.

The standard seat position is that of Greg Lemond and was analysed from the photos taken of him when in the final time trial of the 1989 Tour de France. The forward seat position is that of duathlete Shane Cleveland and was analysed from photos published of him in the 1991 Desert Princess Race in California. The figures (figure 4.5a/b) show that although Cleveland is sitting well forward with his hips almost vertically above the bicycle bottom bracket and Lemond is sitting well behind the bottom bracket, the trunk and arm posture is similar in both. Both these positions display the characteristics of good aerodynamics with respect to the trunk and the arms. This analysis shows that the forward seated position is not a prerequisite for achieving a good aerodynamic position.

The results of our wind tunnel tests with the Australian Road Time Trial Team at the Royal Melbourne Institute of Technology in conjunction with the results of tests carried out in the US have provided clear

Figure 4.5(b): Schematic diagram of the time trial position of Greg Lemond.

guidelines on how to best achieve the optimum aerodynamic position. There are two main aspects that have to be considered in achieving an aerodynamic position on the bicycle. The first is flatness of the back, both relative to the horizontal and to reduce any arching of the spine. Bringing the trunk down so that the top of the back is more horizontal reduces the frontal surface area, while flattening the back to decrease any arching reduces the turbulence behind the rider. Both these changes have significant effect on the wind drag. The other component of position is that of the arms. In general, the closer the arms are together the lower the wind drag. By bringing your arms up in front of the body and having them closer together the frontal surface area projected to the wind is smaller. With the elbows wide the arms catch a lot of air, which increases the resistance. As the elbows are drawn closer towards the centre, the body drafts in the arms' slipstream thereby decreasing turbulence.

The other aspect of the time trial position that has not been clearly defined is the setting of the angle of the bars relative to the horizontal. Many athletes achieve the basic requirements of an aerodynamic time trial position by getting the back flat and low and having the arms narrow. However, there is still much debate amongst time trial cyclists and triathletes as to what is the optimum angle of the bars. Most frequently a position with the forearms at an upward tilt from 15° to 30° is suggested. Our wind tunnel tests indicate that the angle of the bars with the least drag was with the forearms between 5° and 20° above the horizontal. Of the four athletes tested in the wind tunnel, two showed substantially lower drag with the forearms at 5° of upward tilt compared to 20°, while the other two showed similar drag with the forearms at 5° and 20°. In all athletes, drag increased dramatically when the forearms were tilted up to 40°. These findings suggest that setting the bars so that the forearms are tilted slightly upward from the horizontal should get you close to the optimum position.

The basic characteristics of the time trial positions of Lemond and Cleveland and the measurements used to describe them are outlined here to give an indication of what characterizes a good aerodynamic time trial position. In both riders the trunk is low with the upper part of the back being flat. The angle of the upper body above the horizontal is approximately 20° for Lemond and 26° for Cleveland. This is measured by a line from the large bone just under the skin at the side of the upper thigh (the greater trochanter) to the vertebra that stands out most prominently beneath the skin at the base of the neck when the head is tilted forward (first thoracic vertebra). The arm position is not excessively stretched out in front. The upper arms are slightly forward, making an angle of 18° with the vertical for Lemond and 9° for Cleveland. The line of the upper arm joins the centre of the shoulder (acromial process) to the large bone on the outside of the elbow (lateral epicondyle of the humerus). The forearms are slightly tilted up so that they make an angle of 8° to the horizontal for Lemond and 17° for Cleveland. The line of the forearm joins the same bony prominence on the elbow (lateral epicondyle of the humerus) to the bony prominence on the back of the wrist on the side opposite the thumb (head of the ulna).

To assess your own time trial position, the measurements described can be taken with a little care using a level, a protractor, a straight edge and a plumb bob. You will also need a few extra hands.

Other Considerations in Refining Riding Position

When changing the fore–aft position of the seat, because the bicycle seat tube (see figure 4.1) is angled to the horizontal (usually between 72° and 75°, but in some triathlon bikes this angle is much greater) moving the seat backward puts you further from the centre bracket and effectively increases seat height. Conversely, moving the seat forward effectively reduces seat height. With a typical seat tube angle of 74° and a measurement of 750 mm (29½ in) from the centre of the bottom bracket to the top of the seat, moving the seat forward 10 mm (⅜ in) will effectively reduce seat height approximately 3 mm (⅛ in). This needs to be considered if you are one of those triathletes who does choose to have a radically forward position.

Getting your position low at the front of the bike (i.e. with the handlebars) requires flexibility of the spine and may cause your pelvis to tilt forward, which will transfer your weight a little further forward onto your pubic area. This can get uncomfortable, particularly as you usually have little chance to stand up on the pedals to relieve the pressure on this area when riding a flat course. To compensate for this the seat may need to be tilted slightly downward at the front.

Improved Pedalling Technique

Getting the correctly sized bicycle, choosing a suitable crank length for your body size, optimizing the riding position and using the most appropriate aerodynamic equipment will maximize the contribution made by equipment to your riding performance. But what of the pedalling action that produces this cycling performance? How do you optimize that?

Becoming a skillful pedaller involves much practice and, without a means to assess pedalling technique, it is difficult to identify 'good' technique and to know if improvements are being made. It has been the lack of objective information on pedalling technique which has made it difficult for cyclists to know if they are pedalling effectively and what to do to improve. By assessing the biomechanics of pedalling technique, using force sensitive cranks or pedals to measure the forces applied during pedalling, improvement may be gained if information on inefficiencies is available to the cyclist.

Biomechanical analysis of the forces applied to the pedals and cranks during pedalling has provided valuable insight into pedalling technique and produced some interesting findings. One surprising finding was that the widely held belief that cyclists 'pull up' in the

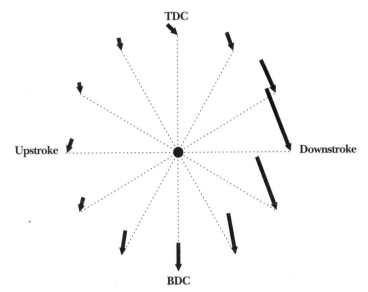

Figure 4.6: Typical pattern of force application on the pedal at different positions of the pedal stroke. The arrows indicate the size and direction of the pedal force.

recovery portion of the pedal stroke and thereby produce a useful propulsive force on the cranks throughout the entire pedal stroke is generally untrue. In a study in our laboratory the force application on the pedals was compared between elite and recreational cyclists. Both the recreational and the elite cyclists showed negative or counterproductive forces in the pedal upstroke. Even the elite cyclists did not pull up in the upstroke. The presence of this counterproductive force effectively means that during the downthrust of the pedal stroke the cyclist is lifting the other leg to the top of its stroke. Thus, retarding force has first to be overcome before the resultant propulsive force moves the bicycle.

Shown in figure 4.6 is a typical pattern of force application on the pedal during one crank revolution while cycling at steady state. Note that throughout the stroke there is a generally downward acting force on the pedal. Maximum force occurs in the middle of the downstroke at around 90° past the top dead centre of the pedal stroke. At this position the pedal force is almost perpendicular to the line of the crank and consequently nearly all of the force applied is used to spin the crank. At the bottom dead centre of the pedal stroke the force applied to the crank remains quite large but still acts almost directly downwards. Thus little or no useful force is applied in the direction of movement of the crank. For nearly all of the upstroke the pedal force acts primarily downward, which is opposite to the direction of travel of the crank, and opposes forward movement of the bicycle. Although this pattern is typical of most steady state cycling, under some conditions such as sprinting and during hill climbing the downward forces during the upstroke are greatly reduced and pedal forces may even become productive all the way around the stroke.

Even though the elite and recreational cyclists studied showed negative torque in the pedal upstroke there were differences in the pedalling technique between the groups. The elite cyclists started pulling backwards on the pedals before the cranks reached bottom dead centre and continued pulling on the back of the pedal for much of the pedal upstroke. Consequently, although both groups had negative force in the upstroke the elite cyclists by pulling backward on the pedal had less negative force in the upstroke than the recreational cyclists. This was particularly evident in the portion of the upstroke from the bottom dead centre of the pedal stroke to 270° past the top dead centre.

Further work carried out in our laboratory has shown that highly trained cyclists can improve their pedalling technique by reducing the counterproductive forces in the pedal upstroke. This was achieved by using a system of computer-assisted feedback of the forces developed on the cranks.

The retarding effect of negative forces on the crank in the upstroke was monitored during pedalling so that an attempt could be made to reduce them. The cyclists rode at 90 rpm at a workload that would produce a speed of about 35 km/hr (22 mph), while watching a computer screen which continually indicated the inefficiencies in their technique. As they rode, the cyclists attempted to decrease counterproductive forces in the pedal upstroke which were highlighted by the computer feedback.

By using this system these cyclists were able to reduce the counterproductive forces occurring in the pedal upstroke. Because these negative forces were reduced this meant that less force was then required during the downthrust to overcome the counterproductive forces produced by the other limb during its upstroke. Not only was counterproductive force reduced, but the change in pedalling technique caused productive work to be continued for a greater period beyond bottom dead centre. Despite these improvements, in all cyclists

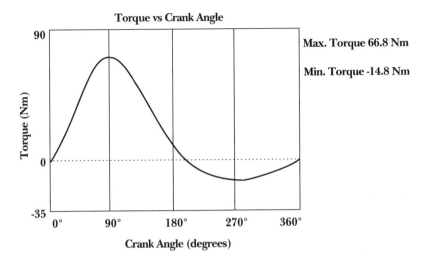

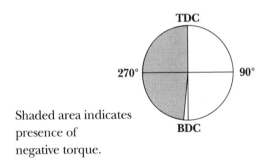

Shaded area indicates presence of negative torque.

Figure 4.7(a): Representative pattern of crank torque characteristics: before feedback training.

counterproductive forces consistently occurred in that section of the upstroke 90° before top dead centre (figure 4.7b).

The cyclists continued the computer feedback training for four weeks with continual improvement in pedalling technique throughout this period. Athough these cyclists were instructed to attempt to eliminate negative forces no cyclist was able to accomplish this goal. Even after four weeks of feedback training negative forces remained in the 90° of the upstroke before top dead centre. What this indicates is that these cyclists were more able to improve their pedalling in that part of the pedal stroke which involved pulling back across the bottom of the stroke.

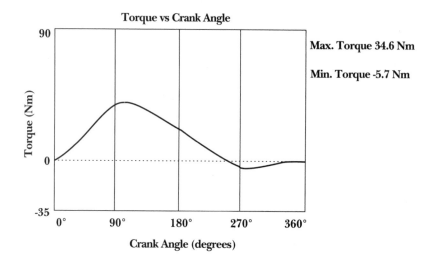

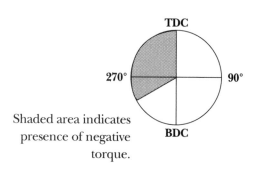

Shaded area indicates
presence of negative
torque.

Figure 4.7(b): Representative pattern of crank torque characteristics: following four weeks of feedback training.

The results of these studies have highlighted the differences between the pedalling techniques of elite and recreational cyclists and demonstrated that even highly trained cyclists can improve their pedalling technique by reducing the counterproductive forces in the pedal upstroke. It would appear that for cyclists attempting to improve their technique most benefit would be gained by concentrating on pulling back across the bottom of the pedal stroke (figure 4.8).

EQUIPMENT CHOICES

To make informed decisions about which equipment to choose to enhance cycling performance it is necessary to once again examine

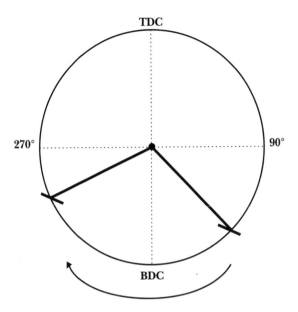

TDC

270°   90°

BDC

Figure 4.8: Improvements in pedalling technique are most likely to be gained by pulling backwards across the bottom of the pedal stroke.

some of the basic physics that underlies cycling.

Pedalling a bicycle at any given speed requires different amounts of physical effort depending on whether you are riding on a flat road into a cross wind, speeding down an incline with the wind at your back, or struggling up a hill. In each situation the forces that retard your efforts are a varying combination of rolling resistance, wind drag and the effect of gravity. An understanding of these forces and how each affects different riding conditions allows a cyclist to make decisions that will either conserve energy or let him ride faster.

Rolling resistance is encountered as the tire deforms to pass over the road beneath it and is influenced by body weight, tire pressure, wheel diameter, and tire tread. Of these factors body weight has the largest effect on rolling resistance, being directly related to its magnitude. For two athletes riding the same wheels and tires, pumped to the same pressure, rolling resistance will be greater for the heavier cyclist.

The type of tire and the tire pressure will also affect rolling resistance. Tubulars and high quality clinchers have the lowest rolling resistance. The new models of clinchers have rolling resistance that is comparable to tubular tires when compared at the same tire pressure. A factor often overlooked, however, is that good quality singles can usually be pumped to a higher pressure than clinchers, thereby reducing their rolling resistance even further. Another advantage of single tires and rims is that, combined, they will weigh less than clincher tires and rims. These two factors explain the 'life' that you feel in good singles.

Wheel diameter also affects rolling resistance. The larger the diameter the lower the resistance. Why then is a 24-in wheel used on some time trial bikes? This really has to do with wind resistance as a smaller wheel has a lower wind resistance. It can also allow the cyclist to get lower at the front thereby improving the aerodynamics of the rider position. The real advantage of wheels smaller than 26-in only becomes apparent in team cycling events where it allows the cyclist to draft closer to the rider in front, thereby reducing the required power output. In individual events the increased rolling resistance will offset the advantage of lower wind resistance to some extent, and with wheels less than 26-in the increase in rolling resistance may be greater than the reduction in wind resistance.

Once rolling resistance has been determined by the type of tire, the pressure, wheel diameter and weight of the rider, it will remain constant, independent of the speed of the cyclist. Wind resistance as we have already seen does not remain constant but increases with the square of the velocity and consequently at time trial speeds wind resistance is the dominant resisting force to be overcome.

Because the majority of time while cycling is spent sitting, and the wheels transform your energy into movement along the road, the effect of gravity does not become important until you begin climbing. When riding on the flat no force is required to overcome gravity, but when climbing, the force is proportional to the steepness of the climb and the weight of the cycle and rider. Further, as the velocity during climbing drops markedly the wind resistance also drops dramatically, and the forces due to gravity can become the major resistance to be overcome. It is here that the smaller rider comes into his own but, conversely, during the descent the extra weight of the larger cyclist will give him an advantage and he will descend faster.

However, if the climb and the descent are of the same distance then the climb will take much longer than the descent because of the large difference in speed. Thus, the time lost by the larger cyclist cannot be recovered during the descent and the smaller rider consequently has the advantage in hilly courses. For both athletes any reduction in weight will be advantageous.

So what conclusions can be made by understanding how these forces retard your cycling effort? The effect of weight is important in rolling resistance, climbing and accelerating. Lower total weight in the frame, component parts and most importantly, body weight, will reduce the forces needed to be overcome, and consequently the power output required to cycle at any speed. It should be noted with respect to body weight that it is only excess fat that should be reduced. Extra muscle will give you the capacity to produce more power.

When cycling at speeds greater than 15 km/hr (10 mph) on the flat, wind resistance becomes the dominant force to be overcome, and in these conditions component aerodynamics and the aerodynamics of bike position have their largest effect. The changes that can be made to your bike by replacing components with lighter or more aerodynamic parts can provide a significant advantage in the cycle time trial performance. However, the largest influence you can have on cycling performance is by optimizing your position on the bicycle. This aspect has been covered already in position setting, but it is repeated here to emphasize the importance of getting a good aerodynamic position on the bicycle. The thousands of dollars spent on optimizing the aerodynamics of the bicycle may be wasted if the gains made here are offset by a poor riding position.

These aspects should be kept in mind when considering the equipment choices that are discussed in this section.

Wheels

After getting an optimum position on the bicycle the next factor that can have a large effect on cycling performance is the choice of wheels. Wheels have a double effect on aerodynamic load because not only are they moving in a straight line through the air, but they are also rotating. That is, a certain amount of power would be required to spin the wheel at 40 km/hr (25 mph) even if the wheel is stationary. This is caused by the rotation of the spokes in the air and is sometimes known as the 'egg beater effect'. The other aerodynamic drag force is caused by the wheel moving along the road at a given speed.

The types of wheels to choose from include conventional spoke and rim wheels, composite construction 3–5 spoke aerodynamic wheels, and either flat or lens-shaped disk wheels. With conventional wheels, since they are built up from separate components, the choices include: the shape of the spokes, either flat, oval or round; the number of spokes, from 16–36; and the shape of the rim, either box-shaped or aerodynamic.

With conventional wheels, thirty-six round spokes and box-shaped rims are the worst combination of components you can choose. While this choice is probably the most suitable for training due to their toughness and reliability, they are definitely not fast. With these type of wheels the number and shape of spokes has the largest effect on drag. Spoke shape is the first consideration. Bladed spokes are best with oval spokes only slightly worse. Round spokes have a very high drag.

Spoke number is the next consideration. The fewer spokes in a wheel the lower the drag. However, a wheel with less spokes is not as strong and there is obviously a trade-off in reliability. A super fast wheel is of no benefit if it does not get you to the finish. Although spoke number is important, shape is more important. A wheel with eighteen round spokes has higher drag than one with twenty-eight bladed spokes.

The other consideration is the shape of the rim. Aero rims are more aerodynamic than flat box-shaped rims and are also strong due to their shape. This advantage in strength can help compensate for fewer spokes. Due to their strength they are also suitable on training wheels.

Composite 3–5 spoke aerodynamic wheels. These wheels have less drag than conventional spoked wheels. This is caused partly by the smaller number of spokes and partly by the aerodynamic shape of the spokes and rim. However, the best of the conventional wheels with 16–18 bladed spokes and aerodynamic rims are not a lot worse in drag characteristics than some of the composite-spoked wheels. Differences in drag between these wheels may only be of the order of 20 grams (0.71 oz), which corresponds to a performance difference at a power output required to ride at 47 km/hr (29 mph), of only approximately .14 seconds per kilometre. The mass of the spoked wheel may be up to a kilogram lighter however, and this may actually provide a performance advantage, especially if on a hilly course. A kilogram (2.2 lbs) of extra weight will increase the rolling resistance by as much as 6 seconds in 40 kilometres (25 miles). This will occur on a dead flat road, but once climbing is involved the weight penalty becomes more significant. On a circuit course containing equal up and down sections, a lighter wheel will provide a significant advantage. Only if the course is mostly downhill will a heavier wheel be an advantage.

There is some variability in the aerodynamic drag of different composite construction wheels and this is based on the number of spokes as well as the shape of the rim and spokes. The most efficient aerodynamic shape is teardrop shaped, with the width more than three times greater than the thickness. All composite-spoked wheels do not conform to this specification. Also, as with conventional wheels, the less spokes the lower the drag. Another aspect not to be overlooked is the weight of the wheel. These composite construction wheels can vary in weight by as much as half a kilogram (1.1 lb). We have already considered the effect this can have on performance. When choosing a composite-spoked wheel the considerations are number of spokes, shape of the rim and spokes, and the weight.

Disk wheels. Disk wheels generally have the lowest drag of all wheels. However, the best of the composite-spoked wheels have drag that is comparable to these. Lens-shaped and flat disks have similar drag characteristics when tested in the wind tunnel with the wind approaching straight on to the wheel. When the wind is a cross wind however, the lens-shaped disks have lower drag due to their shape which provides a lift component of force in the direction of the wind. This is the same effect seen with a wing and in this instance the lens-shaped disk is acting like a wing to some extent. Because lens-shaped disks are equal in performance to flat disks in headwinds but superior in cross winds, the lens-shaped disks can be considered the better choice on most occasions. As with composite-spoked wheels, disks vary a lot in weight with up to a kilogram (2.2 lb) difference between some brands. Extra weight, as we have seen, will provide a substantial penalty.

Tires

Although often overlooked, the choice and installation of tires can affect performance. The matching of tire size to the rim size is important in optimizing the aerodynamics of the wheel. Ideally tire and the rim cross section width should be the same. If the tire is narrower than the rim, air will separate from the rim as it leaves it, causing turbulence and reducing the advantage of the aerodynamic wheel. A tire that is wider than the rim increases the frontal-surfaces area of the wheel, which again reduces the advantage provided by the aerodynamic wheel.

In the introduction to this section the factors affecting rolling resistance were considered. Another factor that can have a very significant effect on the rolling resistance of tubular tires is the way they are fitted to the rim. Since tubular tires are glued to the rim there is the opportunity to fit them crookedly. If the tire is not aligned on the rim so that the tread runs straight, the rolling resistance of the tire will be much larger than what it would be if correctly fitted. This increase in rolling resistance can be such that an incorrectly fitted racing tubular containing twists or an off-centre tread, can have a higher rolling resistance than a correctly fitted training tubular. Take care to get tubulars properly aligned on the rim.

Clothing and Accessories

Apart from the athlete's position on the bike, and the wheels and tires, what other modifications can be made to the bicycle to improve performance? Loose fitting clothing that is wrinkled or flaps in the wind is an aerodynamic disaster. A flapping or gaping singlet is the equivalent of an air brake. The advantage gained by $2000 spent on aerodynamic wheels can easily be lost by a poor choice of clothing. Clothing should be close fitting if not tight, and made from smooth shiny material such as lycra which has lower aerodynamic drag than rougher material.

The correct choice of helmet can also have a dramatic effect on performance. An aerodynamic helmet can have as significant an advantage as a disc wheel. At 47 km/hr (29 mph) the difference in drag force between a good aerodynamic helmet and a helmet not designed for aerodynamics can be as high as 150 grams (5¼ oz). This is equivalent to the difference in drag force between a good quality disc wheel and a standard thirty-six round spoke wheel with a box-shaped rim. An adequate aerodynamic helmet will have a smoothly contoured teardrop shape, and either no vents or vents placed to the side or rear of the helmet.

Those shapes that are less aerodynamic are rounder, squatter, and have larger and more numerous vents. These helmets do however have the advantage of being cooler and in long events such as the Ironman there may be some trade-off between cooling and aerodynamics. For shorter or cooler events the advantage provided by an aerodynamic helmet should make the choice straightforward.

There is another consideration of aerodynamic helmets which perhaps should be considered under the topic of cycling position or riding form. As with loose clothing, an aerodynamic helmet can act as an air brake by dramatically increasing drag if the helmet is turned sideways into the wind. Turning the head to look behind, talk to another competitor or rest the neck will increase the air drag. Similarly, even when looking straight ahead there is an optimum tilt of the head which will minimize drag. Having the tail of the helmet point upwards, or in contrast sit on the rider's back, increases the drag. The best position is to have the bottom of the helmet in line with the rider's back, leaving a space between the base of the helmet and the back. Fortunately, this is a reasonably comfortable head position and encourages the cyclist to look ahead.

Water Bottles and Gear Changers

Two other simple alterations to the bicycle that can influence performance by improving aerodynamics are the addition of 'flite-control' gear levers and the use of an appropriate aerodynamic water bottle.

Flite-controls, while not actually improving the aerodynamics of the bicycle, allow the rider to shift gears while in the aerodynamic riding position. Moving out of the aerodynamic position to reach for the gear levers attached to the bicycle's down tube will increase drag and thus reduce the speed. Gear changes can be frequent depending on the course and the conditions, and each change will slow you down as you reach down for the gear levers.

The standard round water bottle attached to the bicycle down tube or seat tube is another aerodynamic liability. The shape of the bottle and its position on the bike can add up to 45 grams of drag which can mean a reduction of 15 seconds over 40 kilometres (25 miles). By using an aerodynamic bottle that is oval in shape the drag can be halved. However, as with changing gears, reaching down for the bottle will increase the drag of the system and reduce speed. The bike stream system which is housed behind the seat, will partly be protected from wind drag by drafting behind the seat and the rider's legs. Although no test data is available on this system it should have low drag and it has the added benefit of allowing the rider to stay in the aerodynamic riding position while taking a drink.

THE ALLSOP SUSPENSION SYSTEM

With this system the standard seat post and saddle is replaced by a cantilevered carbon fibre beam that is attached to a backwards sloping top tube. The beam system was designed to absorb some of the road shock that is transmitted up through the seat tube to the rider. This goal is achieved very effectively as the beam allows up and down movement at the seat of up to 50 mm (2-in) when under load. Although the Allsop softride system was designed primarily with comfort in mind, some triathletes have begun using it and have reported subjective performance advantages. Currently no data is available on how these bicycles may affect performance. As with other components on a bicycle, aerodynamics and weight should be considered when assessing the possible effects on performance. With this system the lack of a seat tube would not make a large difference to the aerodynamics in still conditions or in a headwind, as the frontal surface area of the bicycle is basically similar to a conventional bicycle. There may be some slight advantage in a crosswind, but the actual aerodynamic characteristics of the bicycle and rider together in this riding condition would most likely be similar to that of a conventional bicycle because the legs are moving in the area where the seat tube would normally be. Wind tunnel tests frequently show that the measured aerodynamic advantage of an aero bicycle is not maintained when it is tested with a cyclist on it. Weight, as we have seen, is also an important consideration. If the overall weight of the bicycle is heavier than a conventional bicycle this will be a disadvantage to performance.

The effect on pedalling mechanics is hard to assess. If seat height is set optimally, similar power outputs should be achieved as on a conventional bicycle. However, it is not clear exactly how much up and down movement occurs during normal riding and excessive movement would affect the efficiency of pedalling. Anecdotal reports suggest that initially the bicycle is difficult to ride with a smooth pedalling technique, particularly at high cadence. An adapted pedalling technique is required and it will be some time before the system feels comfortable. However some triathletes are using the system and reportedly feel positive about its benefits. One aspect of the system that may work favorably for the triathlete is the added comfort provided, particularly in long events. This may allow the athlete to use a little less energy, which can be utilized elsewhere, and may also make the transition from the bike to the run a little less painful. For those athletes who choose to ride the Allsop suspension system, I would suggest that attention is paid to obtaining an optimum seat height as described earlier. In this case, however, the seat height should be set with the rider sitting on the bike to allow for the lowering that occurs as the body weight is absorbed by the carbon fibre beam.

Chapter Five

Physiological Considerations in Cycling

Rod Cedaro

While sports may change, the basic physiological principles of endurance training remain constant as mentioned in the previous chapter, namely:

1. Build an aerobic base
2. Enhance central cardiovascular fitness.
3. Emphasize high quality, anaerobic threshold work.
4. Allow a period of restoration.
5. Cycle weekly microcycles and training sessions so as to avoid physiological/psychological burnout and associated over-training syndromes.

The type of cycle training that a triathlete must endure is different from that of a typical road cyclist. The energy system demands associated with road cycling tend to stress the aerobic system to 'sit in the bunch' and, to some degree, explosive anaerobic power to 'break away', or 'surge' or 'sprint' to the finish line. With triathlon, however, the triathlete must establish the ability to maintain a constant work output for the duration of the cycle leg. Consistent with this line of reasoning, the triathlete doesn't want to make the mistake of going all out in the first 10–15 kilometres (6–9 miles) of a 40 kilometre (25 mile) time trial only to find that the accumulation of lactic acid forces him/her to slow down over the remainder of the ride to dissipate this waste product and 'repay' the oxygen debt that has been established early on in the cycle leg. Therefore, the specific training for triathlon cycling needs to develop a sound aerobic base and push back the triathlete's anaerobic threshold to greater percentages of absolute maximal oxygen uptake. For example, see figure 5.1

What has transpired in figure 5.1 is that the triathlete's absolute aerobic capacity—70 ml.kg.min.—has not changed within the six-week training period. However, the triathlete's anaerobic threshold which

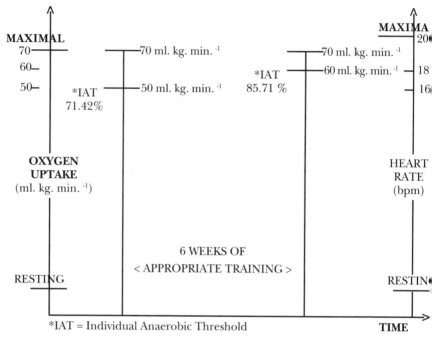

Figure 5.1

initially occurred at 50 ml.kg.min. (or 71.42% of maximal oxygen uptake) has, with effective training, been forced back to 60 ml.kg.min (or 85.71% of VO_2). Therefore this triathlete can now work approximately 14% harder and still not accumulate lactic acid and be forced to slow down. With appropriate testing and equipment (see Appendix C) it is possible to establish at what heart rate this anaerobic threshold occurs. Having established this in EACH of the THREE SEPARATE DISCIPLINES, the triathlete is then able to optimize training time to enhance this anaerobic threshold capacity.

It is wrong to assume that the various energy systems operate in a mutually exclusive fashion from one another. What does transpire, however, is that the emphasis of demands placed on the different energy systems change as the intensity of exercise does. That is to say as the triathlete starts to work harder the contribution to energy metabolism starts to favor glycolytic and the ATP–PC systems more and more, with resultant decreases in intramuscular and extracellular pH, increased concentrations of lactic acid and increased reliance on carbohydrate to meet energy requirements. If the triathlete attempts to maintain this degree of exercise intensity for too long, the degree of slowdown as a result of the need to stabilize the changes in homeostasis based on decreasing pH and lactate accumulation will be far greater than if the triathlete cycled at or slightly below anaerobic threshold for the entire duration of the event.

With more experienced and better conditioned triathletes, 'surging' can be a useful means by which to break away from an opponent, set up a better position going into the run transition or simply climb a hill without breaking one's pace. However, such a practice is not without its costs—those being that the triathlete must ease back at some stage in order to alleviate the accumulation of metabolic by-products that accrue within the working muscles as a direct consequence of the higher intensity exercise. Therefore, it is probably better for elite triathletes to endeavor to cycle at, or slightly less than, threshold for the majority of the ride, picking up intensity towards the end of the cycle leg and then allowing the change of muscle groups going into the run to provide the body with the recuperation that it requires. Highly trained elite triathletes are able to do this by virtue of their well-developed aerobic bases which become extremely efficient at dissipating these waste products. Lesser trained triathletes without as large a background or base may find that after exercising beyond threshold they require far longer periods at much lower exercise intensities to clear metabolic by-products. In other words they need to slow down more and for a longer time, which is obviously an ineffective way in which to complete a time trial as quickly as possible without unduly affecting the run component of the race.

In view of what has been discussed above, the triathlete should be aiming at preparing him/herself for a sustained, constant power output for the duration of the event. This will mean building a sound aerobic base and subsequently forcing back anaerobic threshold to greater percentages of VO_2 max. This is precisely why the use of heart rate monitors have become so prevalent in triathlon and a number of other endurance-based events. By establishing the heart rate—which is directly related to exercise intensity (see figure 5.1)—at which anaerobic threshold occurs the triathlete is able to cycle or run most effectively at the corresponding heart rate which is within a couple of beats of this critical intensity. As such, homeostasis is better maintained and optimal pacing obtained.

Looking at training specifics for cycling the same macrocycle breakdown as was used for swimming is still applicable here. That is (i) base

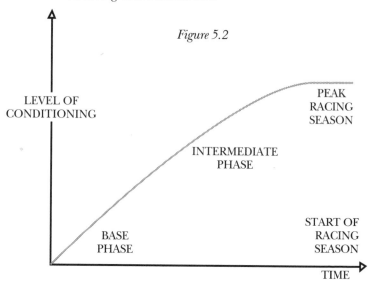

Figure 5.2

(off season), (ii) intermediate (pre-season), (iii) peak (in-season) and (iv) restoration. Once again the emphasis in training should shift from base aerobic work to high intensity speed development in order to develop a performance curve (see figure 5.2).

In the endurance (base) phase of the training cycle triathletes should be looking at breaking down their training into approximate percentage ranges as follows:

Level of Exercise Intensity	Lactate Concentration	Percentage of Total Training Time
1. Compensation	2	17–30
2. Aerobic endurance	3–4	39–50
3. Anaerobic endurance	4–7	15–37
4. Speed endurance/ simulation	Max.	5–10
5. Sprinting	N/A	2–3

Figure 5.3

From the outline shown in figure 5.3 it is obvious that the onus is firmly on the peripheral aerobic component (approximately 56% of total training time) with a blend of threshold work (approximately one-third of total training time) and only a very small percentage of training (less than 10%) being of an intense quality nature. The following example would be indicative of the type of training that a triathlete may engage in during the base phase of a training regimen in preparation for a standard Olympic distance triathlon.

Monday
Rest day.

Tuesday
Warm up at level 1 exercise intensity for 10 minutes.
Pyramiding session: Small chain ring (42 tooth), combination work attempting to hold a cadence of 90–100 rpm while increasing the gearing:

42/18	10	minutes—level 2 exercise intensity
42/17	8	minutes—level 2–3 exercise intensity
42/16	6	minutes—level 3 exercise intensity
42/15	4	minutes—level 3–4 exercise intensity
42/14	2	minutes—level 4 exercise intensity

Repeat twice.
Cooldown at level 1 exercise intensity for 10 minutes.
TOTAL TRAINING TIME 2½ hours (moderate to hard session).

Wednesday
Warm up for 10 minutes at level 1.
Steady state ride at levels 2–3 with a cadence of approximately 90–100 rpm for 1½ hours.
Cooldown as per warm up for 10 minutes.
TOTAL TRAINING TIME 1½ to 2 hours (moderate session).

Thursday
Rest day.

Friday
Warm up at level 1 exercise intensity for 10 minutes.
Intervals: 2 to 1 rest to work ratio (for each time period that the triathlete pushes at equal to or greater than level 3, twice that duration of time is taken at level 1):

ON	OFF
1	2
2	4
3	6
4	8
5	10
6	12
7	14

The fourteen-minute 'off' period at level 1 can double as the session cooldown, or the triathlete may choose to do an additional ten minutes at this intensity. The triathlete should choose a gear that allows him/her to recover when the cadence is low and is large enough to increase heart rate to appropriate levels when the triathlete is called upon to work harder. In other words this session should be completed in a 'fixed gear' with rpms being used to vary intensity levels between compensation and speed endurance/simulation.

TOTAL TRAINING TIME 2 hours (moderate to hard session).

Saturday

Rest day.

Sunday

Long ride with other cyclists in a 'bunch' for 2½ to 3 hours with the majority of time spent at an exercise intensity level 2. Exercise may be increased to level 3 when the triathlete 'takes a turn' or goes to the front of the bunch for approximately one-quarter of the total riding time, whereas levels 4 and 5 should only form a negligible amount of training time in this phase (e.g. when climbing short hills).

TOTAL TRAINING TIME 2½ to 3 hours (easy to moderate session).

TOTAL CYCLING TIME FOR THE DURATION OF THE WEEK 8½ to 10½ hours.

If we look at the total percentages of time spent at each level of exercise intensity:

Level	Total Time (hours)	Percentage of Weekly Training Time
1	3½	30
2	4¾ to 5¾	46
3	1¼ to 1½	12
4	¾ to 1¼	9
5	¼ to 1½	3

Figure 5.4

You'll notice that the above training percentage breakdown fits nicely into the model previously presented. Now, as was the case with the previous chapter, let us go through, dissect, discuss and justify each of the training sessions as prescribed.

Monday

Since the Sunday session was a longer ride which places demands upon the triathlete's energy stores, Monday is taken as a rest day from cycling to allow the specific cycling muscles time to recover, regenerate and re-establish their glycogen stores.

Tuesday

The Tuesday session incorporates a combination which emphasizes aerobic-based activity while introducing some anaerobic threshold/ speed simulation work to tax the triathlete's central component of the cardiovascular equation. The harder (levels 3–4) work, however, forms less than half of this session.

Wednesday

This session has more of a specific triathlon bias. The triathlete is required to warm up gently at a low level of activity, then choose a gear which allows the legs to 'spin' at 90–100 rpm (slightly faster than should be targeted as an ideal time trialling cadence for in-season competition—a cadence, however, that will help teach the triathlete to 'pedal circles' effectively rather than simply pushing on the pedals) and produces a work intensity that works both the aerobic and anaerobic endurance components of energy metabolism. Here the triathlete should endeavor to sit at a 'steady state' heart rate (i.e. +/- 5 bpm) around anaerobic threshold. The 'perceived exertion' produced by such a workout should be such that the triathlete finds it difficult to carry on a conversation and is 'short of breath' without having to ease off. The discomfort should be appreciable, but at the same time bearable. Once again, to ensure adequate dissipation of any accrued metabolic waste, allow a cooldown period at an exercise intensity corresponding to level 1.

Thursday

On the Thursday the triathlete should have a choice. Early on in the base phase this should be taken as a complete rest. However, as conditioning improves and the triathlete adapts to the training load, this Thursday session can be added in. It should incorporate low level activity for recovery purposes (active recovery) while at the same time stimulating peripheral cardiovascular function which helps improve blood supply to the working muscles, increases aerobic enzyme concentrations and energy stores, etc.

Friday

This workout is of moderate intensity. The triathlete is required to work at much greater than anaerobic threshold for one-third of the session interspersed with recovery bouts at level 1 exercise intensity. This should provide stimulation of the anaerobic threshold, while at the same time placing demands on the aerobic system to dissipate metabolites prior to the commencement of the next interval. Because the triathlete is in a base phase of training and aerobic fitness isn't as well established due to the preceding down time (the restoration phase) a relatively long rest is taken and the exercise intensity while recovering is lower than that which will be required later in the training cycle. This will allow stimulation of the anaerobic threshold and adaptation of the aerobic system to deal with a lactate load and dissipate it as efficiently as possible.

Saturday

Since the triathlete has ridden 3–4 of the preceding days, Saturday is taken as a rest day to allow a full 24 hours for muscles to recover their glycogen stores prior to the long Sunday session.

Sunday

This is the longest ride of the week. By riding with a group of other cyclists/triathletes the triathlete is forced to learn basic cycling skills (cornering, braking, etc.). Additionally, by riding in a 'bunch' the triathlete has the opportunity to intersperse harder efforts at the front of the bunch (level 3 exercise intensity) with aerobic recovery (level 2) while 'sitting on' the bunch. The only time the triathlete should force the exercise intensity above level 3 is when climbing hills. The triathlete may force the exercise intensity up occasionally if the bunch decides to sprint to particular road markers (e.g. signposts); however, exercise intensity in excess of level 3 should only constitute a very small percentage of the total training time and adequate recovery should be afforded the triathlete following such exercise efforts.

As the triathlete forms an adequate training base—after about 15–25 weeks of training, particularly for novice triathletes—and the racing season looms closer (within 2–3 months) the training emphasis must change in order to more closely mirror the demands of the upcoming competition. The triathlete needs to develop a well-balanced blend of high intensity work (levels 3–5) to stimulate the central portion of the cardiovascular equation, while at the same time allowing adequate recovery time between high intensity workouts for the muscular and skeletal systems to recover prior to loading the body once more. Additionally, this lower intensity active recovery exercise (levels 1–2) allows the triathlete to maintain peripheral cardiovascular function. In this instance the training percentage breakdown should progress to the following approximates:

Intensity Level	Percentage of Total Time Spent at Intensity Level
1	10–15
2	30–35
3	20–25
4	28–30
5	7–10

Figure 5.5

In this phase approximately 40% of total exercise time is spent training at or in excess of exercise intensity 3, compared to a mere 24% during the base phase. On the other side of the equation the low intensity work, while still predominating, has been curtailed from 76% of total training time to 50% and the emphasis has been shifted during this type of training onto level 2 intensity and away from the level 1, compensatory-type work. In general, the theory of 'progressive over-load' has been applied to the triathlete's training routine by manipulating exercise intensity, frequency and duration. In general the triathlete won't be training as often or for as long during each exercise bout; however, the training that is completed will be at a greater intensity than the sessions during the base training phase. Whereas the base phase was categorized by the notions of duration and generality, the intermediate phase places greater emphasis upon intensity and specificity. An example of such a training regimen as a progression from the previous program may incorporate the following:

Monday

Rest day.

Tuesday

Warm up and cooldown for 10 minutes each at level 1 exercise intensity.

Pyramiding session: Large chain ring (53 tooth).

Attempt to hold a cadence of 80–90 rpm while increasing gearing:

53/17 6 minutes (level 2–3 exercise intensity).

53/16 5 minutes (level 3 exercise intensity).

53/13 4 minutes (level 3–4 exercise intensity).

53/14 3 minutes (level 4 exercise intensity).

53/13 2 minutes (level 4–5 exercise intensity).

Repeat x 2.

TOTAL TRAINING TIME 1 hour (moderate to hard session).

Wednesday

Warm up for 10 minutes at level 2 exercise intensity.

Steady state heart rate at levels 3–4 exercise intensity with a cadence of 80–90 rpm for 1 to 1¼ hours.

Cooldown as per warm up.

TOTAL TRAINING TIME 1½ to 1¾ hours (hard session).

Thursday

Rest or ride at level 2 for 1 to 1½ hour

TOTAL TRAINING TIME up to 1½ hours (easy session).

Friday

Warm up at level 1 exercise intensity for 10 minutes.

Intervals 1:1 rest to work ratio. For each training period the triathlete pushes at or greater than level 4, an equal amount of time is taken at levels 1–2.

ON	OFF
1	1
2	2
3	3
4	4
5	5
6	6
7	7
8	8
9	9
10	10

The ten-minute 'off' period at level 2 can double as the cooldown period. Once again the triathlete should choose a gear that is appropriate to force heart rate to a level at or in excess of level 4 while spinning at a cadence of 80–90 rpm, preferably in the big chain ring, and allows recovery at exercise intensities of levels 1–2 when the cadence is dropped to 60–70 rpm for the recovery phase.

TOTAL EXERCISE TIME 2 hours (moderate to hard session).

Saturday

Rest day.

Sunday

Long road ride.

This should be completed in a small group of 3–5 riders. Aerodynamic handle bars should be fitted to the bike, if normally used when racing. The total duration of the ride should be between 2 to 2½ hours inclusive of the level 1–2 warm up and cooldown. The exercise intensity during this training set should vary between levels 2–3 with intermittent periods at exercise intensity level 4, when the triathlete goes to the front of the bunch, and level 5 when pushing up short hills. An ideal scenario for achieving such a workout would be for the group to form a pace line (see figures 5.6 a, b, c, d) in which triathletes 'roll the bunch' every two minutes,

Figure 5.6 a,b,c,d: The pace-line formation is an effective way to work hard and then recover during a group training session.

i.e. rider one takes the lead for two minutes sitting in an aerodynamic position then pulls out to the right to expose rider two to the wind to 'take his/her turn'. In this manner the triathletes gain both central conditioning, while leading the bunch, as well as peripheral stimulation, while recovering behind the leading rider.

As the triathletes become better conditioned he/she can take a longer spell at the front of the pace line or roll the bunch continuously, i.e. the triathlete goes to the front of the bunch and immediately 'pulls off' to the right to allow the next rider to take the lead who immediately follows suit. In this manner the pace line more closely resembles an individual time trial, which is the specific type of preparation that the triathlete is ultimately working towards (see figure 5.7).

TOTAL TRAINING TIME 2 to 2½ hours (hard session).

Viewing the training on a daily basis will provide justification/ reasoning behind the training completed each day. This concept of 'justification' should be a central concern for the triathlete. Prior to

Figure 5.7 a,b,c,d,e: Continuously 'rolling the bunch' more closely simulates the individual time trial situation.

each training session the triathlete should have a basic idea of what each training session is working to achieve—compensation, central/ peripheral stimulation, etc. In other words, the triathlete shouldn't simply be training for training's sake.

Monday

The Monday session follows the Sunday long ride and should be taken as a rest to allow recuperation from the hard Sunday workout. This will provide the opportunity for the muscles to fully replenish their glycogen stores and overcome any muscle degradation.

Tuesday

This particular workout is designed to improve anaerobic threshold. With such a session the triathlete attempts to spin a progressively larger gear while maintaining efficiency. Increasing the gearing will provide the extra resistance necessary to increase heart rate to appropriate intensities and provide the stimulation to promote muscular strength and endurance at a peripheral level. A comprehensive cooldown is required after such a session to dissipate any accumulating lactate.

Wednesday

Many of the race day demands are replicated in this session. Following the warm up the exercise intensity should be close to what the triathlete experiences while actually competing. This particular session is largely designed to promote central stimulation and improve the anaerobic threshold by having the triathlete exercise at threshold for almost the entire duration of the session. It places great demands upon the body's skeletal system which must subsequently be given adequate time to recuperate—approximately 24 hours in reasonably well-trained individuals. That is why the triathlete is given the Thursday as a complete rest day or an easy (levels 1–2) compensatory-type workout.

Friday

Once again this session is designed to force back the triathlete's anaerobic threshold by demanding progressively longer periods of time at or in excess of anaerobic threshold followed by an equal duration at levels 1–2 which will allow ample time to dissipate the lactic acid that accrues while exercising at intensities greater than anaerobic threshold. As a consequence the triathlete is forced to become efficient at metabolizing these metabolic by-products. As almost half of this session is at or in excess of anaerobic threshold, the demands that are placed upon the triathlete's musculature in order to force the heart rate to adequately high levels are extreme and must be compensated for by low intensity exercise or, as has been the case in the example cited here, rest to allow adequate recuperation prior to further stimulation. This brings us to the Sunday workout.

Sunday

This is again the triathlete's longest training session. A blend of aerobic endurance (level 2) through to speed endurance simulation (level 4) is incorporated into the training program here in order to maintain peripheral cardiovascular function, while at the same time simulating the demands that will be placed upon the triathlete during competition. Additionally, the triathlete should adopt the same type of cycling

Figure 5.8: The trailing riders in a pace-line shouldn't ride in an 'aero' position if inexperienced, as the bike is far harder to control in this position.

position (aerobars) during exercise at levels 3–4 so as to develop the necessary lumbar flexibility required to maintain such a riding position for extended periods of time during competition (see figure 5.8). Once the triathlete eases off or goes to the back of the bunch, a more relaxed riding position can be adopted so that the triathlete can (a) recover and (b) maintain better control (braking and steering) while slipstreaming the triathlete directly ahead.

Looking at the total training times spent at each exercise intensity it is obvious that the onus of training has shifted away from lower intensity, longer duration workouts, as were demanded during the base phase, to higher intensity workouts of a shorter time span:

Exercise Intensity Level	Total Exercise Time (hours)	Percentage of Total Exercise Time
1	1	11
2	2¾	31
3	1¾	22
4	2½	28
5	¾	8

Figure 5.9

In comparison to the base training phase it is apparent that two distinct changes have transpired, (a) the duration of time spent in training has been culled significantly by between 1¼ to 2¾ hours per week and (b) previously—in the base phase—only 24% of total training time was spent at or in excess of level 3 exercise intensity, while in the intermediate training schedule this total has increased to account for some 58% of total training time. It is therefore obvious from this comparison that the objectives of the triathlete's training regimen have changed significantly and are now more biased towards the specific race preparation. This trend is continued during the in-season or peaking phase of the training regimen. Here the triathlete must strike a subtle balance between high intensity racing/training, aerobic base maintenance and adequate rest, recovery and restoration. Studies suggest that it is during the high intensity exercise periods of training regimens that athletes are generally at the greatest risk of injury/illness. It is therefore imperative that triathletes work to an organized, structured regimen and learn to 'listen' to their bodies. For example, slight kinks that the triathlete may attempt to simply train through may develop into full blown injuries. Minor problems should be curtailed early so as not to jeopardize the triathlete's racing aspirations. The following peaking phase need not be greatly different from the previous intermediate phase; however, some subtle changes are necessary primarily to ensure adequate recovery. The triathlete should be aiming at achieving training intensity percentages within the following ranges:

Training Intensity	Percentage of Total Training Time
1	15–20
2	37–43
3	0–15
4	35–40
5	10–12

Figure 5.10

Here the triathlete may complete almost half of his/her total training time at or in excess of anaerobic threshold. It is therefore imperative that both active (level 1 exercise intensity) and passive (massage/rest) recovery are scheduled into the triathlete's training regimen to ensure that the skeletal system (muscles, tendons, ligaments and bones) is given ample recuperative time prior to further stressing, otherwise maladaptation (overtraining syndrome) and injury will almost certainly result. *Note:* This can often be monitored by the triathlete. For example, the commencement of disturbed sleep patterns, elevated morning heart rates (+5 bpm) and the inability to force the heart rate up to normal rates during 'efforts' are generally indicative of the need for more rest and recovery.

The following training regimen is a progression of the previously cited examples and illustrates practically how the emphasis of the training program can be subtly altered so as to achieve the requirements of the peaking/in-season training macrocycle.

Monday

Rest day.

Tuesday

Warm up at level 2 exercise intensity for five minutes.

Intervals 1:2 rest to work ratio.

ON	OFF
2	1
4	2
6	3
8	4
10	5
12	6

'On' efforts should be at or in excess of level 4 intensity and recovery at level 1.

Cooldown for five minutes at level 1 intensity.

TOTAL TRAINING TIME 1¼ hours (moderate to hard session).

Wednesday

Aerobic ride (level 2 exercise intensity) for 1 to 1½ hours incorporating 8–12 x 15–30 second level 5 efforts interspersed throughout the duration of the ride.

Cooldown for five minutes at exercise intensity 2.

TOTAL TRAINING TIME 1–1½ hours (easy session).

Thursday

Warm up for five minutes at level 2 exercise intensity.

Threshold session at exercise intensity level 4 for 1 to 1¼ hours.

Cooldown as per warm up.

TOTAL TRAINING TIME 1½ hours (hard session).

Friday

Rest or one hour's easy ride at exercise intensity 2.

TOTAL TRAINING TIME 0–1 hour (easy session).

Saturday
Rest day.
Sunday
Race: 1–1¼ hours at exercise intensity levels 4–5 (hard session).

Looking at each session individually:
Monday
The Monday session allows for a passive recovery following the intense exercise experienced on the Sunday.
Tuesday
Tuesday places demands upon the aerobic system to dissipate accumulated lactate as quickly as possible prior to the commencement of subsequent lactate efforts. This is similar to that which the triathlete may experience during races, e.g. supra threshold efforts followed by short recovery periods prior to having to repeat such an intense effort.
Wednesday
Wednesday endeavors to maintain the aerobic base while 'priming' the ATP–PC system with short, sharp explosive efforts followed by long recovery periods. It is envisaged that the ATP–PC (or alactic anaerobic) system may be called into play during competition—while climbing hills so as not to break rhythm or lose contact with fellow competitors.
Thursday
The Thursday session stresses the triathlete by working at anaerobic threshold and simulating the demands that will be experienced on race day. *Note:* If the triathlete was to be racing an important race the following Sunday this Thursday session should be modified by (a) replacement with a lower intensity workout of the same duration—levels 2–3 or (b) decreasing the duration of the session to 20–30 minutes at exercise intensity 4.
Friday
Once again depending upon race commitments and the importance of the race, the triathlete either rests completely or completes an easy aerobic session.
Saturday
The day prior to the race should allow for passive recovery and recuperation to ensure that muscle glycogen stores are optimized.
Sunday
Even if this session is only used as a 'training race' it should be used to stress the triathlete to levels not usually experienced during training. This should be the most demanding workout of the week, with the

triathlete maintaining exercise at an intensity of around level 4 with intermittent periods at level 5. Since this session places such comprehensive demands upon the periphery (muscles, tendons, ligaments and bones) and central components (heart and lungs) of the cardiovascular fitness equation, sufficient recovery time (both passive and active) must be allowed prior to again stressing the triathlete. Let's now study the demands of this training phase from a numeric perspective so as to allow comparison to the preceding two macrocycles:

Exercise Intensity Level	Total Exercise Time (hours)	Percentage of Total Exercise Time
1	½	8
2	1¼–2¼	35
3	—	—
4	2¾–3½	49
5	½	8

Figure 5.11

What becomes obvious from the above numeric explanation of the training regimen is (a) that the total time spent has been decreased by between 1½ to 4 hours per week and (b) the 'transitory-type work' (level 3) which is too intense to really allow the triathlete to recover from a hard session, but isn't intense enough to force the triathlete's anaerobic threshold effectively, is eliminated from the training routine. Here the objectives of the triathlete's training program are succinct and precise: (a) improve time trialling capacity by forcing back the anaerobic threshold with higher intensity efforts (levels 4–5) and (b) allow adequate recovery from such workouts and maintain a sound aerobic basis with low intensity training bouts at exercise intensity 1–2. In such a scenario the triathlete removes any surplus training time that isn't directly contributing to the demands of competition and as such optimizes training time availability and decreases the possibility of overtraining and the potential for injury and illness. The regimen becomes more task specific and, as such, time efficient.

PART FOUR
ON THE ROAD AGAIN

Chapter 6

The Biomechanics of Running

Dr. Peter Larkins

Biomechanics is the science of studying man in motion. It has developed as a specific sub-branch of sports medicine to analyze correct technique in sport and help identify faults which may be limiting an athlete's performance. It is especially useful in those events such as jumping and throwing sports, but is also helpful for running, swimming and cycling.

Runners come in all shapes and sizes. I have often stood at the end of a marathon race and watched with a mixture of amazement and admiration the number of different running styles. Many people manage to complete marathons and other significant running races with a running style which would not be considered technically correct by many of the biomechanical specialists of the world. Nevertheless, these people enjoy their running and manage to participate injury free. All this makes me realize that there is probably no one absolutely correct running style but there is probably a best running style for each individual.

Evaluation of running style or 'gait' is important when looking for a potential cause of a running injury. In the past there has been a great deal of research done in analyzing runners to determine what constitutes a 'normal' or correct running gait. From these studies a consistent pattern of running gait has emerged. From the time when one foot hits the ground at heel strike until the same foot hits the ground the second time at the end of its next stride there is a complex combination of movements and forces acting through the body, particularly the lower limb. These forces involve areas such as the heel, midfoot, forefoot, ankle, shin, knee, hip and even the low back.

The forces associated with walking and running have been well documented. During normal walking there is approximately one to two times the body weight transmitted through the lower limb at foot impact. When running, this is increased to three to four times the body weight as a minimum, and this is even greater during downhill running and when running on harder surfaces such as concrete and asphalt.

Gait analysis is a technique of studying running style and is usually performed in a laboratory. Equipment required includes a treadmill with variable speed, a video camera and recorder with slow motion and 'freeze frame' facilities in order for individual components of the running cycle to be studied separately. In particular, gait analysis looks at the foot strike phase of running to observe the interaction between the runner's shoe and the ground during impact and weight transfer. However, other areas such as upper body movement, hip, knee and shin motion can be examined.

In the majority of runners, heel strike occurs on the outer rear area of the heel. Thus, it is quite normal to wear out this heel area in running shoes. If you are one of these runners you are known as a 'heel striker' because the foot should land beneath your centre of gravity at impact and this normal wear area is just on the outside of the mid-point of the heel.

Occasionally runners with tight calves or high arches will tend to land more towards the ball of the foot—these are 'forefoot strikers'. This is also more common as the pace of runs increase with the extreme example being a sprinter who runs primarily up on the toe area.

During the swing phase of running the lower leg is internally rotated at the knee while the foot is airborne. At foot strike the foot should be in a rigid position (supinated) and at this point the lower leg is externally rotated. As the weight is transferred forward from the heel towards the push-off area beneath the great toe, the arch undergoes a flattening process known as pronation. At toe-off position the arch is again raised and the foot adapts a rigid position again (i.e. supinated).

Thus, you can see that it is very important that the foot must act as a mobile adaptor to allow proper contact with the running surface to occur (midfoot pronation) as weight is transferred forward. This allows you to adapt to uneven running surfaces such as a golf course or parklands without causing excessive jarring through the lower limb. Pronation is a normal part of the running gait cycle and is a complex planar movement involving the ankle, subtalar and mid-tarsal joints of the foot.

However, excessive pronation means that more time is taken up with the inward rolling movement of the foot and less time on efficient dynamic transfer of weight towards the front of the foot. This results in increased stresses along the medial (inner) side of the foot and lower leg as the lower leg undergoes excessive internal rotation. This can cause injuries in the region of the foot, ankle, shin or knee.

Failure of this carefully designed chain of foot and lower leg adaptation will lead to excessive stresses on muscles and tendons in an attempt to compensate. Overuse or fatigue injuries then occur. A number of these have been discussed in the specific running injuries section.

A proper biomechanical assessment for a runner should involve both a static and biomechanic component. Static assessment includes measurement of lower limb leg length and flexibility. Leg length differences should be documented and any imbalance or tightness in major muscle groups should be corrected. The arch type (high, normal, low) should also be assessed. The curve of the lower leg should be checked to see whether the main lower leg bone (tibia) is curved inward or outward. The angle of the knee is also important to determine if excessive valgus (knocked knee) or varus (bow legged) is present. The knee cap (patella) should be assessed to see whether there is any patellar squint, lateral tracking, or if the patella is small or situated in an excessively elevated position relative to the rest of the knee. Finally, the hip and lower back area should be checked for mobility and muscle balance.

From this simple static assessment often many problems can be identified and corrections made if they are considered to be relevant to the injury. There are many athletes who do have slight imbalances in many of these areas and yet have been running for years without injury problems. The difficulty then arises as to whether it is necessary to correct these problems and risk interfering with what has been a successful running gait. For instance, it is always worthwhile correcting inflexibility and improving range of movement in those areas that are tight, but small changes such as a few millimetres' difference in leg length may not be of any significance.

The role of sophisticated laboratory gait analysis is debatable. It certainly has specific indications for assessment of injury problems and is best reserved for assessment of complex problems or those chronic running problems which have not responded to previous therapy measures. It should only be conducted by a therapist who is experienced in gait analysis and the various injuries associated with abnormal gait.

There are certain injuries which are associated with specific biomechanical faults. For example, a leg length difference, especially if greater than 1 centimetre, can be associated with problems of low back pain and hip overuse injuries. A high arched foot (cavus) is generally more rigid than normal and does not adapt well to uneven surfaces and this results in a higher incidence of stress fractures and ankle tendonitis. Conversely, an excessively flat (pronated) foot can be too mobile and result in increased stresses such as shin pain and patello-femoral dysfunction (runner's knee). Excessive knocked knee (valgus) condition can result in runner's knee, shin problems and medial (inner) ankle problems. Excessive bow legged (varus) is associated with ankle tendonitis and lateral (outer side) knee and hip problems. These conditions are all discussed more fully in the running injuries section.

During running the buttock (gluteal) and lateral hip muscles work to stabilize the weight bearing leg and maintain alignment and balance through the lower limb. During normal gait the opposite hip rises as weight is transferred to the weight bearing leg. If the musculature is weak this will not happen and pelvic imbalance can occur. There is a complex, yet synchronized series of muscle contraction and relaxation movements occurring to allow for a balanced and efficient gait. Excessive tightness or weakness of these muscles can upset this delicate balance and result in injury and, thus, should always be assessed when the injury is being evaluated.

Finally, a brief word on the value of orthotics. These can vary from a simple heel wedge or heel lift in the running shoe to a fully customized running shoe insert to correct significant biomechanical problems. In between, there are a number of other devices such as a simple arch raise, an 'over the counter' arch support, soft, semi-rigid or rigid orthoses and other shoe adaptations which can alter the biomechanical movement during weight transfer.

The choice of which device may be appropriate should be made by an experienced practitioner who has looked at the other factors which may be contributing towards the injury and can then assess the need for orthotic therapy. This will depend on the nature of the problem, the skill of the practitioner, the facilities available and the previous experiences of both the runner and the therapist in this area. Only then can a decision be reached on the type of orthosis and the likely benefit of proceeding to this stage in therapy.

Chapter Seven

Physiological Considerations in Running

Rod Cedaro

Of the three disciplines triathletes participate in, swimming can be viewed as technically the most difficult; cycling, because of the time that can be spent in training, is the most demanding time wise and psychologically; and running, by its nature, is physically the most demanding and damaging. Of the three, running is the only sport which is totally 'weight bearing' and requires a large component of eccentric muscular contraction, where the muscle contracts while lengthening, which has been reported to produce greater muscular damage than concentric contractions, where the muscle shortens while contracting (Appell et al.,1990). Finally, running is usually the last sport which the triathlete completes, so it is invariably completed in a fatigued state. This often means an increased chance of injury. Therefore, it is imperative that the triathlete is comprehensively prepared for the demands of the running leg. Additionally, because of the greater physiological demands of running—compared to swimming or cycling—the triathlete must apply the basic training principles of (a) progressive overload and (b) hard/easy training sessions.

While it is not recommended, it is possible for triathletes to increase their swimming and cycling training loads quickly or back up hard training sessions on numerous occasions because of the quicker recovery associated with these two sports, but running will not allow the triathlete the same latitude without an increased risk of overuse injury or physiological/psychological burnout. There are, however, a number of ways in which triathletes can improve their running prowess while limiting the possibility of associated injuries and other overuse syndromes. These training adjuncts include running on softer surfaces (trails), choosing appropriate footwear, and incorporating 'water running' into the weekly training routine. All of these considerations will be discussed during the course of this chapter.

As is the case with swimming and cycling the triathlete's preparation for running must commence with a sound aerobic base. This will

Figure 7.1: Running on softer surfaces lowers the incidence of leg injuries and speeds recovery rates.

establish the peripheral fitness necessary to support the later higher intensity exercise necessary to improve performance and progressively strengthen the skeletal musculature in preparation for the rigors associated with racing and intense training. Additionally, this lower intensity, prolonged exercise helps enhance fat metabolism, which increases the intensity at which the triathlete can exercise prior to changing to carbohydrate metabolism, which is limited by substrate availability.

In the preparatory/base phase the triathlete should endeavor to run

per week. At least two of these sessions should be of an over-
low intensity nature (separated by 3–4 days), with 1–2 sessions of
ate intensity/duration. The remaining session should be a quality
out of short duration. As was the case with swimming and cycling, as
e triathlete gets closer to competition the running program is manipulated to place more emphasis upon quality and recovery between the
higher intensity workouts. The following example of a typical weekly
training schedule for a triathlete preparing for an Olympic distance event
provides a comprehensive exam-
ple of appropriate scheduling and
programming through the various
macrocycles.

*Figure 7.2: Racing flats (left) are
lighter, less supportive and more
flexible than training shoes (right).*

Monday

The Monday session becomes a
fartlek workout of between 12–15
kilometres (7½–9 miles) total duration. The triathlete should warm
up for approximately one kilometre at level 1 intensity, then take
some time to stretch the major
muscle groups of the lower limbs
(see Appendix B) prior to the actual training set. During this training session the triathlete should
endeavor to complete 8–12 efforts
at level 3 intensity for 1–2 minutes'
duration on each effort. These 'efforts' should be separated by an
equal amount (1–2 minutes) of
recovery at levels 1–2 exercise
intensity.

TOTAL TRAINING DISTANCE 12–15 kilometres (7½–9 miles) (moderate
session).

Tuesday

Having run two days straight (Sunday and Monday), the Tuesday is
taken as a passive recovery day.

Wednesday

This forms the first of two long/

*Figure 7.3: Water running is a
useful alternative to running on
harder surfaces.*

base runs of the week. Following a brief warm up (five minutes at level 1), the triathlete should repeat the comprehensive stretching routine discussed previously and then complete a run of 18–25 kilometres (11–15½ miles) at exercise level 2.

TOTAL TRAINING DISTANCE 18–25 kilometres (11–15½ miles) (easy to moderate session).

Thursday

This session should be completed at least 24 hours later, e.g. morning run on the Wednesday followed by an afternoon track session on the Thursday. The efforts completed at the track—after a 10–15 minute level 1 warm up—should be of a longer duration (400–1600 metres [440–1750 yards]). The longer repeats should be at a slightly lower intensity (level 3) while the shorter efforts should be executed at level 4, allowing greater recovery between efforts. An example of such a track session would be as follows:

Warm up as indicated above.

3 x 1600 metres (1750 yards) at level 3 separated by a 200 metre (220 yard) 'float' at exercise level 2.

4–6 x 400 metres (440 yards) at level 4 separated by a 400 metre (440 yard) 'float' at exercise level 1.

Cooldown 10–15 minutes at level 1.

TOTAL TRAINING DISTANCE 14 kilometres (8½ miles) (hard session).

Friday

The Friday session should be viewed largely as a recovery day following the Thursday track session. It should incorporate a 12–16 kilometre (7½–10 mile) run at an exercise intensity varying between levels 1–2.

TOTAL TRAINING DISTANCE 12–16 kilometres (7½–10 miles) easy/active recovery session).

Saturday

This should be viewed as a preparatory day for the long run which is to be completed on the Sunday. So a short, easy run of 5 kilometres (3 miles) at level 1–2 can be completed or the triathlete can simply rest.

TOTAL TRAINING DISTANCE 0–5 kilometres (3 miles) (rest/active recovery session).

Sunday

This forms the triathlete's second long run of the week. The total duration should again be 18–25 kilometres (11–15½ miles), ideally on soft dirt trails rather than the road or footpath, and completed at an exercise intensity corresponding to level 2. It is with these longer, lower intensity runs, completed when the triathlete is in a partially fatigued state with lowered glycogen stores (as a result of the training completed earlier in the week), that the triathlete builds his/her ability to metabolize fat more effectively and so spare the limited glycogen stores.

TOTAL TRAINING DISTANCE 18–25 kilometres (11–15½ miles) (easy/moderate session).

Figure 7.4

Exercise Intensity Level	Total Time Spent at Level (minutes)	Percentage of Total Training Time
1	125–157	30–42
2	137–309	46–59
3	26–44	8–21
4	7–10	2–6
5	—	—

TOTAL WEEKLY DISTANCE 74–100 kilometres (46–62 miles)

The breakdown of the weekly training routine is shown in figure 7.4. It is obvious that during the base phase the majority of the training emphasis is on low intensity work with 75% to greater than 90% of the total week being completed at or less than level 2 and a mere 8–27% of total exercise time being completed at or greater than level 3. It should be noted that the program described above is simply an example and should be treated as such. It is not recommended unless a triathlete has a proven record of running over a number of seasons. However, the formula and principles that have been employed, i.e. two over-distance sessions, one to two moderate intensity workouts and one quality session, can be manipulated to the specific circumstances of the individual triathlete. For example, a junior triathlete or a triathlete from a swimming background (with little or no running history) may have to work on one-half to two-thirds of the total durations discussed above. Additionally, the intense track session may have to be supplemented with a pool running session to save the impact shock and resultant potential injuries that the triathlete may experience from such a speed session on the track. As long as general training principles are obeyed, i.e. a sound aerobic base is built and the skeletal muscular system is strengthened in a slow progressive manner in preparation for the more intense training to follow, the triathlete can manipulate the training loads according to his or her own specific circumstances to achieve these objectives.

Depending upon the duration of the event that the triathlete is

Figure 7.5: Intense track running sessions increase the incidence of running injuries.

preparing for and his/her past running background, these factors will dictate the duration of time spent in this base phase of training. Generally speaking, however, the longer the event being prepared for and/or the less experience the triathlete has in running, then the longer the time that should be spent in the base phase. For example, triathletes preparing for ultradistance events may spend up to a year simply developing a sound aerobic basis from which to work. Inversely, for short duration events, triathletes with long running histories are able to re-establish a firm aerobic basis in a relatively short time span, say 6–12 weeks.

Having established, or re-established, this base, the onus of the triathlete's running program must now shift towards developing the central component of the cardiovascular equation by lifting the intensity of the training loads and decreasing the duration in an attempt to improve the anaerobic threshold. As has been noted with the other two disciplines, this transition phase—from base to intermediate-type work—is often a period of increased fatigue and as a consequence there is increased risk of injury. These constraints are nowhere more apparent than in the activity of running which, as mentioned previously, places the greatest physiological load on the triathlete. If the triathlete experiences a persistent ache or pain that doesn't respond quickly to the basic 'PRICEM' principle (see medical treatment chapter), then training should be curtailed and qualified medical assessment sought. Additionally, just because a triathlete is ready to make the transition from base training to intermediate-type work in swimming and/or cycling, doesn't necessarily mean that this transition in the training emphasis is also appropriate for the running segment of the training regimen. In fact, triathletes from non-running backgrounds (swimmers or cyclists) should continue their run base work

Figure 7.6: Running on hard surfaces, such as asphalt, can cause leg and back problems in endurance athletes.

long after they have made the change in their training regimens for the other two disciplines. This may mean that the only 'quality work' that such triathletes get in their running is while racing during their actual competitive seasons. This is fine, as the objective of a comprehensive training regimen should be to develop the triathlete over an extended period of time. Rather than looking for short-term glory the triathlete/coach should be focusing on long-term objectives and performances. Once the triathlete develops a running prowess, which may take a number of seasons of well-structured, progressive and consistent training, then training loads can be manipulated to 'peak' the triathlete's running abilities. While the same is true for both cycling and swimming, i.e. novice triathletes must be trained slowly and progressively, the importance of this progression is paramount in the discipline of running, as this is by far the most demanding physiologically on the triathlete's body and so has the greatest potential to cause debilitating injuries.

Progressing through from the example cited earlier in this chapter (an established triathlete preparing for an Olympic distance race), a logical progression for such a training routine may incorporate some of the following elements—after at least 8–12 weeks of base work—bearing in mind that the fundamental objectives of this phase are to improve anaerobic threshold while maintaining peripheral function.

Monday

Once again the fartlek method of training is employed; however, the total duration and exercise intensities are modified in comparison to the previous phase. The session should be 8–12 kilometres (5–7½ miles) total duration, not including the warm up and stretching as discussed previously. Ten to fifteen 'efforts' of 45–90 seconds at an exercise intensity of levels 3–4 should be completed. These efforts should be separated by equal time duration recoveries at exercise intensity 2.

TOTAL TRAINING DISTANCE 9–13 kilometres (5½–8 miles) (moderate session).

Tuesday

Rest day (easy/passive recovery).

Wednesday

The emphasis of this session still remains upon maintaining peripheral, base aerobic fitness; however, a number of short, brief surges may also be incorporated to simulate the rigors of competition, e.g. attempting to break away from a fellow competitor. The total distance of this training session should be 16–20 kilometres (10–12½ miles) with 80–90% of the running being completed at level 2 intensity and the balance (e.g. striding the hills for 1–2 minutes) being completed at exercise intensities 3–4. Since the emphasis of such a workout is still upon maintaining base aerobic function, the triathlete should be fully recovered from each individual surge prior to commencing a subsequent effort.

TOTAL TRAINING DISTANCE 16–20 kilometres (10–12½ miles) (moderate session).

Thursday

Once again the Thursday session is a high quality session designed to enhance glycolytic energy metabolism and, during this phase, explosive power to a limited extent. Since the exercise intensity is so high, and the stress placed upon the body considerable, the duration of this session should be limited. A progression from the program detailed previously for the base training phase could include the following intervals and recoveries:

> Warm up at levels 1–2 for 10–15 minutes followed by stretching routine.
> 4–6 x 600–800 metres (660–880 yards) at level 3–4 separated by 100–200 metre (110–220 yard) floats at level 2.
> 8–10 x 200–300 metres (220–330 yards) at level 4–5 separated by 200–300 metre (220–330 yard) floats at level 1.
> Cooldown for 10–15 minutes at level 1.

TOTAL TRAINING DISTANCE 10–19 kilometres (6–12 miles) (hard session).

Friday

Unlike the previous program in which this session was viewed as nothing more than an 'active recovery' session, during this intermediate phase the onus of this workout changes slightly in an attempt to work on improving anaerobic threshold by having the triathlete work consistently at anaerobic threshold (level 3 intensity) for 5–8 kilometres (3–5 miles) after a five-minute warm up at level 1.

TOTAL TRAINING DISTANCE 6–9 kilometres (4–5½ miles) (moderate session).

Saturday

This session remains a passive recovery day in preparation for the long training day on the Sunday (rest/passive recovery).

Sunday

As was the case with the Wednesday session, the total duration of this run—in comparison with the base phase—is curtailed significantly while, at the same time, a small quantity of higher intensity work is added. The aim of this session should, however, remain upon maintaining base aerobic function. The total distance covered during this session should amount to 18–22 kilometres (11–13½ miles) with 80–90% being completed at level 2 intensity with the remaining 10–20% being accounted for by hills and surges which increase the exercise intensity to levels 3–4.

TOTAL TRAINING DISTANCE 18–22 kilometres (11–13½ miles) (easy/moderate session).

For comparative reasons the breakdown of this intermediate training phase is shown in figure 7.7.

Figure 7.7

Exercise Intensity Level	Total Time Spent at Level (minutes)	Percentage of Total Training Time
1	23–38	11
2	137–189	59–63
3	38–59	17–19
4	20–30	9
5	2–3	1

TOTAL WEEKLY DISTANCE 58–82 kilometres (36–51 miles)

As can be seen from the breakdown in figure 7.7 the following changes are obvious in comparison to the run training that was undertaken during the base training phase: (a) total exercise duration has been decreased by between 26–39%, (b) while previously 75% to greater than 90% of total training time was spent exercising at or less than level 2 intensity, this percentage now decreased to 70–85% of total exercise time, (c) as a direct result of this change in emphasis, whereas 10–30% of total exercise time was spent at or in excess of level 3 exercise intensity, the duration spent at these workloads now increases to account for approximately 25–30% of total run training time. Because of the more intense nature of the exercise during this phase it is imperative that the triathlete get adequate rest intervals between hard training bouts so as to adequately recover and allow the physiological adaptations to occur which will improve performance. This helps to avoid the possibility of suffering some type of debilitating overuse injury or syndrome, common in poorly trained/coached endurance athletes.

As the triathlete moves into the third active training phase (peak or in-season), training should be worked in such a manner as to complement racing. Here the triathlete needs to pay particular attention to high quality training/racing sessions tempered by adequate recovery, while still maintaining some aerobic base work. Consequently, as was the case with the bike routine, much of the level 3 training—which is too intense to simply maintain base aerobic fitness and allow adequate recovery from hard, quality sessions—is curtailed so that the more highly specific requirements of this training phase can be addressed and adequate recovery time ensured. A typical progression of the example utilized thus far is as follows:

Monday

Fartlek session, total distance to be covered 6–10 kilometres (4–6 miles). Here the triathlete should attempt to incorporate 15–18 efforts at level 4–5 exercise intensity for a total duration of 30–60 seconds for each effort. The rest between each effort should be approximately half as long as the work phase (15–30 seconds) and conducted at level 1–2 intensity. Such a session teaches the triathlete to be able to 'surge' and recover quickly prior to 'attacking' once more. This simulates the type of running the triathlete may experience under race conditions. The short recovery phase between efforts will ensure that the triathlete's aerobic capacity is maintained and the ability to dissipate and metabolize lactate is optimized.

TOTAL TRAINING DISTANCE 6–10 kilometres (4–6 miles) (moderate to hard session).

Tuesday

Rest day (passive recovery session).

Wednesday

Anaerobic threshold session. The triathlete should ensure an adequate warm up and attempt to force back the intensity at which running can be maintained. This session should be of a relatively short duration (3–5 kilometres [2–3 miles]) and run as a weekly/fortnightly time trial at close to race intensity (levels 4–5).

TOTAL TRAINING DISTANCE 3–5 kilometres (2–3 miles) (moderate to hard session).

Thursday

If the triathlete is racing on the weekend this track session should be dropped completely and replaced by the Friday run.

Track session: Warm up at exercise intensity 1–2 for 4–5 kilometres (2½–3 miles), followed by:

6–8 x 400 metres (440 yards) at level 4 separated by a 200 metre (220 yard) float at level 2.

10–12 x 100–200 metres (110–220 yards) at level 5 separated by a 100 metre (110 yard) float at level 1.

Cooldown for 2–4 kilometres (1¼–2½ miles) at level 1.

TOTAL TRAINING DISTANCE 16.3 kilometres (10 miles) (hard session).

Friday

Rest if racing on Saturday OR 5–8 kilometres (3–5 miles) at level 2 if racing on Sunday.

TOTAL TRAINING DISTANCE 5–8 kilometres (3–5 miles) (easy session).

Saturday

Rest if racing Sunday OR race10 kilometres (6 miles) at levels 4–5 OR long run of 16–20 kilometres (10–12½ miles) with 80% of the distance at level 2 and the remaining 20% of the session at levels 4–5, if not racing on the weekend.

TOTAL TRAINING DISTANCE 10–20 kilometres (6–12½ miles) (moderate to hard session).

Sunday

As per Saturday.

The totals breakdown for this peaking phase are as shown in figure 7.8.

Figure 7.8

Exercise Intensity Level	Total Time Spent at Level (minutes)	Percentage of Total Training Time
1	40–45	19.5
2	110–130	55.5
3	—	—
4	27–30	13
5	23–28	12

TOTAL WEEKLY TRAINING DISTANCE 46.5–59.5 kilometres (29–37 miles).

In this phase there has been a significant change of emphasis. Level 3 training has been dropped from the routine entirely while running at an intensity of greater than level 3 makes up one-quarter of the total run training time, with a far greater percentage of this exercise at race pace compared to the intermediate phase. Consequently, a greater amount of training time must be spent in recovery-type activity. For this reason level 3 exercise intensity has been removed from the routine; as was stated previously in chapter five, level 3 is too great to allow active recovery, but not intense enough to improve central cardiovascular function.

At the completion of a racing season, or following an important single race which the triathlete may have been training specifically for, the triathlete should move into a 'regeneration/restoration' phase. Suffice to say at this point that this macrocycle allows the triathlete to 'exercise at leisure' in an unstructured, non-specific manner in order to allow complete recovery from the rigors of the previous specific training/racing phases. This concept will be elaborated on further in chapter eleven, 'Putting It All Together'.

REFERENCES

Appell, Soares & Duartle, 1990, 'Exercise, muscle damage and fatigue', Proceeedings of Fatigue Symposium, Footscray Institute of Technology, Victoria, Australia, pp. 42–47.

PART FIVE
HEALTHY MIND,
HEALTHY BODY

Chapter Eight

Fuelling Your Body

Dr. Louise Burke

TRAINING NUTRITION—THE PRINCIPLES OF EVERYDAY EATING

Each triathlete needs a training program that is unique and specially tailored to his/her situation. Your eating program should be the same. There is no single diet that can fit the needs and goals of all triathletes. Nutritional requirements vary according to your physiological make-up (e.g. your age, your sex, your size) and your training load. And, of course, no two people share the same food likes and dislikes.

Eating well in training is vital to ensure optimum return from all your hard work. A good training diet can be achieved with a variety of different foods and meal plans, all following a common thread or link. The following checklist summarizes your goals for everyday eating.

Is your body weight and body fat level suitable for your competition goals?

Do you provide your body with all its nutrient needs—remembering that the requirement for some nutrients will be increased by a strenuous training program?

Do you promote recovery between training sessions—refuelling and rehydrating as rapidly as possible and allowing your body to adapt to the training load?

Do you think about the future and take into account the nutrition guidelines for long-term health?

Do you enjoy what you eat and enjoy the company of others over meals? No diet needs to be so restrictive that it removes these pleasures.

Do you experiment with ideas for competition eating in the safety of your training program?

STAYING TRIM, TAUT AND HEALTHY

When success depends on propelling your body over long distances, it is an advantage to carry little 'dead weight'—or more specifically, body fat. Therefore, elite triathletes are noted for their low levels of body fat, particularly those who compete in Ironman and long-distance races.

Most triathletes achieve their lean frames 'automatically', due to a combination of heavy training, healthy eating and inheriting the right body characteristics from their parents. Others may have to consciously manipulate their training and diet to reach or maintain their ideal body shape. For some the goal is to speed up the loss of excess body fat. However, others struggle to eat enough to maintain their body weight, especially during periods of heavy training.

Although the general trend is to low body fat levels, the 'ideal' level varies with individuals. This will depend on your training and competition goals and your natural body type. Your ideal level is one that lets you perform well, stay healthy, and be able to eat and exercise sensibly to maintain it. While you will undoubtedly be held back by too many bulges in or over your shorts or swimsuit, there are also problems associated with trying to achieve body fat levels that are too low—intolerance to the cold, reduced stamina, reduced immunity to infections and, perhaps, a higher risk of amenorrhea (loss of menstrual periods) in female triathletes. These symptoms may result from your body struggling to cope with body fat that is well below its 'natural' healthy level, or from the tactics that allowed you to lose too much body fat.

Body fat levels are not always easily appreciated by athletes. While you may be aware of some excess fat deposits on your body (e.g. 'love handles'), most people rely on the bathroom or gym scale to tell whether they are in shape. However, body weight reflects the sum of all your body components (including muscle, body fat, body water, bone and undigested food) and often provides a confusing picture of body fat levels. For example, the scales may fail to pick up losses of body fat if your muscle mass has increased over the same time. Or, alternatively, you may think you have shed 2 kilograms during a long training session, not realizing that body water lost through sweat will be quickly replaced as soon as you have a drink. Body fat levels can be estimated by a variety of techniques including underwater weighing, measurement of subcutaneous fat with skinfold calipers (the 'pinch test') and by using a Futrex machine based on infra-red rays. Each method has advantages and disadvantages and sources of error. An exercise physiologist or sports dietitian can provide the expertise to take such measurements reliably and to interpret the results.

ACTION
Assessment and Advice
• If you are unsure whether you are in shape, or have a concern that your body fat is not at an ideal level, consult an exercise physiologist or sports dietitian for assessment and advice. A sports dietitian can also provide expert advice on the dietary changes needed to achieve your body fat and body weight goals.

• Periodic reassessment of your body fat level may provide useful information, particularly to monitor the progress of your training and dietary program.

• A food diary is a favorite method used by sports dietitians to assess a diet. You may also find it is helpful for self-assessment, when you want to work on your own eating patterns. It is a good way to identify what you *actually* eat and drink, instead of what you *think* you eat and drink. This information can help you to decide strategies both to lose body fat or to maintain/gain weight.

Hints to Lose Body Fat
After looking over your food record you may find that you need to work on three basic issues—the quantity you eat, the type of food you eat, and the reasons that you eat.

Quantity of food. Decide exactly how much you *need* to eat, instead of what you would *like* to eat or what everyone else eats. This may mean reducing your usual serving by a half or a third, or stopping yourself from going back for seconds.

• Avoid letting yourself get too hungry before a meal. A small but well-timed snack may prevent you from eating everything in sight later on. Eat slowly so that you enjoy your food and can stop before you overeat.

• Make your meals as filling as possible:
Drink water (or a low-joule drink) before and during your meal.
Choose high-fibre versions of food.

Eat fruit rather than drink juice. Take care with all high-energy drinks (milk and fruit smoothies, liquid meal supplements). It is easy to quaff quarts of these when you are thirsty. Enjoy your special or favorite foods, but in smaller quantities. For example, share a dessert in a restaurant.

Type of food. Target fat, alcohol and sugar in your diet. These are high-energy foods that contribute little other nutrient value. Fat and oil intake is the most significant problem—see figure 8.1 for hints to reduce your intake.

Eating behavior. From your food record, take note of the reasons that you eat without feeling hungry or really needing the food. Change this behavior to get on top of this unnecessary eating. For example:

- Eating when depressed or upset: Tackle the problem that is causing you to feel depressed. Think up other activities to pamper yourself that don't involve food.
- Eating when bored: Find a non-food activity to enjoy and keep you occupied.
- Eating because the food is around: Either remove yourself or remove the food.
- Eating at social functions: At a restaurant, order exactly what you want and don't be afraid to make special requests. Eat just what you want, and don't be afraid to say 'no thank you'. If dining with friends, let your host know your needs. At some functions, you may choose not to eat at all (eat before you go, or when you get home).
- Find non-food ways to reward yourself for successful changes in your food habits and success with your loss of body fat!

Hints to Gain/Maintain Body Weight

How to Ensure a High-Energy Intake. Make the most of all opportunities throughout the day to eat high-energy nutritious foods. Above all, be organized. You will need to apply the same dedication to your eating program that you apply to your training. A haphazard approach—eating what is available, when it is convenient—is no way to guarantee the quantity or quality of food that you need.

- Increase the number of times that you eat rather than the size of the meals. A 'grazing' pattern of six to eight meals/snacks over the day enables greater intake while reducing gastric discomfort compared to the conventional pattern of three large meals. Build this into your day to suit your schedule.
- Avoid excessive intake of fibre, and replace some of the wholegrain foods in your diet with less bulky 'white' cereal choices (e.g. white bread, white rice). You may find it impossible to chew your way through a diet that is based solely on wholewheat and high-fibre fluids.
- Increase the energy content of nutritious carbohydrate foods by adding

a little sugar. For example, add jams to toast or syrup to whole wheat pancakes to boost the total kilojoule intake.

• Drink high-energy fluids. Make low-fat milkshakes and fruit smoothies, or try liquid meal supplements. These drinks provide low-bulk nutritious kilojoules and can be consumed with meals, or as snacks between meals, even quite close to training.

• Plan to have food on hand for every eating opportunity. Portable snacks are most useful (fruit, sandwiches, dried fruit, protein bars), and an emergency food supply in your car or sports bag is a great idea.

Figure 8.1

WAYS TO REDUCE YOUR INTAKE OF FAT AND OIL

- Choose lean cuts of meat, fish and chicken and remove all fat and skin, preferably before cooling.
- Try low-fat dairy products—skim milk, cottage cheese, reduced-fat hard cheese and low-fat brands of yoghurt and icecream. Make these protein foods accompany the meal rather than dominate it.
- Use cooking methods that add minimal or no fat—steam, grill, microwave, dry fry or bake on rack.
- Minimize the fats and oils that you add in food preparation, e.g. margarine or butter on bread, oils on salads, creams and buttery sauces on dishes.
- Use alternatives such as low-oil dressings and low-fat yoghurt, and adapt recipes to make sauces and gravies with low-fat ingredients.
- Enjoy high-fat foods such as pastries, cakes and chocolate as a treat, seeking quality rather than quantity. It is often possible to modify your own cake and dessert recipes to reduce the oil/butter and to use other low-fat ingredients.
- Be selective in your choice of takeaway fast foods. Most are high in fat, particularly those that are battered, fried or covered in pastry. There are other choices that are more suitable, e.g. a sandwich, lean hamburger with salad or souvlaki. When in doubt, have only a small serving.

ACTION-PACKED EATING—ACHIEVING NUTRIENT NEEDS

Our everyday living requires the intake of many nutrients, including protein, carbohydrate, vitamins, minerals and water. A heavy exercise program increases the requirements for many of these nutrients and a triathlete must aim for an 'action-packed' diet to match these increased needs. In general, two factors assist a triathlete to achieve nutrient needs:

A high energy intake: The more you can eat, the greater potential for eating carbohydrate, protein and micronutrients.

A wide menu of nutritious foods: Spreading your energy intake across a variety of nutrient-rich foods ensures the quantity and depth of nutrient intake.

While these principles will generally help you to achieve your nutritional goals, certain nutrients should be singled out for extra care. Two nutrients immediately affected by a heavy training program are water and carbohydrate. Significant sweat losses result from hot weather, intense and lengthy training sessions and a combination of these factors. Triathletes may be unaware of the extent of fluid losses during training, especially during swimming where sweat is masked by the pool water and during road cycling where sweat is quickly evaporated by the rush of wind. When two or more training sessions are undertaken back to back it is difficult to rehydrate fully. A gradual dehydration can build up over days, thus reducing training performance.

Carbohydrate requirements are also tied to exercise output, since muscle glycogen stores must be continually replaced after each workout. The carbohydrate needs of a triathlete will vary according to the training load. Even when training for an hour or less per day, the typical Western diet falls short of muscle fuel needs. Triathletes are encouraged to increase carbohydrate intake from about 40–45% of total dietary energy to at least 50–55% of total intake. This represents a change in the focus of everyday eating plans. However, some triathletes undertake a workload that calls for maximum glycogen synthesis each day. When loading up for a race, or simply recovering from a 4–6 hour training day, muscle glycogen stores may require the daily input of up to 9–10 g of carbohydrate per kilogram (.16 oz of carbohydrate for each pound) of body weight, i.e. 550–600 g (19–21 oz) of carbohydrate for a 60 kg (132 lb) triathlete, 700–800 g (25–28 oz) for a 80 kg (176 lb) triathlete. To achieve these intakes, the triathlete may have to devote 60–70% of total energy intake to carbohydrate. This will obviously require even greater dietary changes. Triathletes who fail to meet these carbohydrate goals will face a fuel crisis, often in the form of a gradual fatigue and failure to respond to training. Whether you 'hit the wall' in a single race or over a series of heavy workouts, the lack of muscle fuel has an overwhelming effect on performance.

Although endurance athletes rarely recognize it, protein requirements are increased by a strenuous training program. While many athletes think of protein in connection with strength, athletes and bulging muscles, in fact protein plays a more important role in contributing to the fuel mixture for prolonged endurance exercise. Up to 10% of the total energy expended during aerobic exercise comes from body protein stores, representing a small proportion of total energy but a significant amount of body protein after hours of daily training. The protein needs of a triathlete undertaking a strenuous training program may be double those of a sedentary person, i.e. 1.3–1.6 g (.045–.056 oz) of protein per kilogram (2.2 lb) body weight each day instead of 0.8 g/kg/day (.013 oz/1 lb/day).

Interestingly, some endurance athletes may overlook protein foods in their diets believing that carbohydrate-rich foods are all-important or that fat-containing foods should be shunned. The optimal training diet must be planned to meet the requirements for all nutrients, achieved through clever mixing and matching of a variety of foods.

Likewise, requirements for minerals such as iron and calcium should not be overlooked. Both have important roles in optimal sports performance—iron having a crucial role in the transport of oxygen in the blood and muscle, and calcium being needed to protect the integrity of bones which 'pound the pavements'. Iron requirements are also increased by heavy training, possibly to cope with increased iron losses from the gut, from sweating and from the chronic destruction of red blood cells during the physical traumas of training. Females already have greater requirements for iron than males to cover their menstrual blood losses, and adolescents need more iron during their growth spurts. Iron-rich foods should be an important consideration in the triathlete's diet to prevent and combat the threat of poor iron status. Iron deficiency, with or without anemia (low hemoglobin levels), is thought to reduce training recovery, if not competition performance.

While a high calcium intake does not guarantee strong bones, conversely a chronically low calcium intake can increase the risk of low bone density, especially if coupled with menstrual irregularities such as amenorrhea (loss of periods). Low levels of the hormone estrogen, a hallmark of this condition, are associated with the loss of bone density. Adolescents and females are important target groups for high-calcium eating.

Maintain Fluid Levels

• Organize a drink plan to cover before, during and after workout fluid-needs. This is crucial when strenuous training is undertaken in hot weather or when a sudden change in climate or environment is experienced. Ideas are provided in other sections of this chapter.

• Check fluid balance by monitoring acute changes in body weight, e.g. before and after a training session. If your body weight is stable (i.e. you are not on a weight loss or weight gain plan), then your 'early morning' body weight can tell you if you are maintaining hydration levels from day to day. Weigh yourself first thing in the morning after you have been to the toilet. The color and frequency of urine output is also a sign of hydration status.

High Carbohydrate Eating

• Be prepared to be different. A typical Western diet is NOT a high-carbohydrate diet. You will need to plan ahead, be organized, and on occasions stand apart from the crowd.

• Plan each meal around a carbohydrate food or foods, making it the centre of attention and adding the rest of the meal to it. For example, add filling to a bread roll, put sauce on pasta, add a topping to breakfast cereal. Make the carbohydrate food (or combination of carbohydrate foods) take up more than half the room on your plate or bowl and cut the traditional serve of protein food in half.

• Choose nutritious carbohydrate foods as the basis of your dietary plan—bread (and all its varieties), breakfast cereal, potatoes, corn, legumes, fruits, rice, pasta and other grains.

• Become versatile with cooking, try pasta in all its shapes and forms. Experiment with different types of rice and grains such as couscous or cracked wheat. Try legumes (kidney beans, chick peas, lentils etc.) in pasta sauces and casseroles, soups and salads. You may be able to replace some or all of the meat, fish or chicken in these dishes. Look for vegetarian and 'healthy eating' recipe books as a source of new ideas.

• Note that most vegetables, including salads, are not a significant source of carbohydrate. Always ensure that starchy vegetables, bread or pasta/rice are included to 'fuel up' cooked meals.

• Make nutritious 'carbo smoothies' from low-fat dairy products and fruit. Skim milk powder may be added for an extra boost.

• Boost carbohydrate intake further by adding a little sugar to your nutritious carbohydrate base. For example, a little jam on toast, syrup on pancakes or sweetened low-fat yogurt all provide a compact carbohydrate addition.

• A dietary list of carbohydrate-rich foods may be useful in gauging carbohydrate intake, or in swapping one carbohydrate source for another. See figure 8.2.

Boosting Protein Intake

• Protein foods should not be banished but carefully incorporated in your high-carbohydrate eating plans. Figure 8.3 provides a dietary list of protein foods, showing the high-protein content of animal foods as well as the valuable protein contribution of many of the high-carbohydrate foods themselves.

• Combine a small serving of high-quality animal protein with your high-carbohydrate dish. Low-fat protein foods (as found in figure 8.3) provide a valuable addition to protein and mineral requirements while allowing your emphasis on carbohydrate foods to be maintained. Examples include low-fat milk on cereal, fruit salad with low-fat yogurt, lean meat or chicken in a pasta sauce, seafood in a low-fat paella, chili con carne combining beans and lean beef.

• Alternatively, combine two types of vegetable protein foods to mix and match the amino acid profile of the meal. Examples include peanut butter on bread (no margarine) or a kidney bean sauce on pasta.

• Milk-based smoothies provide compact high-carbohydrate–protein combinations.

Iron Rich Nutrition

• Many of the protein-rich foods listed in figure 8.3 are also good sources of iron. Clever food combinations as cited above will also ensure iron-rich high-carbohydrate eating.

• The most accessible or well-absorbed source of iron is the 'heme'-type found in animal foods such as liver, red meat, shellfish and dark cuts of poultry. The total amount that you eat is less important than how frequently you can combine it with other foods at a meal. Thus, plan your meals to include a small amount of these high-iron foods frequently, rather than relying on a monthly splurge with a big steak. Good combinations include a slice of lean roast lamb in a sandwich, lean beef in a chili con carne, a spread of paté on toast and shellfish in a pasta sauce or rice stir fry.

• Vegetable sources of iron include breakfast cereals (fortified packaged cereals are a consistent food source), wholegrain breads and grains, legumes and green leafy vegetables. The iron in vegetable food sources, as well as eggs, is known as 'non-heme' iron and is poorly absorbed in comparison to the animal 'heme' form. However, its availability can be improved by combination with vitamin C foods or the animal iron food itself. Add to your list above, the following clever food combinations: glass of orange juice with your bowl of breakfast cereal, tomatoes in an omelet, peppers in a kidney bean casserole.

• Athletes at risk of iron deficiency include menstruating female triathletes, those in heavy training, adolescents and vegetarians or dieters who exclude animal iron foods. These athletes should regularly check their iron status with a sports medicine doctor and ensure that optimal dietary patterns are followed.

Achieving a Calcium Boost

• Various animal protein foods also provide the best sources of calcium. Low-fat dairy products are by far the most valuable calcium sources and can be easily included in the high-carbohydrate diet. At least two servings of dairy products should be consumed each day, e.g. skim milk on cereal, low-fat yogurt as dessert, a high-carbohydrate fruit/milk smoothie.

• Other useful sources of calcium include the fish bones found in sardines and tinned salmon. These can be incorporated into toast toppings or sauces for rice and pasta, thus continuing to meet the high-carbohydrate theme.

• Missed or irregular menstrual periods are not a healthy sign for a female athlete. Check with your doctor to ensure that proper care is taken to protect your bone density. Your efforts will need to include a high-calcium diet.

Figure 8.2

DIETARY LIST OF CARBOHYDRATE-RICH FOODS

Approximately 2 oz carbohydrate is supplied by the following:

Cereals	bread	4 slices (4¼ oz)
	bread roll	1 large or 2 small (4¼ oz)
	muffin	2 (4½ oz)
	breakfast cereal	=2.5–3 cups 'light' cereal
		=1–1.5 cups granola
		or 'heavier' cereal
	rolled oats	3¼ oz (1 cup)
	untoasted granola	3¼ oz (1cup)
	oatmeal/cornmeal	21½ oz (2.5 cups)
	scones/pancakes	4¼ oz (2 average size)
	wholemeal cake, low-fat	4¼ oz (1 large/2 small slices)
	cracker	3¼ oz (16)
	rice cakes	1¾ oz (3)
	plain granola bar	2 bars
	cookie	2¾ oz (8 plain, 4 cream)
	popcorn	3½ oz
	rice	6 oz (1 cup)
	pasta noodles	7 oz (1.5 cups)
Vegetables	potatoes	13 oz (1 large, 3 small)
		13 oz mashed (1.5 cups)
	carrots/pumpkin/peas	28½ oz (4 cups)
	corn	10¾ oz (1.5 cups)
Legumes	kidney beans, soybeans	10¾ oz (1.5 cups)
	baked beans	18 oz (2 cups)
	lentils	10¾ oz (1.5 cups)
Fruit	fresh fruit	3 medium apples, oranges
		2 medium bananas
	juice	15 oz sweetened
		21 oz unsweetened
	dried fruit	2¾ oz (4 tablsp)
	canned/stewed fruit	14¼ oz sweetened (2 cups)
		28½ oz unsweetened (4 cups)
	fruit salad, fresh	14¼ oz (2 cups)

Figure 8.2 (continued)		
Dairy	skim milk	1 q
products	fruit non-fat yogurt	14¼ oz (2 cartons)
	plain non-fat yogurt	28½ oz (4 cartons)
	low-fat ice cream	9 oz (2 cups)
Sweets	sugar	1¾ oz (2 heaped tablsp)
	jam and honey	2¼ oz (3 tablsp)
Drinks	soft drinks/	
	flavored mineral water	15 oz
	fruit juice	15–21 oz
	low-fat milk/fruit smoothie	10½–15 oz

RAPID RECOVERY

Being an athlete in the 1990s means pushing yourself hard and long, striving to go beyond your best and hold it together until the finish, and then to do it all over again tomorrow. Your ability to train once or twice a day, or to race each weekend, is dependent on your ability to recover from one session and present yourself at your best for the next.

The demands of your training program require you to take an active role in your recovery. You should no longer consider recovery and adaptation as passive events that happen in their own time, rather you should undertake special strategies to speed up these processes. Recovery techniques include massage, relaxation and sleep. Nutritional processes include the following:

Replacement of fluid and eletrolytes lost in sweat.
Refuelling of muscle glycogen stores.
Repair of any damage which occurs during training or racing, and the building of new structures to adapt to the workload.

In general, your nutrient-packed training diet should provide all the building blocks and the vitamins/minerals necessary to build and repair. Many of these processes probably occur over a longer time frame than the acute challenges of rehydrating and refuelling. Recent studies have focused on enhancing the acute recovery phase—examining not just

Figure 8.3

DIETARY LIST OF PROTEIN-RICH FOODS

Approximately ⅓ oz of protein is provided by the following foods:

Low-fat animal foods

grilled fish	1¾ oz (cooked weight)
tuna or salmon	1¾ oz
lean beef or lamb	1¼ oz (cooked weight)
veal	1¼ oz (cooked weight)
turkey or chicken	1½ oz (cooked weight)
game meat (rabbit, venison)	1¼ oz (cooked weight)
eggs	2 small
cottage cheese	2½ oz
reduced-fat cheese (11% fat slices)	1 oz
non-fat fruit yoghurt	7 oz
skim milk	9 oz
liquid protein meal supplement	5¼ oz

Vegetable foods

wholemeal bread	4 slices (4¼ oz)
corn flakes	3 cups (3¼ oz)
granola	1 cup (3½ oz)
cooked pasta or noodles	2 cups (10¾ oz)
cooked brown rice	2 cups (12½ oz)
cooked lentils	¾ cup (5¼ oz)
cooked kidney beans	¾ cup (5¼ oz)
baked beans	⁴⁄₅ cup (7¼ oz)
cooked soybeans or tofu	4¼ oz
nuts	2¼ oz
seeds (e.g. sesame)	2¼ oz

what to eat and drink, but when to do it! In the previous section the importance of a high-carbohydrate diet has been discussed setting you a daily goal of up to 9–10 g of carbohydrate for each kilogram (.16 oz of carbohydrate for each pound) you weigh. However, it is not just the total amount of carbohydrate eaten that determines muscle glycogen recovery. A recent study led by an American physiologist, John Ivy, has reported that the timing of carbohydrate intake is a crucial factor in the recovery process. These researchers found that when carbohydrate was eaten immediately after exhaustive exercise, there was immediate and rapid resynthesis of muscle glycogen—twice as fast as when carbohydrate intake was delayed until two hours after the session. Physiological features of exercise which are sustained for a period of time (e.g. 60–90 minutes) after the session has finished may help to explain this finding. Features such as increased blood (and nutrient) flow to the muscles and an accentuated uptake of glucose into the muscle cells would help to promote the conversion of post-exercise carbo-hydrate meals into muscle glycogen. It is recommended that 50–100 g (1¾–3½ oz) of carbohydrate be eaten within the first thirty minutes following a heavy exercise session.

Of course, this crucial time is usually when a triathlete has the least opportunity or desire to eat. You may not have access to food at the pool or running track, and you may have a busy schedule of stretching, showering and scurrying to your next commitment after training. Often fatigue and mild nausea after a hard training session make the thought of eating, let alone preparing a meal, an unwelcome idea.

Rehydration after a training session is also a practice that doesn't happen 'automatically'. Even when you have looked after your fluid intake before and during an exercise session, it is likely that you will finish with some degree of dehydration. Many triathletes will be unaware of their total fluid losses and should use scales to provide an indication—a loss of 1 kilogram is approximately equivalent to 1 litre of fluid (1 lb is approximately equivalent to ¼ pint of fluid). It is useful to plan a 'drink schedule' in the hours following heavy training sessions and races, particularly when the level of dehydration is moderate (2 kilograms [4.4 pounds] or more), the weather is hot and further exercise sessions are looming. Thirst is not a reliable reminder of the need to drink in these situations. Although water is a suitable rehydration fluid, there is some evidence that a sports drink containing electrolytes will achieve a speedier restoration of fluid balance. Since these sports drinks also contain carbohydrate they can have a dual advantage in promoting recovery.

There is some new evidence that early intake of other nutrients involved in repair and recovery (e.g. protein) can also enhance the time-course of these processes. Thus, clever planning and organization of nutritious meals/snacks to tie in with your training schedule may help you to bounce back quickly and strongly from each session.

ACTION
• Plan your meals/snacks to fit in with your training schedule, particularly to enhance recovery after hard training sessions and races. Aim to eat a nutritious meal within 15–60 minutes of these sessions, or alternatively have a quick snack straight after and a nutritious meal later on.
• Immediate requirements are fluid intake, some carbohydrate (at least 50–100 g [1¾–3½ oz]) and perhaps a general intake of protein and nutrients. While this may all be found in a nutritious meal, a quick and light snack may be the most practical choice in many situations. Ideas include:

Protein drink or fruit juice plus a sandwich.
Low-fat yogurt and some fruit.
Protein bar plus water/fruit juice.
Bowl of granola with low-fat milk plus glass of fruit juice and extra water.
Low-fat fruit smoothie made with low-fat milk, fruit (e.g. bananas/strawberries) and low-fat yogurt.

• Many of these snacks are portable and can be taken with you to your training or race venue. Figure 8.2 lists high-carbohydrate foods that will allow you to choose other 50–100 g (1¾–3½ oz) carbohydrate servings.
• Follow up recovery snacks with nutritious high-carbohydrate meals and adequate fluid intake thus continuing to restore fluid and fuel needs as quickly as possible.

EATING FOR THE FUTURE
Many of the chronic diseases of Western civilization (e.g. diabetes, cancers, cardiovascular disease) are now known to be associated with the Western lifestyle. Dietary risk factors include a low intake of fibre and a high intake of fat and salt. There is also evidence that a healthy consumption of certain vitamins and other food chemicals may provide a measure of protection from some of these diseases. Thus, nutrition experts in many countries have formulated dietary guidelines to steer people towards a healthier lifestyle and reduced risk of disease. The Australian dietary guidelines are presented in figure 8.4.
On examination, the guidelines for a healthy diet well encompass the dietary recommendations for top performance in sport. The emphasis on high-carbohydrate, nutrient-rich meals is a shared goal as is the focus on

reduced fat intake. A committed athlete will drink alcohol in moderation (if at all), knowing that a couple of glasses may be enjoyable or celebratory but that excess intake erodes fitness, skill and health.

In the past, many athletes have thought that training and exercise 'excused' them from needing to watch their diets. It was considered that as long as you 'burnt up calories' on the road then you could 'eat whatever

---

Figure 8.4

DIETARY GUIDELINES

1. Enjoy a wide variety of foods from four food groups.
2. Eat plenty of breads and cereals (preferably wholegrain), vegetables, legumes and fruit(s).
3. Eat a diet low in fat and in particular, saturated fat.
4. Balance a nutritious diet and physical activity to keep your weight within a healthy range.
5. If you drink alcohol, limit your intake.
6. Eat only a moderate amount of sugar and foods containing added sugar.
7. Use salt sparingly and choose low-salt foods.
8. Drink plenty of water.

Companion guidelines:
10. Calcium—make sure you eat foods containing available calcium. This is particularly important for girls and women.
11. Iron—make sure you eat foods containing available iron. This applies particularly to girls, women, vegetarians and athletes.

---

you like'. In fact, all of us are guided by the recommendations for a healthy eating plan. As you eat to perform at your best, consider yourself a good role model for the rest of the community and 'sell' them on the benefits of a nutritious diet.

FUN WITH FOOD

Triathletes are known for their enthusiasm and dedication. They don't do things in half measures and that often includes dietary practices. Some triathletes interpret nutrition advice to mean that all 'bad' foods must be eliminated from their diets and only 'good' foods eaten. They throw their efforts into dietary restriction, removing any food sources of fat, sugar or salt. The result of excessive food restriction is an unbalanced diet, often low in kilojoules, important nutrients and enjoyment value. The possibilities for social eating, and even for sharing meals with the family, are also sacrificed by dietary extremists.

While a healthy training diet means a modification of present Western eating practices, no diet needs to be so extreme that it removes the pleasure of eating. The most important dietary guideline is to enjoy a variety of foods, balancing 'a little of what you fancy' with 'a lot of what you need'.

PRACTICE MAKES PERFECT

In the next section, nutrition strategies for competition will be explored, including pre-race meals, eating and drinking during races and post-race recovery nutrition. A well-prepared triathlete should experiment with these strategies in training sessions. This offers the opportunity to learn practical skills (e.g. drinking on the run), identify problems (e.g. gastrointestinal problems from some foods, dislike for some drinks) and refine the perfect race plan. Not only will this boost your confidence and ensure smooth performance on race day, but the special strategies may also improve your training performance. For example, lengthy training rides and runs will be assisted by a planned intake of fluid and carbohydrate. Many triathletes head out for long training sessions with a token supply of food and/or drinks. While it is hard to mimic the network of aid stations that cater for competitors during races, at least target some training sessions for a dress rehearsal of race day strategies.

COMPETITION NUTRITION—EATING TO WIN

Race nutrition should be planned to combat the factors that are likely to cause fatigue or loss of performance in your event. As outlined in previous chapters, various physiological causes of fatigue are likely to come up during the race, subject to factors such as your level of training, the length of the race, the environmental conditions and your race pace. Dietary strategies can help to reduce, prevent or delay the effects of many of these factors. Issues to consider include gastrointestinal discomfort, dehydration, depletion of muscle fuel stores, hypoglycemia (low blood sugar levels) and in ultra-distance races, hyponatremia (low blood sodium levels).

Your checklist for competition eating involves strategies before, during and after the race:

Do you fuel up before the race to ensure that your muscles are prepared with adequate carbohydrate stores?

Do you eat a pre-race meal that fine-tunes your body's carbohydrate stores without causing gastrointestinal upset during the race?

Do you maintain hydration by drinking appropriate amounts of fluid before, during and after the event?

Do you supplement your fuel stores during long distance events by consuming carbohydrate as you race?

Do you promote recovery and remember your nutrition goals even when the race is over?

FUELLING UP—GENERAL RACES

Racing hard to the finish line is dependent on your ability to continue to generate energy, particularly from your carbohydrate stores. A common cause of fatigue and loss of performance is the exhaustion of muscle glycogen stores. Therefore an important goal of race preparation is to build up adequate fuel supplies to last throughout the event. 'Carbo loading' has become a term almost universally used by athletes to describe this process. Unfortunately, in many cases tradition has overtaken the science behind 'fuelling up' and some triathletes indulge in over-eating rituals that neither do justice to the true meaning of carbohydrate loading nor to the physiological needs of competition.

By strict definition, carbohydrate loading is a special program undertaken prior to endurance or ultra-endurance length races, aiming to maximize muscle glycogen levels to cope with these extreme duration events. This strategy will be covered in the next section. Generally, events of less than two hours (races up to and including the Olympic distance) do not require such elevated fuel stores. Unlike a single discipline sport (a marathon or a cycle race), different muscle groups will be recruited in turn throughout the triathlon—for the swim, the ride and then the run. Thus, your total fuel needs will be shared by a number of muscle groups. In addition, your training will have fine-tuned these muscles into very efficient fuel stores; a trained muscle adapts to be able to store greater amounts of glycogen and to utilize it more slowly at the same relative work load.

Fuelling up for short distance races is simply a matter of giving your muscles sufficient time (24–36 hours) and sufficient carbohydrate

(400–600 g [14–21 oz] per day) to recover their 'trained' glycogen storage capacity. Daily training is actually a mini-cycle of loading up and expending glycogen from one session to the next. The luxury of extra time—a small break before your race—should look after the refuelling needs of most triathletes. The length of your break will depend on how often you are racing and how important the race is. Triathletes who need or choose to train hard right up to the event, or to compete every week, will find their race preparation a greater challenge. Not only is their time for fuel storage cut short, but the presence of muscle damage or soreness from recent heavy training will slow down the rate of glycogen synthesis. These triathletes are advised to further increase carbohydrate intake during the final fuel-up phase.

ACTION

• Your training diet is already based on high-carbohydrate eating and provides a good plan for pre-race fuel storage. You might like to further emphasize your carbohydrate intake over the last twenty-four hours prior to the event. Above all, make sure that you are fuelling up on true high-carbohydrate foods. Many athletes mistake 'junk foods' and other high-fat foods as good carbohydrate sources and look to these foods in their pre-race preparation. See figure 8.5 for a comparison of some badly chosen high-fat foods and some suggested high-carbohydrate alternatives.

• Organize a training break that will leave adequate time for muscles to store glycogen fuel, 24–36 hours or more. This may require careful planning if you intend to race each week.

• If you plan to train heavily right up to race day, accentuate your carbohydrate preparation further. Muscles that are well depleted or damaged will require greater carbohydrate intake to restore fuel levels.

• If you like to race 'light', see comments on preparing an empty gut in the next section on carbohydrate loading.

LOADING UP FOR LONG DISTANCE RACES

Races of half-Ironman distance and greater may challenge the carbohydrate stores of various individual muscle groups. Muscle glycogen stores may become depleted and/or blood glucose levels may fall causing you respectively to 'hit the wall' or 'blow up'. Triathletes undertaking these events are encouraged to maximize their pre-race glycogen stores by undertaking a carbohydrate loading preparation. The modern-day carbohydrate loading program is based on seventy-two

---

Figure 8.5

CHOOSING LOWER-FAT VERSIONS OF CARBOHYDRATE FOODS

High-Fat Carbo Food	Reduced-Fat High-Carbo Food
Lasagna	Pasta with a small amount of low-fat sauce—lean meat, seafood, chicken or vegetarian sauce (low-oil cooking)
Pasta with rich creamy sauce	Pasta as above
English muffin soaked with margarine	English muffin with honey or jam
Pancake soaked with whipped butter/cream	Pancake with honey, jam, syrup or fruit (and perhaps a little low-fat ice cream or yogurt)
Croissant	Bagel or bread roll
Pizza with everything Pizza with extra cheese	Thick crust pizza with low fat toppings (lean meat/seafood/vegetarian) and less cheese.
French fries	Baked potato
Cupcake or pastry	Scone, fruit loaf, reduced fat muffin recipes.
Toasted ham and cheese sandwich	toasted banana or baked bean sandwich—thick sliced bread
Ice cream—especially specialty types	Low-fat ice cream, Low-fat yogurt
Thick shake	Fruit smoothie made with low-fat milk, fruit, low-fat ice cream/yogurts

---

hours of high-carbohydrate intake and exercise break. When the technique was first devised in the 1960s, this seventy-two hour period was preceded by a three-day 'depletion phase'.

During this phase muscle glycogen levels were exhausted by heavy exercise and a low-carbohydrate diet. Recent studies have shown that the depletion phase (an uncomfortable experience) is not necessary to stimulate the muscles to overfill with glycogen, at least for trained athletes. Trained muscle has already undergone physiological adaptations that will allow it to store higher than normal glycogen levels, particularly when given a longer break and high-carbohydrate intake. The modified loading program is not only effective, but is more convenient and pleasant to undertake than the original depletion-loading schedule.

Carbohydrate intake goals during the loading phase are set at approximately 10 g per kilogram (.16 oz per pound) of body weight each day, e.g. 600 g (21 oz) of carbohydrate per day for a 60 kg (132 lb) triathlete or 800 g (28 oz) for a 80 kg (176 lb) competitor. This is believed to be the threshold for glycogen synthesis, i.e. the maximum amount of carbohydrate that can be stored as glycogen each day.

ACTION

• Identify whether you really need to carbohydrate load for your race. Is it likely that muscle glycogen stores will be depleted by the event? While an Ironman event may be a clear-cut decision, there may be shorter races that are less certain. Ask yourself, have you experienced severe fatigue during previous races over this distance? Does your training program allow you to take three days for break and loading? If so, you may be helped by a carbohydrate loading program.

• Organize the week leading up to the event carefully. The first 3–4 days of the week may still involve a reasonable training load. Eat a normal diet during this period. Don't push extra carbohydrate foods at this stage, but neither starve yourself of muscle fuel.

• Over the last 72 hours/3 days, switch to a very high-carbohydrate diet—a daily carbohydrate intake of 10 g per kilogram (.16 oz per pound) of your weight. Sample menus to achieve these carbohydrate levels are provided in figure 8.6. Further ideas can be achieved by substituting foods from figure 8.2 or by consulting a sports dietitian. Training should be interrupted for breaks during this loading phase to maximize the opportunity for muscle glycogen storage.

• To help meet your carbohydrate quota, and to save on the bulk of high-fibre complex carbohydrate foods, you may find it helpful to increase your sugar intake above the level normally found in your training diet. Be careful to choose foods that are good carbohydrate sources, whether complex carbohydrate or sugar, rather than high-fat foods. Many triathletes 'garbo-load' rather than carbo-load. Again, see figure 8.5 to help with appropriate food choices.

• High-carbohydrate supplements (often called carbo-loaders) can also be useful during the high-carbohydrate phase. Like sugar, they provide a compact, low-bulk form of carbohydrate and the instructions on the container make it easy to calculate just how much carbohydrate you have consumed. For example, a litre (4 pints) of a typical carbo-loader provides 250 g (9 oz) of carbohydrate, a significant contribution to your daily needs. Remember, however, that large amounts of sugar or these high-carbohydrate supplements do not make up a 'balanced' diet, i.e. they do not supply adequate amounts of other important nutrients such as protein, vitamins and minerals. Nevertheless, for the three days of carbohydrate loading your focus should be on meeting carbohydrate goals. You can return to your healthy training diet once the event is over.

• Many athletes like to race with a light 'empty' feeling rather than a full stomach. By switching to greater amounts of simple carbohydrate foods and reducing your intake of high-fibre carbohydrate foods over the last twenty-four hours pre-race, you will be able to simultaneously top off muscle glycogen stores as well as reduce your gastrointestinal contents. 'Carbo-loaders' and liquid meal supplements can be useful for this purpose. The switch to a low-bulk diet will leave you feeling 'light and fast' on race morning. Experiment in training to see if this has merit for your race.

• Drink plenty of fluids during your loading days. You will need to be well hydrated for a long event, especially in hot weather. Your muscles will also store water along with the glycogen.

• Enjoy official carbo-loading banquets or pre-race functions but take care not to lose your focus, even if others around you are indulging in eating frenzies. Save your competitiveness for the race and stick to sensible types and amounts of food. Hopefully the event organizer or caterer has consulted a sports dietitian to arrange a suitable low-fat carbohydrate feast.

THE PRE-EVENT MEAL

The goals of the pre-race meal are to top off fluid and glycogen levels (particularly liver glycogen which needs refilling after a night's sleep) and to keep you comfortable during the event. Eating too little or too much before racing can both cause problems—hunger during a race can be just as unpleasant as a stomach jostling with undigested food. In most cases your race preparation should be well completed and the pre-race meal is simply a fine tuning of fluid and carbohydrate levels. Since most races are conducted early in the morning there is usually little time for a large meal to be eaten and digested. Each triathlete will have their own likes, dislikes and even superstitions about pre-race eating. Experiment, particularly in training, until you have found a successful routine.

Figure 8.6

SAMPLE MENUS FOR CARBOHYDRATE LOADING

These menus provide about 700 g (25 oz) of carbohydrate per day—allowing a 70 kg (154 lb) triathlete to meet the recommendation of 10 g of carbohydrate per kg ($^1/_6$ oz per lb) per day. You may need to adapt the menus to eat more or less carbohydrate. A carbo-loader can be used to quickly boost total carbohydrate intake while avoiding 'bulky' eating.

These menus are proposed for carbohydrate loading only—while meeting carbohydrate requirements they do not generally meet all nutritional goals for everyday eating.

Menu 1:

breakfast 2 cups corn flakes + 1 cup of skim milk
1 cup sweetened canned peaches
250 ml (7½ oz) orange juice

snack 2 thick slices toast + Tbsp honey (slight smear of margarine if any)

lunch 2 large bread rolls with 2 bananas as filling
50 g (1¾ oz) jelly beans
375 ml (11¼ oz) can soft drink

snack large coffee roll (unbuttered)
250 ml (7½ oz) fruit juice

dinner 3 cups of boiled rice (made into light stir fry with vegetables and a little ham)
2 cups fresh fruit salad

snack 2 biscuits + Tbsp jam (smear of margarine if any)
extra water during day

Day 2

breakfast 2 cups oatmeal + 1 cup skim milk
2 Tbsp raisins
250 ml (7½ oz) fruit juice
2 slices toast (smear of margarine) + 1 banana

snack 2 muffins + Tbsp jam (smear of margarine if any)

lunch stack of three pancakes + 60 ml (1¾ oz) maple syrup + small scoop ice cream

snack protein energy bar
250 ml (7½ oz) fruit juice

Figure 8.6 (continued)

dinner	3 cups cooked pasta + 1 cup tomato pasta sauce
	2 slices bread (smear of margarine if any)
	250 ml (7½ oz) cordial
	1 carton low-fat fruit yogurt
snack	protein energy bar
	extra water during day

Figure 8.7

PRE-EVENT MEAL IDEAS

- Breakfast cereal with low-fat milk and fresh/canned fruit
- Pancakes and syrup
- Muffins or biscuits with jam or honey
- Toast and baked beans or canned spaghetti
- Creamed rice (made with low-fat milk)
- Boiled rice
- Spaghetti with low-fat meat or vegetarian sauce
- Rolls, bagels or sandwiches with banana filling
- Fruit salad with low-fat yogurt

ACTION

• Base your pre-race meal on high-carbohydrate low-fat foods. Experiment with the type, timing and amount of food that works best for you. As a general rule, eat at least two hours before the race. Very early race starts may leave you with the option of a light snack or liquid meal supplement. A later start may allow a larger meal to be eaten with more time to spare before the gun sounds.

• While some triathletes are content to eat a smaller version of their everyday breakfasts, other competitors like to eat special pre-race meals. Food ideas are presented in figure 8.7. While a low-fat intake should be followed by everyone, some triathletes may also need to limit fibre intake in the pre-race meal. Recent studies have reported that triathletes who reported gastrointestinal upset during a race were more likely to have eaten a high-fat/high-protein or high-fibre pre-event meal.

• Liquid meal supplements provide low-bulk high-carbohydrate nutrition for triathletes who have limited time before the race start, or for those who suffer from 'sensitive stomachs' due to pre-race nerves.

• If you are competing away from home you may need to organize your own food supplies for the pre-event meal. The hospitality industry does not always cater to early rising athletes, so think ahead to ensure that you are not caught without your pre-race food requirements. Liquid meal supplements are also handy as a portable 'meal in a can'.

• There is no real value in consuming large amounts of sugar or sugary foods in the hour before your race, despite the tradition that lingers in some circles. There is no quick 'energy boost' to be gained and a few athletes are actually disadvantaged by this practice—by gastric upsets or by a quicker burning of carbohydrate fuel during the race. Trust that your dietary preparation over the last days and race morning has looked after your fuel needs. Try any pre-race meals or pre-race snacks in training to ensure that your competition strategies are problem free.

EATING AND DRINKING DURING RACES

The 'walls' that are waiting to be 'hit' during the race include dehydration and lack of carbohydrate fuel. Even though your race preparation has optimized your fuel and hydration levels, race conditions and your race pace may cause a steady depletion.

Dehydration is an important problem, since a hard-working triathlete in hot weather can sweat in excess of a litre (1½ pints) per hour. (In extreme conditions, such as the Ironman race, sweat losses may be considerably higher). Even moderate fluid losses (1–2 kg/2.2–4.4 lb) can impair race performance—both physically and mentally—and on hot days severe dehydration is a major risk for heat injury (e.g. heat exhaustion, heat stroke). In sprint events and races up to the Olympic distance, fluid needs are the principle issue of race nutrition and water is probably the most widely used fluid. Of course, a sports drink is also suitable—in fact, a pleasant tasting drink may encourage you to take better care of your fluid needs. Race rules generally insist (or advise) that competitors start the race with a full bottle of fluid on their bikes, and aid stations are usually provided in transition areas as well as on the run. Those who are out on the course for long periods in hot weather are usually the target of advice to make use of these opportunities, However, even top competitors need to be warned of the disadvantages and dangers of dehydration. A drinking pouch, consisting of a pressurized sack with a plastic tube running along the top tube to the triathlete's mouth, can provide easy access to fluid for those who worry about wasting precious seconds reaching down to the bottle cage.

Longer races require a more definite plan of fluid intake to combat mounting sweat losses. In addition, there becomes a more obvious advantage to supplementing body fuel reserves during the race. As your various glycogen stores become exhausted during long-course and Ironman length races, your trained muscles become glad to take up any carbohydrate that you can eat or drink. Your goal is to anticipate the depletion of your body stores and then maintain an adequate supply of additional carbohydrate to take over your muscles' fuel requirements. A ball-park figure of 30–60 g (1–2 oz) of carbohydrate per hour is suggested, starting at a point in the race that will allow blood glucose levels to be well-maintained before your muscles need to call heavily on this supply. At the business end of an Ironman race you may need every bit of a carbohydrate intake of 50–70 g (1¾–2½ oz) per hour.

There are many traditions for consuming carbohydrate during races, ranging from bananas and chocolate bars, to sports drinks and sports bars. A successful plan needs to take into account both carbohydrate and fluid requirements, as well as avoid gastrointestinal discomfort and upsets. Perhaps the most efficient and trouble-free strategy to look after race needs is to use a sports drink. Drinks like this have been scientifically developed to empty rapidly from the stomach, provide moderate levels of carbohydrate and promote intestinal absorption by supplying a small level of electrolytes. A comfortable intake of 600–1000 ml (20–34 fl oz) per hour provides 40–70 g (1⅜–2½ oz) of carbohydrate as well as a sizeable attack on sweat losses. Your race consumption should vary according to your fluid and carbohydrate needs. Solid foods are not necessary (unless you suffer from an 'empty' stomach during long events), but may be used to provide additional carbohydrate. Over-consumption of solid foods, especially those with a high-fat or fibre content can cause gastric distress in some people—particularly during the running leg. Any race plan should be well practiced before the event.

ACTION

Sprint and Short Races
• Begin the race well hydrated, especially on hot days. Drink plenty at your pre-race meal, and in hot weather some extra glasses in the 30–60 minutes pre-race.
• Judge the weather and your expected sweat losses to make good use of fluid intake opportunities during the race. On hot days and in longer races it is important to drink on the bike and run. This needn't slow you down too much; use drinking pouches and a well-practiced technique to

grab a quick drink in the transition area or on the run.
• Rehydrate well after the race

Long Course and Ironman Races
• Consider the anticipated fluid and fuel needs of your intended race. Consult the race instructions to find what the aid station network and menu will have on offer for you, and whether there is opportunity for you to add your own provisions. This will help you to form your race day plan.
• Practice in training with the types and amounts of fluid (or food) that you intend to use so that you become an expert. Make sure that you enjoy the taste of your exercise refreshments, and that your nutritional goals are met by your plan of intake.
• Prepare well for the race so that you are well hydrated and fuelled up. The theoretical nutritional requirements during endurance length events are:

> 30–60 g (1–2 oz) of carbohydrate per hour (increasing as the race develops).
> Fluid to keep pace with sweat losses. Under usual conditions a fluid intake of 500–800 ml/hr (17–27 fl oz/hr) should match about two-thirds of your sweat rate. In extremely hot environments you may need to aim for 1000 ml (34 fl oz) per hour, or as much as can be comfortably tolerated.
> In Ironman length events it may be beneficial to provide a small level of electrolytes in your drinks. Not only will this enhance intestinal uptake of fluids but it may help to offset the small risk of hyponatremia (low blood sodium) in some athletes.

• Fluid intake should start as soon as possible in the race—in the swim-bike transition. Plan to drink regularly, aiming for 150–250 ml (5–8½ fl oz) (half a small bottle or a small glass) each 15–20 minutes. You should be able to keep your bottle supply well stocked from the aid stations on the cycle leg, and help yourself to drinks as you pass through aid stations on the run. Cold drinks are more refreshing and palatable and may add an additional cooling effect. Pouring extra water over yourself may also be refreshing.
• Don't let yourself become dehydrated. Dehydration is known to reduce gastric emptying rate and to retard the entry of any further fluid that is drunk. Not only do you increase the risk of bloating and gastrointestinal upset, but your chance of rehydrating becomes minimal.

• Your stomach empties fastest when it is fullest. In extremely hot conditions you may need to maximize fluid intake to meet extreme sweat losses. Make use of the 'volume effect' by starting the race with the largest amount of fluid in your stomach that can be comfortably tolerated. Top it off each 15–20 minutes as it empties, thus maximizing gastric emptying and your rate of fluid replacement.

• Carbohydrate intake may begin simultaneously with fluid intake or may start later in the event. In any case, begin a significant intake before you anticipate feeling fatigued and continue intake throughout the event.

• Intake of 500–800 ml (17–34 fl oz) per hour of a sports drink supplies fluid and carbohydrate needs as well as a small intake of electrolytes. This can provide the basis of your race intake plan. Additional water can be used to rinse your mouth or add to fluid intake in conditions of extreme sweat loss. Figure 8.2 shows the carbohydrate content of other fluids and foods to allow you to calculate 50 g (1¾ oz) carbohydrate servings.

• Although it is not necessary to eat solid foods to provide carbohydrate requirements, many athletes enjoy the tradition or the convenience. Many races offer choices such as bananas, oranges, chocolate chip cookies and sandwiches, and other athletes like the convenience of protein bars. If you intend to try solid food, experiment in training to ensure that you are not troubled by gastrointestinal side effects. Make sure that your fluid needs are not neglected. The choice of using solid or fluid sources of carbohydrate during a race is not mutually exclusive—a combination of both may be the best strategy for most triathletes (see below).

• In races that last longer than 6–8 hours, it is possible that a 'liquid only' race plan (i.e. sports drinks) will leave you feeling a little hungry and empty in the stomach. If so, a little solid food (a couple of bites from a sandwich or banana) can help to allay these feelings and provide a brief change from the taste of the drinks.

RECOVERY AFTER THE RACE

While the end of a successful race is a cause for celebration, many triathletes are quickly back into the daily grind of training. Maybe there is another race next week, or perhaps you are in the midst of a solid training phase before a longer race. In any case, there is a need to pick yourself up after the race and move on quickly. The nutritional components of recovery have been discussed in the training nutrition section.

These strategies are sometimes harder to put into practice in the competition setting—food opportunities at the race venue are often sparse and there are many distractions (awards ceremonies, race post-mortems, socializing and celebrating). It is great to be able to enjoy the atmosphere of the race, but try not to totally compromise your recovery goals. With a little thought and planning you can start your recovery even as you lie back and bask in the pleasure of a finished event.

ACTION

• Support the efforts of race directors who provide a post-race spread or a race bag containing recovery foods and fluids. Trestle tables may provide a 'quick grab' of items such as fruit, sports drinks, low-fat yogurt, granola bars or sports bars. Alternatively, a finisher's bag may bundle up a selection of snacks and drinks. Foods that are bite-sized, light, or cool and watery are all likely to appeal to tired, thirsty triathletes.

• Take your own drinks and high-carbohydrate snacks to supplement race provisions. This is especially important if the race catering is poor, if the race venue is isolated from food outlets and if you plan to stay around the race for most of the day.

• Remember the value of speedy intake of drinks and carbohydrate foods, particularly when you are quite dehydrated and have some muscle damage/soreness. Even if you are tired, 'on a high', or anxious to catch up with friends, make sure that food and fluid recovery are a top priority. It is possible to do lots of things at once, as long as you keep your food/drink supply handy.

• Celebrate with a small amount of alcohol, if this is your desire, but don't let this interfere with your recovery. Make sure you have rehydrated with sports drinks, fruit juices or water before you start on alcoholic drinks. Enjoy quality rather than quantity with alcohol, perhaps a glass of good champagne rather than a truckload of beer. Low alcohol beers are also a good alternative.

Can Short Cuts be Found in a Bottle?

Every sports magazine is filled with advertisements for pills, potions and bars that promise to make you leaner, stronger, faster or whatever it takes to be a better triathlete. Many triathletes claim to be walking advertisements for these products, both officially and by word of mouth. How can you resist such tempting promises? Or alternatively, how can you afford to let your opponents get a competitive edge over you? Many triathletes are overwhelmed by the conflicting information and the pressure to buy.

The answer to these questions is made easier by dividing the world of supplements into two major categories. The first category can be termed 'dietary supplements' and is characterized by products that address real physiological and nutritional needs arising in sport. Many nutritional requirements of athletes have been identified and discussed in this chapter, e.g. compact and high-nutrient energy sources for 'big eaters', or carbohydrate and fluid mixtures for use during endurance sport. While these nutritional needs can be generally found in food, sometimes a more efficient or compact form can be assembled and commercialized for athletes. Generally, these products are supported by nutrition education material to explain how they should be used in sport. After all, there is no 'magic' behind the product itself, but a triathlete who can utilize the supplement to meet their nutritional goals—the right supplement at the right time in the right amounts—will be rewarded with good performance. Examples of these dietary supplements include sports drinks, liquid meal replacements and 'carbohydrate loader' supplements. These supplements have a high credibility rating among sports science experts.

The other type of supplement might be termed the 'nutritional ergogenic aid', 'ergogenic' meaning to directly enhance work performance. Supplements such as large doses of vitamins, amino acids, ginseng, coenzymes and bee pollen all fall into this category. In general they promise to enhance performance through a pharmacological rather than physiological means, e.g. they often claim to 'speed up' metabolism. In general their mechanism of action is more a theory than a scientifically proven fact. Unfortunately, there is little regulation of the supplement industry and manufacturers are not required to test their products or substantiate their claims, hence the existence of the outstanding and almost unbelievable promises. Anecdotes and testimonials do not offer acceptable scientific proof, since they have not controlled for the many other factors that affect performance, including the 'placebo effect' (the power of positive thinking). Most of these substances remain largely untested, both for advantages or for side effects, and where studies have been undertaken they generally fail to support a beneficial effect on performance. Of course, it is difficult and expensive to conduct tests that will confirm tiny improvements in exercise results. While a 'significant' change to an athlete may be an improvement of seconds or less, a statistician requires a larger margin to satisfy their definition of 'significant'. Nevertheless, more thorough scientific testing is required before sports scientists will rate most of the current range of 'nutritional ergogenic aids' as credible sports supplements.

So where does this leave the triathlete? The good news is that many dietary supplements have a valid and practical role in sports nutrition. Supplements such as sports drinks and meal replacements can be utilized to improve the nutrition and performance of triathletes. Fortunately, most of the manufacturing companies take a responsible role in supporting nutrition education and sports science research to assist athletes to make best use of such products. A sports dietitian can also provide expert advice about the beneficial role of sports supplements, in conjunction with a nutritious diet.

There are still many unanswered questions about the large array of other nutritional ergogenic aids, and we should all join the call for scientific testing of these products. In the meantime, there is the possibility that one or more of them might actually improve your performance, whether by real action or by the placebo effect. It is up to each triathlete to judge the cost of being a human 'guinea pig'. The downside includes the possibility of side effects from the long-term and heavy use of some products. All nutritional ergogenic aids, including vitamins, are chemicals, and too much of any chemical can cause problems. Your wallet will certainly be affected, as many products are expensive and a high dosage is recommended. Finally, don't pin your hopes on the supplement and overlook factors that definitely influence performance. There is no factor that can replace good training, an optimal training diet, the right equipment, a strong mental attitude and adequate sleep and recovery.

SEEKING ADDITIONAL HELP

This chapter has provided you with some theories of sports nutrition and some ideas to help turn the theory into practice. If your interest and scientific understanding has been challenged you might like to follow up with some additional reading from the reference list at the end of this chapter. Alternatively, you may have nutritional problems or questions that require personal attention. Perhaps you would simply like an assessment of how well you have used the nutrition advice in this book. The expert you seek is a sports dietitian, trained in the science of exercise physiology and nutrition and well practiced in the art of education and counselling. Contact your local sports medicine centre or the Dietitians Association in your State. A sports dietitian can help you to move further along the road to optimal nutrition and champion performance.

SUGGESTED READING

General

Burke, L. 1992, *The Complete Guide to Food for Sports Performance*, Allen and Unwin.

Inge, K. and Roberts, C. 1989, *Food for Sport Cookbook*, Simon and Schuster.

O'Connor, H. 1991, *Fitness Food*, Better Living Collections, Fairfax Press.

Advanced

Brodie, D. A. 1988, 'Techniques of measurement of body composition' Part 1 *Sports Medicine* 5, pp. 11–40.

Brodie, D. A. 1988, 'Techniques of measurement of body composition' Part 2, *Sports Medicine* 5, pp. 74–98.

Brotherhood, J. R. 1984, 'Nutrition and sports performance', *Sports Medicine* 1, pp. 350–389.

Brouns, F., Saris, W. H. M., Rehrer, N. J. 1987, 'Abdominal complaints and gastrointestinal function during long-lasting exercise', *International Journal of Sports Medicine* 8, pp. 175–189.

Brownell, K. D., Steen, S. N., Wilmore, J. 1987, 'Weight regulation in athletes: analysis of metabolic and health effects', *Medicine and Science in Sports and Exercise* 19, pp. 546–556.

Burke, L. M. 1992, 'Protein and amino acid needs of the athlete', *State of the Art Review* 28, Australian Sports Commission.

Burke, L. M., Read, R. S. D. 1987, 'Diet patterns of elite Australian male triathletes', *Physician and Sports Medicine* 15 (2), pp. 140–155.

Burke, L. M., Read, R. S. D. 1989, 'Sports nutrition: approaching the nineties', *Sports Medicine* 8, pp. 80–100.

Burke, L. M., Read, R. S. D. 1993, 'Dietary supplements in sport', Part 1, *Sports Medicine* 15, pp. 43–65.

Coggan, A. R., Coyle, E. F. 1987, 'Reversal of fatigue during prolonged exercise by carbohydrate infusion or ingestion', *Journal of Applied Physiology* 63, pp. 2388–2395.

Coggan, A. R., Coyle, E. F. 1989, 'Metabolism and performance following carbohydrate ingestion late in exercise', *Medicine and Science in Sports and Exercise* 21, pp. 59–65.

Costill, D. L. 1988, 'Carbohydrates for exercise: dietary demands for optimal performance', *International Journal of Sports Medicine* 9, pp. 1–18.

Costill, D. L., Flynn, M. G., Kirwan, I. P., Houmard, J. A., Mitchell, J. B., Thomas, R. T., Park, S. H. 1988, 'Effects of repeated days of intensified training on muscle glycogen and swimming performance', *Medicine and Science in Sports and Exercise* 20, pp. 249–254.

Costill, D. L., Pascoe, D. D., Fink, W. J., Robergs, R. A., Barr, S. I., Perason, D. 1990, 'Impaired muscle glycogen resynthesis after eccentric exercise', *Journal of Applied Physiology* 69, pp. 46–50.

Coyle, E. F., Coggan, A. R., Hemmert, M. K., Ivy, J. L. 1986, 'Muscle glycogen utilization during prolonged strenuous exercise when fed carbohydrate', *Journal of Applied Physiology* 61, pp. 165–172.

Devlin, J. T., Williams, C. (eds), 'Foods, nutrition and sports performance', *Journal of Sports Sciences* 9 (special edition).

Haymes, E. M., Lamanca, J. F. 1989, 'Iron loss in runners during exercise: implications and recommendations', *Sports Medicine* 7, pp. 277–285.

Highet, R. 1989, 'Athletic amenorrhea: an update on aetiology', *Sports Medicine* 7, pp. 82–108.

Ivy, J. L., Katz, A. L., Cutler, C. L., Sherman, W. M., Coyle, E. F. 1988, 'Muscle glycogen synthesis after exercise: effect of time of carbohydrate ingestion', *Journal of Applied Physiology* 64, pp. 1480–1485.

Ivy, J. L. 1991, 'Muscle glycogen synthesis before and after exercise', *Sports Medicine* 11, pp. 6–19.

Lamb, D. R., Brodowicz, G. R. 1986, 'Optimal use of fluids of varying formulations to minimize exercise-induced disturbances in homeostasis', *Sports Medicine* 3, pp. 247–274.

Lemon, P. W. R. 1991, 'Effect of exercise on protein requirements', *Journal of Sports Sciences* 9 (special issue), pp. 53–70.

Loucks, A. B., Horvath, S. M. 1985, 'Athletic amenorrhoea: a review', *Medicine and Science in Sports and Exercise* 17, pp. 56–72.

Maughan, R. 1991, 'Carbohydrate-electrolyte solutions during prolonged exercise', in Lamb and Williams (eds), *Perspectives in Exercise Science and Sports Medicine*, Vol. 4, 'Ergogenics: enhancement of performance in exercise and sport', pp. 35–85, Brown and Benchmark, USA.

Murray, R. 1987, 'The effects of consuming carbohydrate-electrolyte beverages on gastric emptying and fluid absorption during and following exercise', *Sports Medicine* 4, pp. 322–351.

Newhouse, I. J., Clement, D. B. 1988, 'Iron status: an update', *Sports Medicine* 5, pp. 337–52.

Noakes, T. D. 1990, 'The dehydration myth and carbohydrate replacement during prolonged exercise', *Cycling Science*, pp. 23–29.

Noakes, T. D., Rehrer, N. J., Maughan, R. J. 1991, 'The importance of volume in regulating gastric emptying', *Medicine and Science in Sports and Exercise* 23, pp. 307–313.

Robergs, R. A. 1991, 'Nutrition and exercise determinants of post-exercise glycogen synthesis', *International Journal of Sport Nutrition* 1, pp. 307–337.

Sherman, W. M., Costill, D. L., Fink, W. J., Miller, J. M. 1981, 'The effect of exercise and diet manipulation on muscle glycogen and its subsequent utilization during performance', *International Journal of Sports Medicine* 2, pp. 114–118.

Sherman, W. M., Lamb, D. R. 1988, 'Nutrition and prolonged exercise', in Lamb, D. R., Murray, R. (eds), *Perspectives in Exercise Science and Sports Medicine*, Vol. 1, 'Prolonged exercise'. Benchmark Press, Indianapolis, pp. 213–280.

Short, S. H. 1989, 'Dietary surveys and nutrition knowledge', in Hickson, J. F., Wolinsky, I. (eds), *Nutrition in Exercise and Sport*, CRC Press, Florida, pp. 309–344.

Telford, R. D., Egerton, W. J., Hahn, A. G., Pang, P. M. 1988, 'Skinfold measures and weight controls in elite athletes', *Excel* 5 (2), pp. 21–26.

van der Beek, E. J. 1985, 'Vitamins and endurance training: food for running or faddish claims?' *Sports Medicine* 2, pp. 175–197.

Williams, M. H. 1989, 'Vitamin supplementation and athletic performance', *International Journal for Vitamin and Nutrition Research*, Suppl 30, pp. 163–191.

Chapter Nine

Psychology: Mind Matters

Gayelene Clews

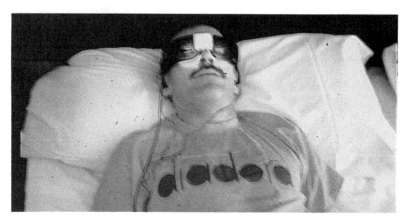

Athletes can have a great deal of technical and physiological skill, but without the ability to channel their talents they may never produce the performances they are capable of. Sports psychology introduces the athlete to techniques that can be used to enhance athletic performance, in a balanced environment. At the elite end of any sport, the difference between the top competitors is marginal. The very best athletes have above average physiologies, good biomechanics and sound psychological profiles. Some of these characteristics we are born with, but many can be improved through learning and practice. To gain the competitive edge, the triathlete needs to:

> Develop a supportive environment
> Communicate with others
> Set goals
> Increase body awareness
> Master concentration
> Control stress
> Focus attention
> Stop negative thoughts
> Learn relaxation
> Image success

A healthy psychological approach to one's sport can be enhanced when the athlete has an effective social support network. Social support is an exchange of emotional resources between individuals designed to improve the well-being of the athlete through encouragement, to increase self-confidence and decrease the stress in the athlete's life.

It is difficult to excel in a discipline as demanding as the triathlon without support. When we choose a goal, the value we place on it is partly determined by our expectations for support and approval for what we do. Social support does not automatically occur in the athletic environment, it needs to be nurtured and developed. Athletes need to seek out and maximize the support available to them from a range of providers.

THE CONDUCIVE ENVIRONMENT

We often hear triathletes singing the praises of different cities as the 'ideal' training environment. In the United States it is a choice between San Diego, California, and Boulder, Colorado. San Diego has the benefits of all year round good weather, while Boulder is an opportunity to train at altitude. In Australia, the Gold Coast is said to be great for swimming, Canberra has safe roads for cycling, while Melbourne has good parks and trails for running.

All of these places offer good facilities, training locations and medical back-up, but what about the social and emotional environment? The location with the best training facilities is not necessarily the best emotional setting for the athlete. The social environment must be conducive to the athlete's psychological needs. The type and level of social support given can increase participation, improve performance, reduce stress and enhance the individual's over-all well-being.

A young triathlete, offered an athletics scholarship at a premier private school with excellent academic and sporting facilities may struggle to perform adequately if she is frustrated, confused and lonely in this environment. A State school with few facilities but a network of friends and teacher empathy for the young athlete's sporting interests may enable her to thrive. Pines, Aronson and Kafy (1981) found six types of social support contribute to a healthy and positive sporting experience:

Listening support
Emotional support
Emotional challenge

Technical appreciation
Technical challenge
Shared social reality

Listening Support

Listening support is given, when an individual listens to the athlete, without giving advice or making judgements.

Listening is a skill. People who talk too much and cannot listen use the sound of their own voice to cover up their own uncertainties. Knowledgeable individuals will first listen, then respond with forethought. In listening, we help the athletes find the answers to their own problems by encouraging them to articulate their concerns and rearrange their thoughts.

In all good athlete/coach relationships, the coach will ask athletes to express their opinions on factors that affect their training and racing schedule. A coach who is too dominant will hinder an athlete's growth by not providing the athlete with the opportunity to develop self-reliance.

Administrators have been known to make unfair selection policies, for State and national representation, because they act without listening to the concerns and needs of the athlete. Similarly, athletes sometimes overreact to policies because they don't listen to the needs of national sporting organizations in fulfilling sponsorship contracts. Effective communication can be enhanced by the development of an athlete advisory committee to bring the needs of fellow competitors to the attention of the administration. Only where there is listening can there be compromise and only with compromise can effective communication take place.

Figure 9.1: A good coach is a good listener.

Emotional Support

Athletes are shown emotional support when another individual helps them through a difficult situation, even if they don't totally agree with them.

Sometimes effective coaching means supporting an athlete in a decision, even when it is not thought to have been the best decision. A parent who supports a son's wish to compete in an Ironman-length event, when common sense suggests it may be beyond the son's capabilities, is giving the athlete emotional support. However, athletes suffer an absence of emotional support when their performances are used to meet the needs of others. Perhaps parents have worked particularly hard to put a son through college, or suffered a financial burden in supporting his athletic career. The athlete may feel indebted for this help and the only way that he knows how to say thank you is through his performances.

In many circumstances, expecting success is extremely motivating. However, if these expectations are not realistic and/or the athlete feels he has disappointed those close to him by not performing well, he is likely to suffer increased anxiety in future events. This increase in pre-competitive stress levels may ultimately have a negative effect on:

Performance
Self-esteem
Motivation
Sporting enjoyment
Persistence
Perceptions of success and failure
Sense of self-worth

When expectations are realistic and success is determined by one's performance and effort, rather than the individual's finishing place, all of the above can be enhanced.

Emotional Challenge
You, the athlete are emotionally challenged when another individual questions the effort you are making to attain your goals.

Friends who challenge you to do your best can help you find the threshold of your own capabilities. They can show you the way, but only you can find it. You will never achieve any more than you believe you are capable of. For example, take the case of two athletes who failed to complete their first Hawaii Ironman. They both failed to finish the event, but one maintained she had the ability to, while the other claimed he did not.

'I have the ability.' This athlete believes that she has the ability, she just wasn't prepared physically for the event, nor adequately acclimatized for the hot humid conditions. Chances are she will come back and attempt the event again, training harder and incorporating an extensive heat acclimatization program into her preparation.

'I don't have the ability.' This athlete believes he failed to finish because he does not have the physical ability to complete such a demanding endurance task. He has a list of reasons to justify his belief: he is too large, not capable of swimming such long distances and is biomechanically a poor cyclist. He is unlikely to attempt the Ironman again.

The different ways in which these athletes perceive their failure affects their future involvement in the sport. Emotional challenge should instil in athletes their ability to succeed if they apply themselves. However, as previously mentioned in Emotional Support, when emotional challenge is offered, coaches, family and friends must be careful not to reflect their own needs onto the athlete's performances. As simplistic as this sounds this is not always accomplished.

In the American college system, sporting scholarships help put a large number of students through college, but this is not always the best for their athletic development. Funding for the different sports programs is dependent upon how well the individual sports do in any one competitive season. It is not unusual for coaches to race injured or ill athletes because their job is on the line if certain standards are not met. A large number of good athletes are lost through this system, burnt out or injured before completing their college degrees.

Technical Appreciation
Technical appreciation can be given by someone who knows the difficulty and effort required to accomplish certain goals in triathlons.

Triathlon goals range from completing a sprint event to winning the Hawaiian Triathlon. At either end of the scale, it is frustrating to be congratulated on a poor performance by someone without any knowledge or understanding of what you were trying to achieve. Athletes appreciate supportive comments that reflect an educated viewpoint. This viewpoint requires the provider of technical appreciation to have knowledge of the athlete's ability, his/her expectations for success and the difficulty of the task.

Teammates and coaches usually provide technical appreciation, but anyone close to the athlete can provide this support if given the appropriate information. The athletic environment in which the individual places himself is his creation. We are all responsible for our own version of the world, our particular reality and our unique experience to it. If you are not receiving the type of support you desire, you have to accept that you have the ability to change it.

If a well-meaning friend tells you what a great race you had and this annoys you, do not dismiss it. Take the opportunity to educate your friend on the requirements of the sport, the strength of competition and the challenge of the event. Inform the friend about the structure of your training, and why you felt you had not accomplished what you had hoped to, in that particular competition.

By taking the time to educate those who care about you, you give them the opportunity to understand more about triathlons, and in doing so help them to develop an appreciation for you and your sport. Similarly, if you do not want negative feedback after a poor performance, find an aspect about your event that you executed well. Perhaps you had a good swim. **If you respond positively about your performance, you set the tone for others to appreciate what was achieved, rather than what was not.** Be prepared to educate family and friends on the requirements of the triathlon, encouraging positive feedback and developing social support.

Technical Challenge
Technical challenge is given when someone encourages you to strive beyond your previous achievements.

Technical challenge comes mostly from coaches and team-mates, who have a sound understanding of the skills and complexities in-herent in triathlons. Technical challenge must come from know-ledgeable and/or experienced individuals who the athlete respects. These individuals may hold high expectations for the athlete, but they must be realistic. By encouraging the athlete to strive harder, the value of succeeding must outweigh the cost. The ultimate goal must be worth the sacrifice of time, family commitments, employment opportunities and other interests or else the athlete will not take up the challenge.

The provider of technical challenge would do well to consider the following. Is achieving a specific goal in the triathlon as important as some other aspects of the individual's life? Perhaps the athlete has the necessary skills to be one of the best athletes in the country, but to him/her the emotional and financial losses may outweigh the benefits of achieving national status.

You may challenge athletes extensively, but only they can determine the persistence and effort they are prepared to make to achieve that goal. When supporting an athlete with technical challenge you must be sure that you are working towards a mutually desirable outcome.

Shared Social Reality
Shared social reality is given by someone who shares similar life experiences and views.

This type of support is most useful in anchoring the overcommitted athlete to the realities of life. Sport is a worthwhile activity to pursue, but to what level and at what cost?

Sometimes in being blessed with more than the average ability, the athlete forgets how to appreciate what she has. Take the elite swimmer who spends hours each day training for national representation, never satisfied with her achievements because someone else is better. One day a group of disabled children comes into the pool for a swim. On the land these children are uncoordinated, but in the water they glide effortlessly, radiating joy and enthusiasm, appreciating their freedom of movement. The elite swimmer looks across at these children and is reminded of the abilities she has—strength, movement, speed and agility—gifts she always wants to be better.

There are times when athletes are so driven by trying to achieve, that they are no longer aware if it is in the striving that they hope to find themselves, or in the striving that they lose themselves. **Some athletes are never satisfied with who they are, always striving to be someone better in the future.**

Athletes need to strive, but they also need to be reminded occasionally of what they have already achieved. It is hoped that the athlete does not place everything good she feels about herself into a single achievement, a single facet of her life. If athletes concentrate everything good they feel about themselves into a single performance, and that performance is not forthcoming, their lives may be shattered. In offering social reality support, we hope to keep perspective and balance in athlete's lives.

The environment which is most conducive to an athlete is one of communication, interaction and support. It is about building a network around the athlete which reflects empathy, appreciation and understanding, but is rooted in reality. It provides people who:

Listen without giving advice or making judgements.
Support even when they don't totally agree with the athlete's decision.
Question the effort the athlete is making.
Appreciate the difficulty and effort required.
Challenge the athlete to strive.
Anchor the overcommitted in the realities of life.

The triathlon is not everything in life, but for many it is a big part of it. Athletes are constantly striving to extend the limits of their own abilities. In doing so they expand not only their physical limits but also their ability to be compassionate towards others who strive. The social support network within the sport of triathlon enables athletes to build relationships, share experiences, develop tolerance and persistence and a strong work ethic. By its nature, the triathlon and its environment attracts many people to its challenge. With a conducive social environment athletes can achieve the goals they set themselves.

GOAL SETTING

Goals come from thought processes, but performances come from physical effort. When an athlete sets herself a goal she gives purpose and direction to the physical effort she puts into her training. Goal setting is one of sport psychology's most discussed strategies. Goals encourage growth and development within the athlete and have been shown to enhance positive changes in confidence, anxiety control, motivation and persistence.

Goals do not automatically stimulate performance. They must be set out thoughtfully, in a systematic fashion, in consultation with those who may be affected by them.

How Goals Help Performance

The relationship between goals and performance enhancement has been described in two ways.

(1) A Mechanistic Theory (Locke, Shaw, Sarri and Lathram, 1981),
(2) A Cognitive Orientated Theory (Burton, 1983).

MECHANISTIC THEORY

The mechanistic theory states that goals influence performance in four ways:

(a) Goals direct the performer's attention to important aspects of the task. For example, an important goal during the triathlon may be to reduce the time taken between the swim-to-bike transition. This focus requires the athlete to concentrate on the details needed for a fast transition. Breaking the event down into components, instead of just concentrating on the whole, requires detailed thought and a carefully planned pre-race strategy.

(b) Goals help the performer mobilize effort. By setting a series of training and racing goals the athlete will exhibit more effort in trying to achieve those goals. For example, if athletes know that a specific training session will raise their anaerobic threshold, thereby increasing the speed they can maintain during races, they will be motivated to do that session well, knowing that each repetition contributes towards a better competitive performance.

When athletes set specific measurable goals in training such as: 5 x 400 metre (440 yards) swimming intervals, to be swum in 5 minutes 30 seconds, with a 30 second recovery, they are given a focus for the session. They can spread their effort evenly over the number of intervals required and can monitor their improvement from one session to the next. Less explicit goals such as 'try your hardest' or no goals at all give little feedback and do not encourage athletes to focus on their work output.

(c) Goals not only increase immediate effort but help prolong work by increasing persistence. It would be difficult for some athletes to maintain the high mileage required for the Ironman, if they did not set themselves some intermediate goals. These goals enable athletes to test their fitness levels, affording them a sense of achievement and progression as they work towards their long-term goal. Athletes need to know that they are doing the right amount of quality and quantity in their training, maximizing both time and effort. Feedback from intermediate goals help athletes persist, keeping their enthusiasm and motivation high.

(d) Athletes often develop new learning strategies through the process of setting goals. Take, for example, the case of a novice cyclist who sets himself a long-term goal of contesting the State Road Cycling Championship. In order to gain the confidence to ride in such a high profile event, he first needs to gain confidence in riding in large groups. He adopts a strategy for achieving this goal, initially riding with small numbers of people, gradually increasing the numbers in the group until the group size is large enough to consider competing.

The process of setting a goal (competing in the State Championships) has required the athlete to adopt an appropriate learning strategy (cycling with increasingly larger numbers of people) to achieve it.

COGNITIVE ORIENTED THEORY

This theory states that athletes' goals are linked to their levels of anxiety, motivation and confidence. Goals are described as being either 'outcome' or 'performance' goals.

Outcome goals. Outcome goals focus on results, such as winning. When you concentrate everything good you feel about yourself into a finishing place, at some point in your career you are likely to feel disappointed. This results in lower confidence, increased anxiety and decreased effort, particularly if your expectations are unrealistic. **Athletes have little control over outcome goals.** They may have performed to their absolute best, but may have been beaten by someone else who was marginally better on the same day.

Performance goals. Performance goals, on the other hand, assist the athlete in forming realistic expectations, increasing levels of confidence because the athlete can control his own effort and improve motivation.

Both of the above theories have important considerations when setting goals. The athlete and the coach need to be aware of the mechanisms between goal setting and performance. **The coach and the athlete should set goals in consultation with each other** and attempt to set performance-based rather than outcome goals, being systematic in their approach to goal setting.

WHAT TYPE OF GOALS TO SET

In consultation with his coach, the athlete should set a range of goals, including his dream goal, and break them down into realistic and achievable goals both in the short term and long term.

Dream goals. A dream goal may be obtainable or it may not; it should merely reflect what the athlete would most like to achieve in the triathlon. For some, the dream goal may become a reality, for others it is just nice to dream about being the absolute best.

Realistic goals. Realistic, obtainable goals enhance the athlete's self-confidence, if the athlete has the resources required to meet the needs of the goal. If the goal is unrealistic and exceeds the athlete's ability he is likely to become frustrated and disillusioned. The coach can help the athlete set realistic goals by keeping them flexible and adjusting the difficulty of the goal, either increasing or decreasing it, in response to the athlete's progress.

Specific training goals. Goals are set to maximize the training effect of each session. However, this is not to say each session is a hard workout; recovery sessions are equally as important. If the athlete is fatigued or unwell training goals should be flexible and adjusted accordingly. What may be

Figure 9.2: Training goals should be kept flexible.

a realistic time for track intervals one day may not be realistic the next, especially if the athlete is tired. In fact, under these circumstances, sticking rigidly to a time frame may flatten the athlete, placing her days behind schedule. Sometimes it is advisable to abandon the stop watch altogether and let the athlete run on 'feel' or with a heart rate monitor—where the athlete runs below a certain heart rate to avoid overtraining.

Short-term goals. The goals we set in the short term help break up the competitive season. Races of less importance give the athlete something to focus on, keeping her motivation and enthusiasm high whilst working towards a long-term aim. Short-term goals enable the athlete to monitor her progression, make adjustments to her training programs and if necessary her goals. If the athlete doesn't have short-term goals it can be difficult to maintain immediate focus in training. She may find work, study, or family commitments become more important so she loses touch with the workload that is needed to maintain a realistic chance of achieving her original goal. As any elite athlete can tell you, 'If you're not out doing a session, you can be sure someone else is.'

Long-term goals. Long-term goals may reflect a performance that we hope to achieve at the end of a season, or a national team that we may wish to make three years from now. Many Olympic athletes have said that their Olympic objectives are comprised of a four-year plan. All goals require a target date. The long-term goal is usually a fixed date the athlete is working towards. Training or short-term racing goals are more flexible. If a target training session or a minor race is missed there are usually alternatives.

Performance versus outcome goals. The triathlon is a wonderful event for setting performance goals. Few people who start the Hawaiian Ironman have visions of winning the event. The vast majority are there to achieve their own goal—a specific time or just to finish. The number of perform-ance-structured goals within the triathlon are many.

One of the biggest enticements of the sport is the variety of distances enabling athletes to progress at their own rate in completing sprint, Olympic, long-course or Ironman distances. Triathlons are gender and age group structured allowing individuals to do well in their specific age groups as opposed to competing against elite competitors.

Each event may be broken down into five components—the swim, swim/bike transition, the bike, bike/run transition and the run—allowing athletes to achieve any number of goals in any given event. For example, take a complete newcomer to the sport. In his first season he may set himself the goal of completing a sprint triathlon: 500 m (550 yd) swim, 20 km (12 mile) cycle, 5 km (3 mile) run. Over a number of seasons he may progress to the Olympic distance format of a 1500 m (1640 yd) swim, 40 km (24 mile) cycle, 10 km (6 mile) run, then attempt a half-Ironman. After several years in the sport he competes in his first Ironman.

In setting these goals the athlete should not be preoccupied with winning but rather in giving his best performance he will achieve the best possible outcome.

Keeping a Diary

Once the athlete's goals have been identified, it is a good idea to record them in a weekly diary. This acts as a constant reminder to the athlete of what her daily training objectives are and whether or not they have been achieved, while keeping her focused on the long-term aim. Recording training and racing goals serves as a good reference point in evaluating the athlete's schedule. In identifying the goals discussed in this section—dream goal, realistic goal, specific training goals short-term goals, long-term goals and performance goals—the coach and athlete are able to assess workouts and strategies. This assessment provides feedback on the success of particular training sessions, or programs, so that a good performance can be reproduced, or a poor one rectified.

Goals are not a magic formula to success, but if implemented effectively they can help improve performance, increase self-confi-dence and provide direction and focus while enhancing athlete and coach communication. There are no short cuts to sporting success, however; **the athlete who achieves the most at the end of the day is usually the one who is the most prepared.**

TRIATHLON SKILLS

The triathlon is the combination of three gross motor sports—swimming, cycling and running—with a little dexterity required in the transition from one sport to the next. Each sport has a specific skill component that is refined through training and practise. The athlete needs to reproduce correct technique in training until it becomes an automatic response that can be executed successfully in stressful, competitive situations.

The more a response is practiced the more likely it will occur under stress. If the skill is correct, simple, or learned, increased arousal should improve performance. However, if the skill is incorrect, complex or not well learned, increased arousal is likely to impair performance (Gill, 1986). Before an athlete can implement changes in his swimming, cycling or running form, he needs to be aware of his current body movements; only with this awareness can he fine-tune his athletic skills.

Body awareness and control are important for improving sporting skills. Changes must be integrated gradually, enabling the athlete to focus on the correct motor movement in each of the sports. Progressive shaping of movements enables the athlete to improve his technique over time. There may be periods when the athlete reverts to his old form, consequently he needs regular feedback to encourage him to persist with the correct technique.

When working on swimming stroke, for example, it is useful to simultaneously identify the athlete's strengths and weaknesses. In doing so the coach can keep the athlete's self-esteem high, encouraging him to maximize his strengths, whilst at the same time correcting his weaknesses.

Bandura (1982) states that athlete confidence can be enhanced when acquiring new skills through four types of information:

> Performance accomplishments
> Vicarious experience
> Verbal persuasion
> Emotional arousal

Performance accomplishments refers to our actual successful sporting experience. If an athlete who is working on improving his swimming stroke finds that he swims faster in competition, he is more likely to persist in maintaining his new swimming form. Successfully executing a new skill is most effective in developing confidence to persist.

Vicarious experience refers to watching another person successfully execute a skill. Demonstrations are often used when teaching sports. The closer the model is to someone with whom the athlete can identify, a person of the same age, size, gender and ability, the more confident the athlete will be that he can do likewise.

Bandura states that the models we observe affect our attention, retention, motor reproduction and motivation (to execute that skill). For example, if all the models used to show a young female cyclist how to take a corner without braking on the bike are professional male athletes, the young female is not likely to see the demonstration as reflecting something she is capable of achieving. She is less likely to value the information given in the demonstration and is less likely to attend to (observe) it. It would be better to present the young female with a model with which she can identify.

To help her retain as much useful information as possible from the demonstration, the coach should direct her attention to critical features in the performance. If she tries to watch the whole performance, she is likely to miss the key elements. However, by directing her attention to several specifics, such as the positioning of the inside knee or the tilt of the bike, the athlete is more likely to retain the appropriate information.

Before asking the athlete to reproduce the skill, have her contemplate what she has just learned, mentally rehearsing the movement in her mind before actually attempting it. The feedback that the coach gives to the athlete is important. He should endeavor to shape the athlete's ability to take corners on the bike with gradual changes. The combination of the coach's feedback and the athlete's self-correction should produce a positive result. **If feedback is positive, the athlete is more likely to persist with mastering the skill.**

Video filming is another form of modeling that can help with correct motor skill acquisition. Filming a swimmer under water enables the swimmer to actually see the roll in his shoulders and hips, as well as the entry, pull and follow through of his stroke. Stop the video at crucial points giving the athlete the opportunity to see his stroke pattern, identifying aspects that can be improved upon, for a more efficient technique.

Verbal Persuasion in the form of encouragement and reinforcement from others helps keep the athlete's spirits high, minimizing the disillusionment that comes from unsuccessful attempts to execute a skill correctly. **It is extremely motivating for the athlete to have others express confidence in his ability to accomplish a new task.**

Emotional Arousal is the fourth source of information that effects skill acquisition. If the athlete feels anxious a negative relationship can develop between his ability to execute a skill and his confidence to do so. This aspect of skill acquisition is addressed more fully in the following section.

AROUSAL AND PERFORMANCE

Most athletes are aware of how high levels of arousal affect their athletic performance. Even the most successful athletes can occasionally tip the scales from being optimally aroused to being over anxious.

It is easier to get to the top in sport than it is to stay there. The 'dark-horse' comes into a race with fewer expectations, while the favorite carries the expectations of his community, his country and sometimes the world. This additional pressure may increase the athlete's pre-race arousal levels to a point where his concentration is affected. Instead of focusing on his performance, the athlete's mind is filled with self doubts, he makes mistakes and loses valuable time because he is not focused on the task at hand.

High levels of anxiety result from self-defeating thought processes that interfere with certain physiological responses (Landers and Boutcher 1986). Arousal is a natural ongoing state but when arousal levels become extremely high the athlete experiences unpleasant emotional reactions associated with the autonomic nervous system. This maladaptive condition is referred to as 'stress' or 'state anxiety'. When arousal levels are inappropriate, reactions can result in ineffective performance, faulty decision making, inappropriate perception, injury or burnout.

The relationship between arousal and performance is best explained

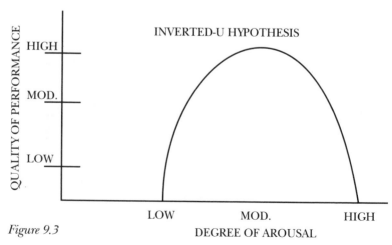

Figure 9.3

180

by the inverted-U relationship (see figure 9.3). This theory suggests that performance is optimal at a moderate level of arousal. If the athlete is under or over aroused his performance will decline.

When the athlete is under aroused or apathetic, he performs below his capability. If he is over aroused, he is likely to become over anxious and tense, making errors and performing below his capability.

Optimal levels of arousal differ between sports and individuals. A golfer, for example, requires low levels of arousal so as not to interfere with his concentration, or affect his fine motor movements. The triathlon requires higher levels of arousal, because of its strength and endurance component. However, because the triathlon is a multi-task event, where attention shifts from the primary (swim, bike, run) to secondary tasks (transitions), it may be appropriate to adjust arousal levels during the event.

If an athlete comes into the transition area 'pumped up' and aggressive, when he should be centering himself to concentrate on his transition, his performance may suffer. He should avoid being distracted by outside influences and focus on his movements. Triathlon transitions require finer movements than the individual swim, bike, run legs, therefore, the athlete needs to adjust arousal during the event.

Figure 9.4: Transition requires greater arousal control than the individual legs.

How Anxiety Affects Performance

Every mental or emotional state is consciously or unconsciously accompanied by an appropriate change in bodily state. Muscle tension that occurs with anxiety and worry interferes with performance because many of the nerves required for coordinated movement are involved with worry messages. Proper form in any movement involves using just the right amount of tension in the muscle; too much tension interferes with the execution of the skill. The athlete needs to learn to only expend those energies necessary to accomplish the task at hand. This is referred to as 'differential relaxation' (Harris, 1986).

Excessive muscular tension can be triggered by mental input generated by worry and anxiety. When the nerves are occupied with impulses in an aroused state of 'fright or flight', they inhibit the impulses needed for coordinated movement. The more muscular tension that occurs in the body, the more difficult it becomes to execute good form or correct coordination in any type of movement task.

Too much stress has a negative impact on athletic performance, with some individuals affected more acutely than others. To assist the athlete to control his anxiety it helps to explain to him how the body/mind connection works. Lynch (1988) in his discussion of athletic injuries gives an excellent outline. Although his article addresses the relationship to injury, it is a good model of how negative thought processes can have a detrimental impact on performance in general.

Outlined opposite is Lynch's flowchart—after having altered entry (F) to reflect a poor performance instead of the injury indicated on the original chart. The chart concerns a hypothetical triathlete.

As a result of a poor performance (F) and the athlete's interpretation of that performance (C), emotions are heightened at (D) causing a stress/poor performance cycle. To break the cycle, psychological interventions need to be introduced at (C) as discussed in the following section.

Controlling Arousal—Improving Concentration, Focus and Attention

Concentration is necessary for optimal sports performance; it enables the athlete to focus his attention on the task at hand, maximizing his energy output. When the athlete learns to concentrate effectively, he eliminates 'internal noise' and distracting external stimuli from his performance, thereby reducing anxiety.

Internal noise refers to those negative thoughts that go through the athlete's mind from time to time; self doubts such as, 'I am so tired', 'I want to slow down', 'I had a terrible bike', 'I'll never catch them on the

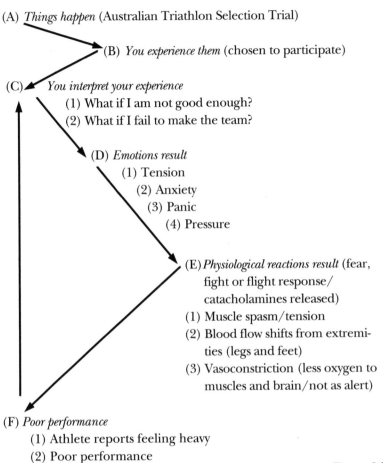

(A) *Things happen* (Australian Triathlon Selection Trial)

(B) *You experience them* (chosen to participate)

(C) *You interpret your experience*
    (1) What if I am not good enough?
    (2) What if I fail to make the team?

      (D) *Emotions result*
        (1) Tension
         (2) Anxiety
          (3) Panic
           (4) Pressure

             (E) *Physiological reactions result* (fear, fight or flight response/ catacholamines released)
                (1) Muscle spasm/tension
                (2) Blood flow shifts from extremities (legs and feet)
                (3) Vasoconstriction (less oxygen to muscles and brain/not as alert)

(F) *Poor performance*
    (1) Athlete reports feeling heavy
    (2) Poor performance

Figure: 9.5

run'. External stimuli refers to distracting elements outside the athlete, such as a noisy crowd, unsportsmanlike behavior from an opponent or a dog running out in front of the athlete in the middle of a competition.

Schmid and Peper (1986) point out that internal noise and external stimuli are continually connected. **Almost every external event will trigger mental or emotional shift in the athlete.** For example, unsportsmanlike behavior, such as a fellow competitor drafting during the cycle leg of a triathlon, is likely to emotionally upset his fellow competitors. Unless the other competitors have mastered concentration under pressure they are likely to lose composure and their performances will suffer as a direct result.

Concentration is the learned skill of passively not reacting to, or being distracted by, irrelevant stimuli. For an athlete to learn to focus his attention, he first needs to become aware of the attentional demands of his sport. Nideffer (1986) identifies four types of attentional focus; these are:

> Broad-External
> Broad-Internal
> Narrow-External
> Narrow-Internal

BROAD-EXTERNAL

Used to rapidly assess a situation. The type of attentional focus that the triathlete needs when he is exiting the water and locating his bike in the bike compound. He needs to be aware of the direction of his own movement amidst the movement of other athletes leaving the water and mounting their bikes.

BROAD-INTERNAL

Used to analyze and plan. The thought process whereby the athlete is assessing his own situation and developing a race strategy.

NARROW-EXTERNAL

Used to focus in a positive way on one or two external stimuli. For example, once the athlete is on his bike he may concentrate on the figure of the cyclist in front of him, as he strives to narrow the distance between himself and the other cyclist.

NARROW-INTERNAL

Used systematically to mentally rehearse a performance situation, or control arousal. During the swim leg, for example, the athlete may image his hand placement in the water to maximize his stroke efficiency and thereby improve his swimming performance. Or, on the cycle leg he may find he talks himself through a controlled breathing exercise, in order to reduce levels of heightened anxiety.

The triathlon places a variety of attentional demands on the athlete. At the beginning of the swim leg a broad-external focus is needed to establish his positioning among the other swimmers in the field. He must be aware of swimmers around him and the positioning of the buoy. This may lead to a broad-internal focus, such as the swimmer he plans to draft in the race. Once the field thins he can narrow his

Figure 9.6: To draft well in the swim you must use all your concentration.

external focus to either the feet of the swimmer in front, or the buoy. At the same time he may oscillate between a narrow-external focus, the position of the buoy, and a narrow-internal focus, such as controlled and relaxed breathing.

The athlete's attention is required to shift across different dimensions within his performance. Athletes have different abilities for shifting and directing focus. Some can take in large amounts of external information from the environment, while others are better at developing narrow, non-distractible types of attention.

To help athletes experience the different attentional styles, Gauron (1984) developed the following exercise:

1. The athlete focuses on his breathing while continuing to breathe normally. For the next minute breathe more deeply and slowly while keeping the chest, shoulders and neck relaxed. Return to normal breathing for 3–4 breaths and then back to deep breathing until the deep breathing is comfortable, easy and regular.

2. Now pay attention to what you hear by taking each separate sound, identifying it, then mentally labelling it, such as footsteps, voices, a cough. Next, simultaneously listen to all of the sounds without attempting to identify or label them. Listen to the blend of sounds as you would music, while verbal thinking drops away.

3. Now, become aware of bodily sensations such as the feeling of the chair or the floor supporting your body. Mentally label each sensation as you notice it. Before moving onto another sensation, let each sensation linger for a moment while you examine it; consider its quality and its source. Next, experience all these sensations simultaneously without identifying or labelling any particular one. This necessitates going into the broadest possible internal awareness.

4. Attend now only to your emotions or thoughts. Let each thought or emotion appear gently, without being forced. Identify the nature of your thoughts and feelings; remain calm no matter how pleasant or unpleasant they may be. Feel one, then another, then another. Now try to empty yourself of all thoughts and feelings. If this is not possible, tune in to only one and hold your attention there.

5. Open your eyes and pick some object across the room and directly in front of you. While looking directly ahead, see as much of the room and the objects in the room as your peripheral vision will allow. Simultaneously observe the entire room and all things in it. Picture now a broad funnel into which your mind is moving, and centered in the middle of the funnel is the object directly across the room from you. Gradually narrow your focus by narrowing the funnel, so that the only thing at the small end of the funnel is the object directly across from you. Expand your focus little by little, widening the funnel until you see everything in the room. Think of your external focus as a zoom lens; practice zooming in and out, narrowing or broadening according to your wishes.

This exercise not only helps athletes experience different attentional styles, but it is a good illustration of shift from internal to external dimensions, from a body awareness to a panoramic focus. With improved concentration the athlete will not become preoccupied with negative self-doubting thoughts, or let external events interfere with his concentration on the task at hand.

FOCUS IN COMPETITION

In general, the ability to concentrate and pay attention to certain aspects of your race, while ignoring others, is critical for an effective performance. Different athletes have different attentional styles. The ability to control and shift one's attention is related to arousal. Becoming aware of your own attentional style is the first step in training yourself to control attention, so that you can match the changing attentional demands of the triathlon.

When competing, many triathletes disassociate—focusing on external objects or ideas, such as singing to themselves, mentally replaying discussions at work, or admiring their surroundings. Not surprisingly, however, research has shown that most elite endurance athletes prefer to associate during competition—concentrating on general body sensations, such as their breathing and feelings in their leg muscles (Morgan and Pollock, 1977).

It is believed that associative or narrow-internal focus is advantageous for endurance events but, as has already been discussed, athletes need to change attentional focus throughout the triathlon for optimal performance.

The athlete narrowing his focus when racing, to concentrate on form and pace judgement is likely to enhance his performance. However, the triathlon is a gruelling sport, where pain and fatigue can become over-riding factors. If the athlete's goal is to just keep going, a disassociation strategy, singing or talking to a fellow competitor, may distract his attention from his physical discomfort enabling him to complete the event.

Elite athletes usually have a time limit on what they are trying to achieve and are concerned mainly with maintaining performance. As such, they are more likely to monitor body sensations to remain relaxed and as efficient as possible in achieving their goals.

Not all internal focus is conducive to optimal athletic performance. As greater demands are placed on the athlete and pressure to perform increases there is a tendency to involuntarily narrow attention. When this narrowing focuses on the negative, performance will be impaired. Arousal causes physical changes such as increased heart rate, muscle tension, blood pressure and respiration rate; the athlete who pays attention to the negative aspects may suffer from the phenomenon that we usually refer to as 'choking'.

A simple technique to help the athlete control anxiety and remain focused is 'thought stopping'.

THOUGHT STOPPING

Once the athlete is aware of his 'internal noise' and his ability to direct and change his focus he can begin to control negative thought processes. A lapse in concentration allows self-doubt and fear to creep into the athlete's mind, resulting in excessive worry and anxiety that can begin a vicious cycle impeding athletic performance.

A lot of athletes find themselves engaging in negative self-talk, asking questions like:

> 'What if I have not done enough training?'
> 'Did I freshen up enough last week?'
> 'I should not have worked late on Friday'.
> 'My legs feel heavy, what if I tie up during the run?'

Thought stopping is a simple way of controlling self-talk. This technique is an effective method of eliminating negative and counterproductive thoughts. **Getting rid of negative thoughts makes it possible to break the link that leads to negative feelings and behaviors** (Bunker and Williams, 1986). Thought stopping requires a brief focus on the unwanted thought, then using a 'trigger' to interrupt or stop the undesirable thought. The athlete may pretend that he has a flick switch in his hand; each time a negative thought enters his mind he activates the switch, replacing the negative thought with a performance-enhancing one.

An athlete, for example, who has lost several days of training with heavy study commitments, and is concerned about his ability to race, may be thinking, 'I won't race well, I haven't trained all week.' When he hears himself thinking negatively, he should make a conscious decision to change it. He can flick his imaginary switch and replace the thought with a positive one, 'I should race well today, because I've had a particularly easy training week.'

Thought stoppage will not work unless the athlete is aware of his undesirable thoughts and is motivated to stop them. Athletes can use this technique in training and in competition. Most negative thoughts occur when the athlete is in a highly aroused state, e.g. negative thoughts while doing a particularly hard training session. The athlete should first identify the thought, then stop and take a deep breath. As he feels himself relaxing he should release the breath slowly and at the same time substitute a self-enhancing thought.

Progressive Muscle Relaxation

Another way the athlete can reduce the effects of stress is through progressive muscle relaxation. Relaxation brings about a reduction in the amount of physiological and psychological arousal an athlete feels during stressful situations. Relaxation can decrease:

Oxygen consumption
Respiratory rate
Heart rate
Muscle tension
Sweating

The purpose of progressive muscle relaxation is to teach the athlete 'muscle awareness', and sensitivity to what muscle tension feels like. Progressive relaxation consists of a series of exercises that involve contracting a specific muscle group, holding the contraction for several seconds, then relaxing. The exercises progress from one muscle group to another. Contracting the muscle lets the individual know what tension feels like before relaxing it. If a muscle is contracted before it is relaxed, it will achieve a more relaxed state.

RELAXATION STRATEGY
Find a quiet room where you can either sit or lie comfortably. Once comfortable, take a moment or two to centre yourself. If lying, you should be on your back with hands by your sides and legs stretched out. If sitting, the back and shoulders should be square, but relaxed, not hunched. Feet should be squarely placed on the floor.

Consciously relax your face, jaw and neck, let your arm and shoulder muscles feel loose. Feel your abdominal and leg muscles relax. Now inhale slowly and deeply, hold it for two seconds and exhale slowly. Repeat this breathing pattern several times. By concentrating on your breathing let go of distracting thoughts and prepare for the progressive relaxation exercises.

1. Starting with your feet, curl your toes tightly, hold for five seconds then relax, feel the warmth of your blood circulating back into your feet.

2. Now flex your feet towards your head, hold for five seconds then relax.

3. Tighten your calf muscles, feel the muscles gripping, hold for five seconds and relax.

4. Contract your hamstring muscles, feel the large muscles in the backs of your legs tighten, hold for five seconds then let go.

5. Tighten your quadricep muscles, feel your large thigh muscles tighten, hold for five seconds then relax.

6. Tighten your buttock muscles, feel all of your pelvic floor muscles contract, hold for five seconds then relax.

7. While holding your abdominal muscles in, count for five seconds then relax.
8. Tighten your lower back, do not strain too hard if you have back problems, feel the tension, hold for five seconds then relax.
9. Raise your shoulders up towards your ears, pushing them up as far as they can go, hold for five seconds then relax.
10. Clench your fists tightly, hold for five seconds then relax.
11. To loosen your jaw and neck muscles, smile widely so that the tendons stand out in your neck, hold for five seconds then relax.
12. Screw up your eyes until you feel your facial muscles tighten, hold for five seconds then relax.

Progressive relaxation exercises relax the athlete both physically and mentally. By concentrating on the above exercises the mind should be closed off to other distractions. This type of training teaches the athlete body awareness and the skills to centre, relax and release the tension in his body on demand. When the athlete is relaxed, a mental imagery exercise can be tried.

MENTAL IMAGERY

Imagery is a psychological technique, involving all senses, to create or re-create an experience in the mind. Most athletes have the ability to use imagery, but just as athletes are different psychologically, so too is their ability to image.

Imagery involves all senses, it does not have to be limited to just 'seeing within the mind's eye'. Vealey (1986) states that it is important for athletes to use all of their senses—visual (sight), auditory (sound), olfactory (smell), taste, tactile (touch) and kinesthetic senses (the feeling we have of where our body is positioned in space) when imaging.

As creative individuals, athletes can use imagery to visualize any event that they would like to re-create in their life. **There is no magic in imagery, the individual has the tools, he just needs to get in touch with himself so that he can use those tools in the most productive manner.**

The imagery most used is based on memory. When an event is re-created it gives the athlete an opportunity to identify both positive and negative aspects of his performance. It is clear, however, that we can also use imagery to create new events in the mind, e.g. a successful bike-to-run transition. There are two main theories on how imagery enhances performance.

(1) Psychoneuromuscular theory suggests that imagery is similar to the experience produced by physical execution. Through imagery, the athlete can actually strengthen the neural pathways for certain movements in his event. Performing a skill is physical but the brain does the organization and coordination. When we train we send signals from the brain to the muscles, clearing the pathways so that training will be performed perfectly. Imaging allows you to travel the pathways without performing the physical movement.

(2) Symbolic learning suggests that imagery facilitates performance by helping individuals blueprint, or code their movements into symbolic components, thus making the movements more familiar and perhaps more automatic.

Generally speaking, triathletes can use mental imagery to actively plan and evaluate their performance at training and in competition. Mental imagery can do the following:

Reinforce and strengthen existing skills.
Speed up learning of new skills or correct 'problem' skills.
Improve mind–body reflexes.
Increase self-awareness and awareness of important cues.
Improve concentration and confidence.
Decrease anxiety.

Webster (1984) suggests the athlete take a four-step approach when using mental rehearsal: (i) Goal setting, (ii) scene creating, (iii) automatic mental rehearsal, and (iv) review.

When the triathlete establishes a training or racing goal he selects an aspect of his event that he wishes to work on. This may be skill related, such as improving his gear changes on the bike, or a mental aspect, such as improving concentration during the swim.

To create the scene, you, the athlete, should spend a couple of minutes relaxing, then, with eyes closed, create in sequence the performance you wish to perfect. This should be done in as much detail as possible, as if you were actually there. Notice what various parts of your body are doing and how you feel. Be aware of where you are performing this skill and who is around you, focusing your attention throughout the movement. For example, you may wish to learn how to draft during the swim leg of the event. You may mentally image the following scene:

See yourself standing at the water's edge, feel the sand under your feet, the cool touch of the water, the fresh breeze on your face, smell the salt if you are by the ocean.

Be aware of the other athletes around you, hear their voices, see their faces.

Feel your body relax, rested and waiting to begin the event. While you spend a moment or two centering yourself at the water's edge seek out a swimmer you believe you can draft, move behind this person on the start line.

Feel the slight tension in your muscles as you anticipate the starter's gun. Hear the gun, smell the smoke.

See yourself entering the water swiftly, acknowledge the bumps and jostling around you but don't focus on them, concentrate on the swimmer you have chosen to draft.

Feel yourself moving through the water, be aware of your breathing, feel it controlled and relaxed, note your ability to keep in touch with your chosen swimmer in the first 200 metres (220 yards).

See and feel yourself out of the chaos, swimming rhythmically and strongly in the wake of another's draft. Feel confident that you have the ability to stay there.

Once you have created the scene in your mind with as much detail as possible, you can continue to rehearse the image at a normal speed making sure that you are executing your performance smoothly and correctly. **The more you rehearse the scene the more automatic your response will become.**

After training or competing, it is important to evaluate the skills you have practiced. Did you perform as planned? What improvements did you make and how would you want to improve on them in the next session?

When competing you need to be as prepared as possible to avoid psychological blocks that may result due to the added pressure of competing. A good time to use relaxation skills and mental imagery rehearsal is the night before competition. Go over your performance in your mind—the goals, strategies and skills that you need to re-create. By doing this you familiarize yourself with the competitive environment or venue thereby reducing some of the anxiety that comes with competing and continuing the suggestion of success.

To summarize the above, triathlon performance can be enhanced through:

Successful athletic experience
Observing others
Constructive and informative feedback
Positive reinforcement
Focusing attention
Increased body awareness
Association
Disassociation
Stopping negative thoughts
Relaxation strategies
Mentally imaging success

Figure 9.7: Sport empowers the female athlete.

THE FEMALE ATHLETE

Psychologically, elite male and female athletes are more similar in their abilities than they are different. **The qualities that culminate in a superb athletic performance are the same irrespective of gender**—an ability to control arousal, to associate during competition, to narrow or broaden attention to meet the needs of competition, a good self-image and confidence in one's ability to meet the demands of the task.

The underlying gender bias of sport in Australia, however, places the female at a distinct disadvantage before she is even old enough to know that she wants to be involved.

Female athletes still receive less than 5% of print and television media, yet they win over 30% of Australia's Olympic medals. Given that they have fewer Olympic events than men, they bring home proportionately more medals.

Young girls don't see women playing sport on television and in the absence of female sporting coverage, fewer women watch it. Consequently, girls learn from an early age that the rules for them are different. In understanding these differences we can learn more about the limited choices of the female athlete—why she may, or may not, choose a sport such as triathlon, her motivation to be involved and her expectations for social approval.

The value females place on their sporting involvement will depend on the positive experiences they have in participating. Why would a young female choose to play sport poorly, if she can play music well? If she does not value a task she is unlikely to persist with it. Males, on the other hand, play sport because they value displaying their athletic competence. Females who want to be seen as feminine do not like to engage in sports that are not considered feminine.

Society expects less from the female athlete and values less what she does achieve. This information is conveyed to girls and women in such a way that they are more likely than males to underestimate their athletic abilities. Males, on the other hand, tend to overestimate their abilities, based on the belief that all males have some sort of innate ability to play sports well (Nelson and Nelson, 1977).

Why do females underestimate their athletic abilities? Research shows that we reinforce males and females differently. There is a tendency to give boys praise for their accomplishments, such as, 'You really moved out front on the bike', while females would be more likely to be told, 'You look great on the bike'. Females more readily attribute a poor performance to a lack of ability, such as, 'I'm a hopeless cyclist,

I'll never be able to ride hills well', while a male is more likely to view failure as reflecting lack of effort: 'I could have won if I had wanted to, I just rolled through this one as a training session'.

Ability is something that we believe to be innate, over which we have little control, whereas lack of effort can be easily controlled and changed by us. The impact of a female perceiving herself to be lacking in ability may adversely affect her self-confidence and motivation. If she loses confidence she may be reluctant to keep pursuing goals in the triathlon. The male on the other hand, preserves his self-esteem by believing he has the ability, he just needs to try harder.

Some of the factors that influence how athletes attribute their success or failure are:

Motivation for doing the task. Sport in general is viewed as masculine and an important activity for all boys; this clearly is not the case for females.

Reward structure for doing the activity. Females in general get paid less for their performances in the form of appearance fees, prize money and endorsement contracts. In non-monetary terms they receive less media attention and fewer athletic scholarships.

Perceived athletic ability. Females have been stereotyped as less competent than males even when they perform equally as well. This results in females valuing less their athletic abilities.

History of athletic success or failure. While females tend to attribute failure to a lack of ability they are more readily affected by previous performances than are males. The saying that 'you are only as good as your last performance' probably has stronger implications for female athletes than for males, who more readily justify a less than ideal race.

Responses made by others. Coaches, friends, peers, family, siblings, the media and teachers all contribute to shaping the athlete's beliefs and perceptions over time. As socializers they provide important reinforcement to the athlete, shaping different experiences for males and females.

When different gender behaviors are reinforced they become reality. If we listen to our athletes we can pick up cues that may threaten their self-confidence and then endeavor to reinforce them in a positive way. **The female athlete needs to be empowered with her ability to succeed.**

Females have shown that while they are equally challenged by competition they deal with winning and losing more appropriately. Females are less likely to be devastated in losing, because they tend to strive for personal standards, while males are more preoccupied with defeating fellow opponents.

What type of females choose to be engaged in sports?
Butt (1987) identifies five types:

The feminine type behaves like an athlete when she is performing, but elsewhere exhibits typical feminine behavior.

The hysteric type only superficially conforms to the feminine role. She is likely to be flirtatious, and sport may, psychologically, be a way for her to gain the attention and admiration of people who are significant to her.

The instrumental (jock) type denies the feminine role, typically epitomizing male role presentation in body structure, manners, style, speech and action.

The image maker participates in sport for entertainment and profit and is encouraged by sponsors to present herself in a manner acceptable to the public.

The liberated/independent type is comfortable with her identity and does not need to play a particular gender role. This is the most adjusted role to which women aspire.

Within each of these five classifications are an additional four personality types a coach is likely to work with and these classifications apply to both males and females:

> Victims
> Rescuers
> Do-ers
> Be-ers

VICTIMS
Victims are the ones who believe that they are helpless and the world acts upon them. These are the athletes who suffer colds and injuries

before major competitions. They are reluctant to take full responsibility for themselves and often feel that others can take away from them what they have worked for.

To change victim psychology the female athlete needs to stop blaming others for her inability to perform. For example, an athlete who believes that she should have been selected in a state or national team may blame administrators for robbing her of this opportunity. However, she must ask herself, 'Did I perform to the best of my ability, were my performances beyond question?' In being responsible for her own performances the athlete should have been familiar with selection criteria and sought to meet those criteria. If the selection policy was inappropriate she should have solicited change before competing. By not acting before the event, she is passively empowering the administration at the expense of controlling her own destiny.

Victims who are frequently ill or injured must ask themselves, why? Sometimes it is easier for athletes to make comebacks in the face of adversity than it is to stay at the top. After a bout of injuries some spectacular performances may result; the athlete then predictably falls victim to another injury, removing the pressure of repeating those performances. This is not a conscious behavior and certainly not a desirable one, but for some athletes it is a maladaptive way of coping with a fear of failure.

Athletes who fall into victim behavior patterns may not want to be there. Ultimately, they need to accept their control and can direct their own sporting experience.

RESCUERS

Rescuers are the athletes who spend a great deal of time taking care of others, while neglecting themselves. In caring for others they fulfill their own needs in an indirect way.

The rescuer is the athlete who offers empathy and support to others—helping a friend deal with disappointment and making positive suggestions to overcome problems—while not dealing with specific problems of her own. The rescuer is likely to accept less than her own personal best while insisting that others should not.

Females, in general, are socialized into rescuer-type care-giving roles. They learn from an early age that it is more appropriate to focus on the needs of others rather than on themselves. Taking the time to help themselves is often seen as indulgent and selfish. To change the rescuer's psychology, females need to know that as long as they focus on the problems of others they ignore their own feelings and needs. Women and girls should endeavor to communicate honestly about how important athletic participation is to them and know that it is perfectly acceptable to spend time on themselves.

Females are more socially oriented than males. Their strong need for friendship is an important contributing factor for female participation in sport. Without an adequate social environment the female athlete is less likely to remain in sport, but because of her nurturing and social tendencies she is more likely to have a rescue personality type.

DO-ERS

Do-ers are primarily action-oriented athletes. They know how to get things done and are not afraid to take risks. They have a lot of outgoing energy, but have trouble receiving. This energy is usually seen as male energy and sometimes manifests itself in athletes who have trouble listening and taking advice from professionals because they always know best.

Athletic coaches have often been quoted as saying that female athletes are easier to coach. They listen more and are receptive to ideas and change. However, the coach working with do-er female energy should be careful not to dominate. Do-ing energy can be constructive and performance enhancing. A coach who is too dominant will hinder an athlete's growth by not encouraging self-reliance.

A do-er may be too analytical, creating unnecessary anxiety by paying too much attention to detail, over-monitoring body sensations, or the profiles of her competitors. However, even the most productive athletes must learn to listen and be encouraged to let others help them pursue their goals.

BE-ERS

Be-ers are those athletes who are in tune with their inner selves. They know how to relax but at times take it too easy. They are not very assertive and have trouble expressing their opinions. They lack the confidence to deal with people. Young females tend to fall into this category; they avoid expressing thoughts, feelings and wishes directly, conforming to gender stereotypes to avoid conflict.

Sport is an opportunity for female athletes to develop assertiveness because it is a more acceptable area to speak one's mind without violating the rights of others. However, the be-ing athlete seeks approval from friends, family and the coach without expressing herself in the first place.

To develop the be-er's psychology encourage her to take more risks, be more impulsive. Engage her in the decision making process so that she has input into her training and racing schedule; in doing so she will develop a sense of control over her athletic participation.

There is not one perfect personality type. The above psychological profiles are discussed to give coaches and athletes more insight into athlete behavior and how best to respond to and help shape positive athletic experiences.

Males and females are not dichotomous. Females have a masculine side and males have a feminine side. Rather than oppressing these opposite aspects in ourselves, we should try to develop both in balance and harmony. The female is seen as the intuitive self, the deepest and wisest part of ourselves. The male is action, the ability to do things in the physical world. The female is inspired to create and communicate through feeling, the male acts on speaking, moving and doing. The best athletes will ultimately reflect a balance of both.

What motivates athletes to achieve is similar for both genders. Achievement behavior is reflected in choice, intensity and persistence (Atkinson, 1974).

Choice refers to the athlete's decision to take on the challenge of an event or to avoid it. In general, female attitudes towards achievement are similar to those of males, with the most successful individuals being those who don't avoid challenging situations. However, it should be pointed out that achievement orientation is a multidimensional construct with four dimensions: mastery, work, competitiveness and personal concern.

While both males and females are equally oriented towards success, males have been shown to be more competitive against other competitors, while females work harder and compete more against themselves—although, among the very elite these differences are minimized.

The athlete is in the unique situation of controlling her destiny; she decides how hard she is prepared to work, how she perceives her experiences and how she expresses herself. She need not play the role of victim. If she feels certain relationships or decisions are not in her best interests, she has the power to change them. The growing awareness of gender equity in sport places the 1990s female athlete in a strong position to transcend social differences. The female athlete may respond to the sporting experience in a positive, thinking and capable way.

Triathlon, being a relatively new sport, has the opportunity to make its administration as equitable as possible—by organizing women-only races, separate swim starts, allocating gender-equitable funding of state and national teams, offering appropriate child care support and equal prize money, as well as coaching and employment opportunities. Gender equity within the sport acknowledges that the male and female sporting experience is different. Not more or less, but different. By learning to understand some of these differences, administrators, coaches, sponsors, family and friends can assist the female triathlete to develop her athletic skills to their fullest.

BURNOUT

The term 'burnout' is a familiar one in triathlon circles. **Burnout occurs when there is an imbalance between the athlete's resources and the demands placed on those resources.** For triathletes there is a fine line between optimal training and overtraining. Athletes may wrongly perceive that their training is not enough and continue to train harder and further in spite of signs that reflect staleness.

Burnout is a combination of psychophysiological signs some of which have been identified by Barron, Noakes, Levy, Smith & Mullar (1985):

> Apathy
> Lethargy
> Appetite loss
> Sleep loss
> Mood changes
> Elevated resting heart rate
> Elevated resting blood pressure
> Muscle pain or soreness
> Performance decline
> Abnormal resting hormonal profiles
> Retarded recovery after exertion
> Weight loss
> Heavy feeling
> Gastrointestinal disturbances
> Lymphadenopathy
> Drawn appearance

The psychological profile of an athlete suffering from burnout is one that includes feelings of anxiety, tension, fatigue and exhaustion. These feelings may be either real or perceived. Exhaustion is usually thought to be physical, mental and emotional reflecting a loss of

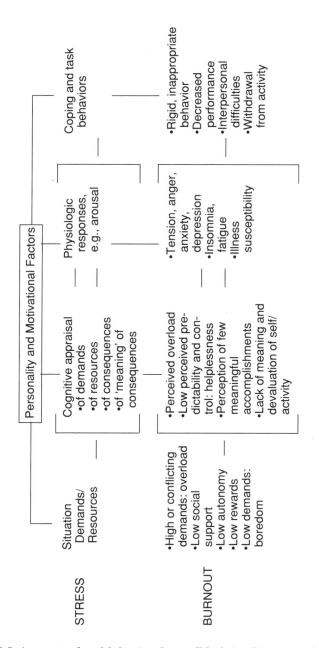

Figure 9.8: A conceptual model showing the parallel relationships assumed to exist among situational, cognitive, physiologic, and behavioral components of stress and burnout. Individual differences in motivation and personality are assumed to influence all of the components. R. E. Smith (1985)

energy, a loss of interest in training and racing, a feeling of drudgery and heightened reactions to daily hassles and concerns.

Burnout often results in athletes who quit, break down or lose competitive drive before they have reached their full athletic potential. Stressful situations result when high expectations placed on the athlete cause a fear of failure, anxiety, frustration and depression.

Smith's (1985) model (figure 9.8) shows the interaction between environmental demands and personal and environmental resources. Demands can be external, such as competing against a strong opponent in an important triathlon or performing up to someone else's expectations. Or, they can be internal, such as having to fulfil a goal or unconscious demand—like performing for love. When demands are not met, costs in the form of anxiety, guilt and anger may occur.

Many athletes respond emotionally to a performance, that is they feel happy, frustrated, proud or depressed about how they have performed. **In sport it is often our thoughts that create the experiences we have.** In Smith's model, cognitive appraisal is central to understanding stress, because the consequences that an athlete anticipates if goals are not met drives his belief system. In other words, how we expect to feel emotionally after a performance influences the amount of stress we experience before that performance takes place.

If an athlete, for example, believes that she has trained well and has the ability to successfully contest a half-Ironman event, pleasing her coach, family and friends, she will suffer little pre-race anxiety. However, if she feels that her competition is more athletically talented and better trained, and her performance will disappoint her coach, family and friends, her pre-race anxiety is likely to be high.

Stress arises from inappropriate responses. Look at an athlete who believes she is not racing well because she is not training hard enough, when in fact she is training too hard. She continues to suffer both increased physiological and psychological stress because she feels she is letting down family and friends with her poor performances.

As the time taken to recover adequately from training and racing increases, she is likely to become frustrated and anxious, with increasing levels of fatigue, insomnia and depression. To stop this downward spiral she needs to assess the negative thoughts that are contributing to her burnout.

Before suffering from burnout she should have been aware of a preliminary state, most commonly referred to as a slump. Psychological factors which may contribute to a slump can be an athlete's misconception about a particular performance. She may exaggerate the severity of a performance, increasing her levels of anxiety and concern, which then impacts upon her beliefs for future success. Athletes may attribute failure to a personal lack of ability, when in fact their opponent may have had a particularly good race. Any negative reactions that the athlete has about her performances can have a detrimental effect on self-esteem, concentration, motivation and anxiety. This creates a downward spiral that makes breaking out of a slump difficult.

External factors can also contribute to a slump—problems at work, with family and friends, financial problems, can all increase stress. Slumps are generally a combination of physiological and psychological problems.

Take the instance of the female athlete who took up triathlon after the birth of her first child. Within her first year in the sport she rose to world class status. To meet the demands placed on her time, caring for her child and training, she kept her training sessions short, but hard. In her second competitive year her performances slumped. Her child was more demanding in its needs and her personal resources were more limited.

Training was less enjoyable, recovery from races took longer and in general her performances were significantly below what they had been the previous year. She was in a slump, but instead of addressing the demands placed on her time and restructuring her training and racing commitments, she worked harder, believing that her poor perform-ances were because she wasn't training hard enough.

As a mother she was anxious about the quality time she spent with her child and worried that she may not be filling that role adequately. She was always tired from training, could not sleep, ached in her limbs constantly and struggled from one training session to the next. She lost confidence in her ability to perform and felt powerless to do anything about changing it. The costs of competing in triathlons, limited time with her child, fear of failure and disappointment began to outweigh the benefits. She was burnd out and quit the sport.

To avoid the burnout stage the athlete first needs to be sufficiently aware of changes in her body's physiological and psychological re-sponses to stress and exercise. The greater our awareness the earlier intervention can take place.

INTERVENTION STRATEGIES

A number of intervention strategies have already been mentioned in this section; they include:

Awareness
Goal resetting
Good social support
Relaxation skills
Arousal control

If athletes are aware of how they feel in a normal physiological and psychological state, they will detect early signs of a slump in their training and racing. Rather than training through difficult periods, an effort should be made to determine changes that have occurred in their environment that may be contributing to a decrease in performance. While some coaches advocate training through this period, the risks are great and, like the female triathlete above, delaying a satisfactory intervention could result in the athlete dropping out of the sport altogether.

By resetting goals athletes can adjust their expectations to a more realistic level, reflecting their current state of health. For example, it may no longer be appropriate for the athlete to do three training sessions a day; they may need to rearrange their schedule to a incorporate longer recovery between sessions. By adjusting daily and short-term goals the athlete may recover from a slump in time to fulfill his/her long-term expectations.

In some situations it may be beneficial for an athlete to take time off. This may break an inappropriate thought cycle that has the athlete believing that he/she has to continue to perform.

An understanding and sympathetic social/emotional environment can help prevent burnout, by reassuring the athlete that **more is not always better.** Or it can help him/her find ways to cope with the demands that have over stretched his/her resources.

Relaxation and arousal control, as previously discussed in this section, can help athletes conserve their resources so that they are able to meet the physical and emotional demands which are placed on them every day.

RETIREMENT

Retirement from elite competitive sport is inevitable for all athletes. The reasons for retirement are varied. Athletes retire because they can no longer sustain maximal performance, they have suffered a debilitating injury, they have burnout, they have suffered financial difficulties, they have other priorities or they have family and/or career demands.

The transition process can be a long one from the initial recognition that retirement is pending, to the actual termination. How the individual copes with retirement depends on a number of factors:

Is retirement a self imposed choice, or a premature one due to external consequences?
Does the athlete have other facets in his life that he can pursue?
Does the athlete have an adequate support network to help him through this transition?

Retirement is often painful for the competitive athlete because it may involve a loss of identity—settling for anonymity after years of recognition—lowering of economic status and a loss of control over one's work output.

The four stages of retirement have been identified by Svoboda and Vanek (1981) as:

1. A high level of motivation to continue
2. Denial/anger
3. Depression/withdrawal
4. Acceptance

In the first stage athletes often report increased training efforts in an attempt to regain former levels of performance. When performances are not forthcoming they enter the second stage of denial and anger. God, fate or life may seem cruel and unfair, and the athlete lashes out at those close to him. In extreme cases athletes may indulge in drugs and alcohol to disguise the pain. Although denial and anger are painful they are usually temporary.

The third stage is depression and withdrawal, where the athlete withdraws from others. He may feel alone and isolated having withdrawn from a lifestyle that once provide so much meaning and purpose to one that is without aim or direction.

No matter how centered the athlete is there are likely to be issues that remain unresolved and a certain sense of loss. The following is a case history of an elite triathlete who took five years to transcend these stages before being able to return to triathlons as a recreational competitor.

As a child this athlete had always been made to feel special; she knew that she was good at sports and she was constantly reinforced for being so. She received the praise of her teachers and admiration of her friends. She felt loved for what she did, and what she did quickly shaped who she was.

While other adolescents struggled with their personal identities, trying to find themselves in the world between independence and authority, she knew who she was. She was an athlete, focused, dedicated and motivated to excel. Every day had a purpose and a direction. Days turned into weeks and weeks into months, training was like putting money in the bank for state, national and international competitions in which she hoped to excel. She suffered injuries and setbacks but they were always only temporary, motivating her to strive more than ever to be as good as she possibly could be.

She swam nationally and represented her country internationally in running, but it was not until the birth of her first child, in her early twenties that she took up triathlons seriously. In her first two years in the sport, she raced every top female triathlete in the world and defeated them all. She had arrived! Within the year, however, she began to struggle and question what she was doing. She was now in the first transitional stage of retirement. Exhausted and tired most of the time because she was overtraining, she believed that she wanted nothing more than to regain the form that had made her one of the best in the world the previous year.

She went through the United States Triathlon circuit, confused and tired. In the second transitional stage to retirement she denied the suggestion that she might want to quit competing and sought medical aid and support in order to regain her lost form.

After finishing a disappointing fifth in one of the series events she commented to a friend that she did know if she wanted to do this anymore. Her friend suggested that it may be time she let it go and for the first time she acknowledged an impending direction towards retirement.

The third stage, which is noted for depression was the most difficult. After a race in San Diego she walked with a friend around the various art galleries on the city's seashore. She saw two paintings that had a powerful emotional impact on her that day. One was by Spanish artist Miro; it was a thick black heavy scribble with two lost eyes seeking out through a maze of confusion, and the painting was titled *Le Captive*. The second painting was by American artist Robert Watson. It was a tranquil painting depicting a solitary figure, alone on a mountain top away from the confusion of the world; it was titled *The Sanctuary*.

Miro's picture suggested to her that she was a captive in the sport of triathlons. At twenty-five years of age she was considered by those close to her too young to retire from competitive athletics. How could she retire when she was one of the best athletes in the world? Everything good she had ever felt about herself was a reflection of her athletic ability. To no longer be an athlete was frightening she would have to find a new identity and a new direction.

Watson's painting suggested to her where she wanted to be—in a sanctuary, tranquil, centred and at peace with herself. She bought *The Sanctuary*.

Her next event was a half-Ironman in Hawaii. Having swum well and in second place on the bike she should have been focused on what she was doing. Instead, negative thoughts kept creeping into her mind, thoughts like, 'I don't want to be here', 'I don't enjoy this any more' 'I just want to stop'—thoughts that she tried to chase away and replace with positive performance-enhancing strategies—but they wouldn't go away. On the crest of a hill 60 km (40 miles) into the cycle leg a realization came to her: 'I don't have to do this, if I really don't want to.' She stopped riding, dismounted her bike, hitched a ride back to her hotel and packed her bike in her cycle bag where it stayed for five years.

She eventually returned to triathlons and enjoys the sport as much as ever. However, five years is a long time not to compete. Total withdrawal from a sporting activity is often easier for an athlete to cope with. Many athletes find it more rewarding to take up an entirely new sport, where they can get satisfaction from their improvements, rather than cope with the disappointment of not being as good as they have been in a sport that was, for a time, the central focus in their life.

Other athletes find remaining in a sport that they love, in an administrative or coaching position, rewarding and they continue to compete as age group competitors. For others still, there is a need to remain involved because of the friendships and social support networks that revolve around the sport. It is a difficult time for all individuals, but perhaps retirement is most difficult for those who do not have academic qualifications, career or family to fall back on. In this sense it is vital that even the most successful athletes give thought to what they will do after competing. Be alert to opportunities that may help make the transition easier when it comes around.

Successful athletes know success because they have a strong work ethic, are ambitious, dedicated, focused and usually have a good sense of self. These qualities, if harnessed, can be applied to future study or employment goals. Athletes may need to do some serious self-reflection to find the type of environment that they wish to work in after sport and know that they have the power to direct their lives to the fulfillment of that goal. Nonetheless the transitional period is likely to be a difficult one.

The following are modified suggestions from Richman, Hardy and Rosenfeld (1989), as a guideline on how social support strategies can be developed for providers and recipients.

LISTENING SUPPORT
- National sporting organizations could include communication training in their coaching accreditation levels. This would provide skills in active listening and increase the awareness of individual differences as they relate to communication patterns and styles (e.g. gender, culture and race).
- Social events for administrators, coaches, athletes and others allow individuals to step out of their roles and invite feedback and listening.
- Emphasize regular informal contacts; this can be done in residence halls, hotel lobbies, common rooms, sports medicine and massage rooms.
- Construct a warm physical environment; offices should be accessible, furniture should be grouped to facilitate interaction, and magazines create an environment with a comfortable feeling.
- Encourage the maintenance of positive relationships with past coaches. Where it is appropriate keep these coaches informed on the athlete's progress and encourage their continued support.

EMOTIONAL SUPPORT
- Encourage athletes to provide emotional support. Athletes should learn to identify feelings and actively listen. This is particularly important for athletes who work together in teams.
- Use a sports psychologist, who can encourage the use of emotional support and help others practice and refine this type of support. Inventories may also be used to assess the social support network of the team or individual.
- Arrange social/academic activities between team-mates. This increases the opportunities for support.
- Stress the importance of emotional support to team leaders, so that they may lead by example.

- Arrange parent interactions; educate parents on how to provide emotional support without pressure.
- Support injured players; physical limitations may change an athlete's lifestyle, remain involved with the athlete and help her recognize and deal with a loss. DON'T ISOLATE HER!
- Encourage inter-team support, i.e. track teams can encourage swimmers; this expands the athlete's pool of emotional support providers.
- Have an open-door policy between coaches and athletes.

EMOTIONAL CHALLENGE

- Provide workshops for parents, family and others, to teach them awareness and empathy and the valued role that they play.
- Maintain relationships with past coaches. The prior coach is in a unique position to provide technical knowledge regarding the sport in her interactions with the athlete.
- Use strategies like restating the team goal, pep talks, quiet time etc., to emotionally challenge the team members to perform to their best.
- Encourage verbal exchange between players during both training and competition. 'Give it your best'. 'You're fit and ready.'

SHARED SOCIAL REALITY

- Create sharing opportunities between experienced and inexperienced athletes, between new and established team members.
- Have team meetings where athletes can discuss pressure, expectations, media, travel, etc.
- Provide a suggestion box where athletes can comment anonymously.
- Train athletes to share social reality, interactions that enable the athlete to interpret their world and decide upon reasonable responses.

TECHNICAL APPRECIATION

- Provide specific information leading to technical appreciation. 'I really thought you concentrated well down the back straight and held firm around the bend', and 'I liked the way you accelerated out of the turn'.
- Recognize daily goal attainment rather than focusing on competition.
- Use athlete status outside of the sporting environment to develop community awareness of issues such as drug and alcohol abuse.
- Encourage parental involvement at athletic meets.

- Highlight good performances and team efforts in event programs, coaching reports, newspapers etc.

Technical Challenge
- Discuss the athlete's perception and the appropriate timing of technical challenge. Technical challenge should be given in combination with other forms of emotional support.
- Use video tapes to provide feedback to athletes on their own performances and to observe the experts.
- Educate coaches on the provision of technical challenge. The goal of technical challenge is to help the athlete hear and assimilate the support. If you give technical challenge immediately after an error is made, it may be interpreted as criticism.
- Create a mentor system to encourage some of the experienced athletes to give feedback on technique, share observations and act as models to the less experienced athletes.
- Encourage team support; athletes should provide technical information and challenge to each other.
- Encourage athletes to assist in coaching others; this helps increase their own perceptions by observing others and offering technical challenge.

REFERENCES
Atkinson, J. W. & Raynor, J.O. (eds) 1974, 'The mainsprings of achievement-orientated activity', *Motivation and Achievement*, pp.13-41.
Bandura, A. 1981, 'Self-efficacy mechanism in human agency', *American Psychologist* 37, pp. 122-147.
Barron, J. L., Noakes, T. D., Levy, W., Smith, C., & Millar, R. P. 1985, 'Hypothalamic dysfunction in overtrained athletes', *Journal of Clinical Endocrinology and Metabolism*, 60, pp. 803–806.
Bunker, L. & Williams, J. M. 1986, 'Cognitive techniques for improving performance and building confidence', *Applied Sports Psychology: Personal Growth To Peak Performance*, Hayfield, Mountain View, CA.
Burton, D. 1983, 'Evaluation of goal setting training on selected cognitions and performances of collegiate swimmers', unpublished doctoral dissertation, University of Illinios, Urbana, Ill.
Butt, D. 1987, *Psychology of Sport: The behavior, motivation, personality and performance of athletes*, (2nd ed.), New York: Van Nostrand Reinhold.
Eccles, J. S. 1991, 'Gender differences in sport involvement: Applying the

Eccles' expectancy-value model', *Journal of Applied Sport Psychology* 3, pp. 7–35.

Gill, D. L. 1986, *Psychological Dynamics of Sport,* Human Kinetics, Champaign, Ill. USA

Harris, D. V. 1986, 'Relaxation and energizing: techniques for regulation of arousal', *Applied Sports Psychology: Personal Growth to Peak Performance.*

Landers, D. M. & Boutcher, S. H. 1986, 'Arousal performance relationships', *Applied Sports Psychology: Personal Growth To Peak Performance,* Mayfield, Mountain View, CA.

Locke, E. A., Shaw, K. N., Sarri, L. M., & Lathram G.P. 1981, 'Goal setting and task performance', *Psychological Bulletin* 90, pp. 125–152.

Lynch, G. P. 1988, 'Athletic injuries and the practising sport psychologist: Practical guideline for assessing athletes', *The Sports Psychologist,* 2, pp. 161–167.

Morgan, W. P. & Pollock, M. L. 1977, 'Psychologic characterization of the elite distance runner', *Annals of the New York Academy of Sciences,* 301, pp. 382–403.

Nideffer, R. M. 1986, 'Concentration and attentional control training', *Applied Sports Psychology: Personal Growth to Peak Performance,* Mayfield, Mountain View, CA.

Nideffer, R. M. 1981, *The Ethics and Practise of Applied Sports Psychology,* Mouvement Publications, New York.

Pines, A. M., Aronson, E., & Kafy, D. 1981, *Burnout.* New York Free Press.

Rushall, B. S. 1979, *Psyching in Sport: The Psychological Preparation for the Serious Competition in Sport.* London, Pelham books.

Schmid, A. & Peper, E. 1986, 'Techniques in training concentration'. *Applied Sports Psychology: Personal Growth to Peak Performance,* Mayfield, Mountain View, CA.

Smith, R. E. 1985, 'A Component analysis of athletic stress'. *Competitive Sports for Children and Youths:* Proceedings from the Olympic Scientific Congress pp. 107–112, Champaign, Ill: Human Kinetics.

Svoboda, B., & Vanek, M. 1981, 'Retirement from high level competition', Proceedings, Fifth World Congress of Sports Psychology pp. 26–31, Ottawa, Canada.

Vealey, R. S. 1986, 'Imagery training for performance enhancement', *Applied Sports Psychology: Personal Growth to Peak Performance,* Mayfield, Mountain View, CA.

Webster, R. 1984, *Winning Ways: In Search of Your Best Performance,* Fontana.

Chapter Ten

Medical Considerations in Triathlon

Dr. Peter Larkins

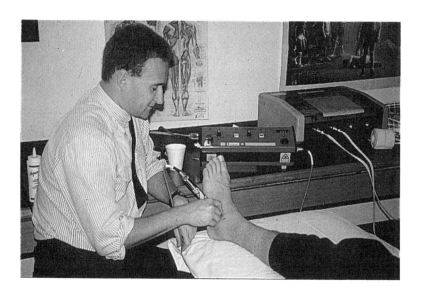

Any injury is an unwelcome interruption to training regardless of the type of sport played or fitness programs being undertaken. This is especially so when an injury occurs in a triathlete preparing for an event at local, state, national or international level.

However, the advantage for an injured triathlete is that it is often possible to continue training in the other two disciplines while allowing the injury sufficient time to recover. Thus, a running related injury may completely prevent all running, yet the triathlete can maintain a well-planned and intensive cycling and swimming program. Similarly, a shoulder injury may prevent swimming but not interfere with running or cycle training. This is just one of the advantages of being a triathlete—even when you are injured!

On the surface it would appear that triathletes are less likely to become injured due to the 'cross-training' program typically followed in the course of a normal training week. That is, in theory the workload for the three disciplines is spread over different days and different muscle groups in rotation, thus sparing the tissues from excessive repetitive loads associated with single-sport training. For example, it could be argued that swimming rests the running muscles and vice versa and cycling, although using similar muscle groups to running, involves different stresses and reduced impact loading on lower limbs.

However, in real life situations many individuals become obsessed with the need to train intensely in all three sports; this is commonly referred to as 'triple training'. Here the risk of injury, especially the overuse variety, is greatly increased, particularly in those competitive athletes who follow a high intensity program.

The secret of an enjoyable triathlon participation is to find a sensible balance in the training program and thus avoid becoming injured. This is where experience and seeking out training advice from qualified individuals is invaluable.

General Presentation of Injuries

Injuries usually begin as either *acute* or *chronic* events. Acute injuries have a clear history of onset associated with a specific traumatic incident, e.g. a sudden muscle pull, spraining an ankle joint or a fall from the bike. In these cases there may be significant soft tissue swelling and bleeding, together with pain and loss of function.

Chronic injuries may begin as mild discomfort, e.g. of the shin, shoulder or knee, without a specific incident; however, over time this discomfort may develop into a more significant disability with pain which eventually affects everyday training leading to the need to seek medical advice. These chronic (or overuse) type injuries may be associated with inappropriate training methods including attempting too much too soon in an effort to get fit quickly, or incorrect technique, e.g. running style, or faulty bike set-up. Management of injuries must therefore also address these faults. (See sections on avoidance and prevention of injury for further discussions of these points.) A chronic injury may also occur if an acute injury is not managed properly and continues to cause symptoms or relapses after partial recovery.

Avoidance of Overuse Injuries

When looking at the causes of overuse injuries in triathlon training it is important to consider three important areas where mistakes can be made:

1. Training program errors.
2. Equipment and footwear problems.
3. Technique and/or structural faults.

1. Training Program Errors

'Training program' refers to the frequency, intensity, duration and environment in which training takes place. Several studies have concluded that as the amount of time and intensity of the training program increases so too does the risk of becoming injured, but there are other factors which may be involved. When assessing if the training program could be at fault there are a number of areas to consider.

(a) Rapid changes in training. A sudden increase in frequency, intensity or duration of training sessions is often associated with the onset of an injury. Examples include the novice runner who begins a running program or the established runner returning to high-level running much too quickly after an injury. This can also occur in swimming or cycling. Thus, by attempting too much, too soon, an overload situation develops and subsequently tissues become stressed and fatigued.

In all situations training should start out at a low-intensity level, concentrating on correct technique in all three disciplines before increasing the volume or intensity. Progressive increases in load can then occur over several weeks allowing the body to adapt to one level of training before progressing on to another of higher intensity.

(b) Running surfaces. There is evidence that running on hard surfaces such as asphalt or concrete is associated with a greater incidence of running injuries. It is preferable to run on a variety of surfaces, including parklands and dirt trails to avoid excessive impact. Running on an uneven ground or a path or

Figure 10.1: Running on softer surfaces such as bush trails or golf courses can lower the incidence of running related injuries.

roadway with a constant slope (camber) to one side will often cause abnormal stresses leading to injury.

(c) Insufficient recovery. Days of complete rest or 'light' training sessions should be included in the regular training program to allow the body to 'absorb' the training and recover from the harder days. These 'body maintenance' days offset the risk of accumulated stresses from successive hard days of training. Similarly, by varying the training sessions throughout the week so that the same training session is not performed on two consecutive days, the various muscle groups and other structures are able to recover.

(d) Single severe session. A sudden change in regular program to include a run, swim or cycle which is much longer or harder than usual can also precipitate an injury. These types of training sessions should be avoided in a well-designed triathlon program.

2. Equipment and Footwear Problems

(a) Bicycle set-up. Many cycling injuries are caused by an incorrect match between bicycle and cyclist. Attention to the bike set up is an extremely important aspect in avoiding overuse injuries. Factors to be considered include frame size, riding position, height, seat position and distance between the seat and handlebars. The type of gearing and selection of gear during training is also important as this will determine the revolutions per minute (RPM) or cadence in cycling. There is a greater risk of overuse injuries if the RPM is low or the resistance is high (i.e. high gears). It is advisable to seek professional assistance when purchasing a bike and to make sure that it is properly set up to suit the body size of the cyclist. Even the type of handlebars selected can be an important factor in determining the risk of certain riding injuries, e.g. neck and wrist (see section on Cycling Injuries for more specific details).

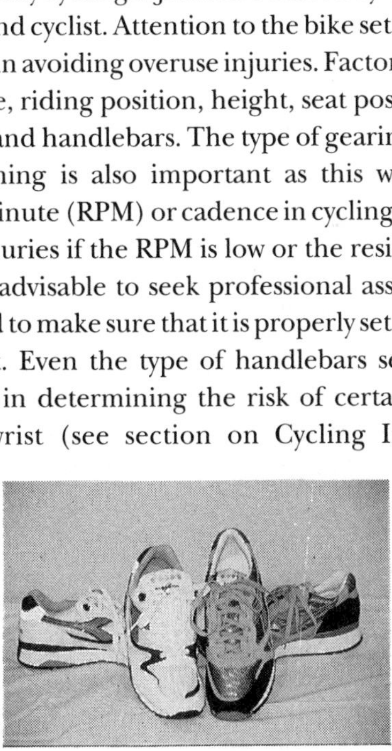

Figure 10.2: Appropriate footwear is imperative.

(b) Footwear. The runner today is faced with dozens of models and brands of footwear from which to select. There is no doubt that there have been major improvements in the design of running shoes as a result of the explosion of interest in this sport.

The two major features in a good running shoe are:

> Adequate shock absorption.
> Stability or control of foot motion.

The pattern of shoe wear on previous running shoes is a good guide when selecting a new pair of shoes. If the shoes have worn out rapidly or the shoe shape is excessively distorted it usually means a better quality shoe with increased motion control (in the rear of the shoe) is needed. The life of the shock-absorbing materials used in most modern running shoes is much shorter than appreciated by many runners. Runners often keep their shoes far too long before changing to a new pair. The addition of modifications to the midsole layer of running shoes, e.g. air or gel, has led to increased shock absorption and extended the useful life of the shoe.

Important features to look for when purchasing a running shoe are:

> Comfortable fit—this includes allowing a little extra length for the foot to slide forward and the increase in foot size which occurs during running.
> Shock absorption in the rearfoot and forefoot zones. These are areas which absorb the impact loading and it is these areas of the shoes which wear out most rapidly.
> Stable rearfoot heel counter (cup) to control foot motion (pronation or inward rolling of the ankle and midfoot).
> Adequate heel raise (12–15 mm or ½–⅝ in) for protection of calf and Achilles tendon strain.
> Adequate room in the toe section to prevent bruised toe nails.
> A flexible midsole.

The features of a good running shoe are shown in figure 10.3.

3. Technique and/or Structural Faults

The importance of correct technique in each discipline has been more fully discussed in the chapters on training for running, cycling and swimming. However, it is important to mention again here that many

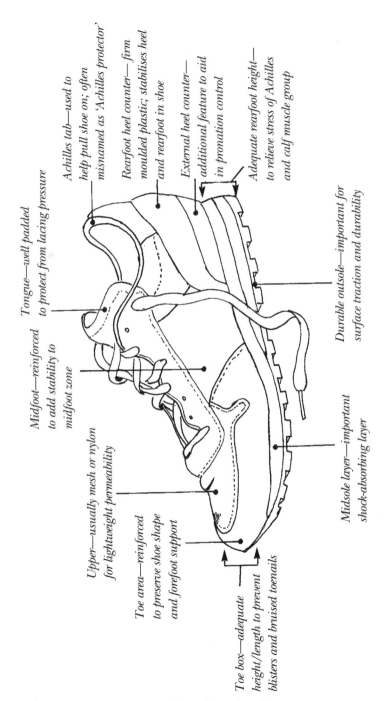

Achilles tab—used to help pull shoe on; often misnamed as 'Achilles protector'

Rearfoot heel counter—firm moulded plastic; stabilises heel and rearfoot in shoe

External heel counter—additional feature to aid in pronation control

Adequate rearfoot height—to relieve stress of Achilles and calf muscle group

Tongue—well padded to protect from lacing pressure

Durable outsole—important for surface traction and durability

Midfoot—reinforced to add stability to midfoot zone

Upper—usually mesh or nylon for lightweight permeability

Midsole layer—important shock-absorbing layer

Toe area—reinforced to preserve shoe shape and forefoot support

Toe box—adequate height/length to prevent blisters and bruised toenails

Figure 10.3: Anatomical features of a good running shoe.

overuse injuries are related to problems in the biomechanics of the athlete due to faults in the running, cycling or swimming style. For example, in the runner with poor strength and flexibility of the lower limb together with excessive pronation (inward rolling of the foot) there is a higher risk of injury to the Achilles tendon, shin or knee area. The swimmer with poor technique in the pull-through and recovery phases of swimming will risk injury to the rotator cuff tendons of the shoulder and other structures related to the shoulder blade and neck area. The cyclist who rides with excessive intoeing or out-toeing of the foot will cause increased stresses in the region of the knee and thigh which can lead to injury in these areas. Correct positioning on the bike, including flattening of the low back during long rides, not only adds to the more efficient aerodynamics of cycling but also eliminates the risk of injury to the lower back and neck area.

Structural abnormalities in the lower limbs will magnify the accumulated stresses during running and cycling and commonly contribute to overuse injuries. Some of the more important areas to consider are:

(a) Arch type. A high arched rigid foot (*pes carvus*) is a poor shock absorber whereas a flat foot which allows excessive sub-talar joint pronation (*pes planus*) may cause additional stresses in the ankle, shin or knee as a result of transmitted loads. In general *pes cavus* leads to problems with lateral (outside) structures, whereas *pes planus* contributes to medial (inside) stress injuries.

(b) Knee alignment. Excessive *genu varum* (bow leg) or *valgum* (knock knees) may contribute to additional problems in the region of the knee. Patella (knee cap) malalignment as a result of lateral tracking or a small high patella is associated with increased patello-femoral joint stresses. Imbalances in knee musculature or tight knee and knee cap structures can result in additional pressures across the knee joint during cycling and running activities.

(c) Leg length differences. Leg length differences greater than 1 cm (⅜ in) may contribute to significant gait abnormalities and cause injury in runners. Minor differences, less than 1 cm (⅜ in), are quite common in the general population and their significance in runners has not been determined.

(d) Inflexibility/strength imbalances. Lack of flexibility in the important

muscle groups involved in running, cycling and swimming together with muscle strength imbalances are important causes of injury. Stretching exercises should be undertaken for the major muscle groups—calves, hamstrings, quadriceps, groin, low back and shoulder (see appendix B) together with identification of any weaknesses or wasting of muscle groups on the injured side. A specific strengthening program can then be designed (see appendix A).

GENERAL PRINCIPLES OF INJURY MANAGEMENT

It is important to have a clear approach to the management of any injury. The following guidelines provide a general outline.

1. Early Assessment

The sooner an injury is seen, the earlier its management can begin. With acute injuries, e.g. ankle sprain, muscle tear, it is usually obvious that these require assessment to plan appropriate treatment. In acute injuries the first six hours may be the most important in determining the recovery time if appropriate first-aid measures are applied. For chronic injuries it is important to have these assessed if the onset of new pain or discomfort persists beyond the second or third day. Early assessment allows for appropriate diagnosis to be made and thus treatment prescribed, if required.

2. Initiation of Treatment

For acute injuries this means appropriate first-aid measures in the first forty-eight hours and definitive follow-up therapy as required (see section on Immediate Care of Injuries).

3. Treatment of Injured Area

Rearrange the training program so that activities which aggravate the injury are avoided and those activities which are not affected by the injury can be increased. For instance, an injured runner will spend more time in the swimming and cycling disciplines, perhaps with the addition of some gym work. This will allow the running injury to be treated without risking further aggravation.

4. Return to Participation at a Suitably Reduced Level

This may be achieved by shorter workout sessions within the limits of symptoms and protection of the injured area, e.g., by strapping an ankle injury or bracing a knee injury. Stressful activities should be avoided until the injured area has returned to full function and the required skills such as coordination strength and mobility have been regained.

5. Immediate Care of Injuries

a. Acute injuries

(i) *Immediate care (first 48–72 hours).* In this phase it is important to control pain, swelling and further damage. A simple checklist is to remember PRICEM—i.e., prevent any further injury, immobilize the injured part, apply ice and compression, elevate and provide appropriate medication (see figure 10.4). It is also important to avoid heat, alcohol, movement and massage which may aggravate bleeding and cause further damage (i.e. do no HARM, see figure 10.5).

(ii) *Subsequent treatment.* After the pain has subsided and the risk of bleeding has diminished (usually 24–48 hours) most soft tissue injuries require a supervised therapy program and modification of training activities. Treatment such as heat and forms of electrotherapy can be introduced safely at this stage. The aims of treatment are to provide pain relief, reduction of swelling and early return of movement.

Massage can often be beneficial after the first forty-eight hours. In addition, massage is very useful in chronic injuries where excessive scar tissue, thickening or adhesions have occurred.

Early movement of soft tissue injuries promotes better quality repair of tissue (collagen). The use of braces or protective strapping will often allow a return to limited activities after initial first-aid therapy.

Taping of an injured joint, e.g. following ankle sprain, will often allow a return to activities during rehabilitation without risking further damage to the injured tissues.

It is important during the treatment phase to pay attention to general body conditioning including the maintenance of cardiorespiratory fitness. Musculo-skeletal rehabilitation should also begin as soon as possible. It is important to pay attention to regaining strength, flexibility and coordination before attempting full training loads. This stage of therapy obviously varies depending on the nature of the injury sustained and it may be necessary to reintroduce training at a more graduated level.

b. Chronic/Overuse Injuries

Pain, swelling and inflammation should be controlled with treatments such as ice and medication. Training levels may need to be reduced to avoid aggravating the injured tissue. Subsequent treatment may involve physiotherapy to promote tissue healing and an exercise program for strength and/or flexibility. Errors in training, equipment or biomechanics (e.g. knock knees, flat arches) should be identified and corrected.

Figure 10.4: First aid for acute soft tissue injury in the first forty-eight hours (PRICEM)

P= Prevent any further injury by removing player from the game or participation as warranted.

R= Rest. Immobilize the injured part. The injured area should be supported by strapping or bracing, together with a sling for upper limb (shoulder, elbow, wrist) and crutches for lower limb injury (knee, ankle, foot) as appropriate.

I= Ice. Apply cold packs for 25–30 minutes every two or three hours during the waking hours over the first forty-eight hours. Do not apply ice directly to skin; wrap it in a damp thin towel or plastic bag, or use a commercially available reusable cold pack. This will help control pain, swelling and spasm.

C= Compression. Between ice applications, a firm compression (elasticized) bandage should be applied over the injured area. This helps to minimize swelling, and immobilize and support the injured area. This is best removed to allow ice treatment and may need to be loosened overnight.

E= Elevation. Where practical, elevate the injured area to encourage venous return and prevent distal edema, e.g. rest the ankle, calf or knee on a pillow or cushion; use a sling to raise the wrist or hand.

M= Medication. Adequate analgesia should be prescribed; however, aspirin should be avoided since it may aggravate hemorrhage. Nonsteroidal anti-inflammatory agents have been shown to be effective in controlling pain, swelling and loss of mobility in soft tissue injury. These should be used in moderate to high doses for at least four to five days beginning on the day of the injury. Most acute soft tissue injuries should be reassessed after forty-eight to seventy-two hours in case further treatment is required.

Figure 10.5: Things to avoid in the first forty-eight hours (do no HARM)

H= Heat—avoid hot baths, ray lamps, hot packs, etc. These all aggravate bleeding and swelling.

A= Alcohol—this causes vasodilation and thus aggravates bleeding.

R= Run—attempts to 'run out the injury' will cause further bleeding, swelling and pain.

M= Massage—in the first forty-eight hours can cause further damage and bleeding.

PREVENTION OF INJURIES

There are many important factors in avoiding injuries; most injuries can be prevented if the individual is adequately prepared ('fit') for the activity attempted, obeys the rules of the sport (written and unwritten) and above all, uses common sense. The following is a list of basic principles to avoid injury:

1. Start Out Slowly

Avoid doing 'too much, too soon'. Remember to begin a training program at low intensity and pay attention to warm up, stretching, strength and stamina. Build up gradually; when attempting a new technique or new activity be sure to start at a level consistent with your level of preparation.

2. Coaching and Technique

Obtain advice before introducing a new technique or attempting a discipline on which you are not experienced.

3. Check Equipment Regularly

Appropriate footware (stability and cushioning features) and maintenance of the bicycle are important in injury prevention. Any signs of excessive wear or faulty function should be attended to immediately.

4. Ensure Adequate Warm Up

A simple routine to increase muscle blood flow, raise body temperature and stretch the appropriate muscle groups is essential. This period will also allow the individual to focus on the tasks ahead.

5. Protective Equipment

This particularly applies to cycling and includes the wearing of a correctly fitted helmet, riding gloves and riding glasses to improve vision and avoid eye damage from road, dirt and wind.

6. Biomechanical Faults

Specific problems such as leg length differences, arch problems or knee alignment may be associated with overuse injuries. Other problems such as muscle wasting or strength imbalances, tight hamstrings or calves can be identified and should be corrected with appropriate exercises.

7. Manage Existing Injuries Properly

This should be self-evident but many athletes suffer recurring injuries or prolong their current disability by attempting to continue or return to activities without seeking adequate treatment or advice.

MEDICAL CONDITIONS

1. Heat Related Illness

Triathlon is an outdoor endurance activity usually taking place in the warmer months. Heat stress and other forms of heat illness can occur even in shorter distance events. These risks are brought about due to the rise in body temperature associated with muscular activity and the environmental effects of exercising in the heat. Problems associated with dehydration include early fatigue, nausea, dizziness, disorientation and collapse. When conditions are severe, heat illness is, potentially, a life threatening condition and should be treated by medically qualified personnel. Prevention includes adequate planning of the event by the organizers, careful preparation by the participants (including appropriate clothing and wearing of a cap or hat) and provision of regular fluids at aid stations during the event.

Fluid losses can be as great as 2 litres (3 pints) per hour during endurance activity and every attempt should be made to prevent dehydration by paying attention to fluid replacement before, during and after endurance events. Water is a perfectly acceptable form of fluid replacement and an amount of 250 mls (8½ fl oz) every fifteen minutes will prevent dehydration during hot weather training and competition. Carbohydrate/electrolyte beverages can be used, particularly if additional energy sources are required during participation. Chapter eight, on nutrition and fluid replacement, has more details on this important area.

2. Asthma

Asthma is a common condition affecting up to 10% of the population. Most asthmatics may experience difficulties with exercise but there is also a form of asthma which occurs in people who do not experience difficulties at any other time apart from during exercise (i.e. exercise-induced asthma). Running is the activity most likely to provoke asthma symptoms while swimming is the least likely. Apart from the obvious symptoms of breathing difficulties and chest tightness, the symptoms of exercise induced asthma may be more subtle and may manifest themselves as cough or chest tightness occurring only after exercise. Asthma is usually aggravated by exercise in cold air, excessive stress or when an infection is present. Good aerobic conditioning, adequate warm up and the use of appropriate asthma medications will assist in the management of the condition.

3. Diabetes

Individuals who suffer from diabetes need not be excluded from participating in endurance sport including triathlon. All sports require muscle energy and the use of glucose for efficient metabolism and thus exercise can be used as a means of treating diabetes (high blood glucose levels). It is important for any diabetic to seek medical guidance regarding the planning of their training and medication but once this is done safe participation is possible. Even diabetics who require insulin injections can participate in long distance and high intensity sports events by careful attention to their dietary needs, insulin dose and training preparation.

4. Gastrointestinal Upsets

It is not unusual for endurance athletes to experience gastrointestinal upsets including stomach cramps and diarrhea. This is believed to be associated with the reduction in blood supply which occurs to the intestinal system when the muscles are requiring the larger proportion of cardiac output. Sometimes dietary errors can result in extra strain on the intestinal system and cause cramps. Avoiding fatty foods and concentrating on easily absorbed carbohydrate meals, especially on race days and high intensity training sessions, will usually overcome these problems. The avoidance of dehydration can also lower the incidence of gastrointestinal upsets. If they should persist then certain medications are available but appropriate advice should be sought regarding this area.

RUNNING INJURIES

Running is the activity most likely to cause an injury when training for the triathlon. Most running injuries are of the *overuse* variety and result from stresses such as shock, friction, traction, torsion or various combinations of these. The impact loading which occurs through the lower limb during the foot strike phase of running can be three or four times body weight. When running down hill, this stress can be increased to six to eight times normal body weight. Thus, it is easy to see how these accumulated stresses can build up to cause one of the more common running injuries.

Although there are a large number of running injuries which can occur in the tissues of the lower limb there are several well-known injuries and these are listed below. They will be discussed individually.

TEN MOST COMMON RUNNING INJURIES

Patello-femoral pain
Achilles tendinitis
Medial tibial (shin) stress syndrome
Stress fracture
Iliotibial band tendinitis
Plantar fasciitis/heel pain
Muscular calf pain
Patella tendonitis
Adductor/groin pain
Trochanteric (hip) bursitis

1. Patello-Femoral Pain

Pain around the front of the knee remains the most common injury seen in runners (see figure 10.6). This condition is known by a number of other terms including anterior knee pain, chondromalacia patellae, lateral patellar pressure syndrome and patellar malalignment syn-

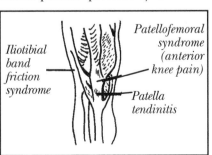

Figure 10.6: Overuse syndromes around the knee joint. Pain around the front of the knee is the most common injury seen in runners.

drome. The injury is due to damage to the articular cartilage (cushioning layer) on the back of the patellar bone. Occasionally there are associated changes on the femur (thigh bone) where the patella makes contact during flexion and extension of the knee. Symptoms will include stiffness and aching in the front of the knee, especially after prolonged sitting or driving and these symptoms are usually aggravated by walking, climbing stairs or any attempts to run, particularly on hilly terrain. The condition may occur purely as an overload phenomenon due to too many miles on hard surfaces, but other factors such as inappropriate footwear or lower limb biomechanical problems must be considered. Squatting is usually painful and any load or pressure around the patella may result in a grating or clicking sensation behind the kneecap. Swelling may be present in some cases. The condition may start gradually or suddenly and although initially present only with running activities may later affect other training, especially cycling. In the latter stages the knee may be sore with general day-to-day activities.

2. Achilles Tendinitis

Pain, stiffness or swelling in the region of the Achilles tendon may result in damage to the Achilles tendon or to its surrounding sheath. It is common to find a locally tender area 2–3 cms (¾–1⅛ ins) above the heel bone insertion of the Achilles tendon and a nodule or lump may be present in this area (figure 10.7). Chronic or recurring inflammation of the sheath may result in thickening and adhesions between the tendon and its surrounding membrane tissues. There are a number of different causes of Achilles pain but the most common causes include acute overload tendinitis, small tissue tear (perhaps microscopic) or chronic degenerative change in the older athlete.

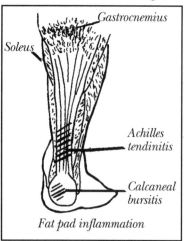

Figure 10.7: The calf and Achilles tendon. In Achilles tendinitis, a locally tender area 2 to 3 cm above the calcaneal insertion of the tendon is common.

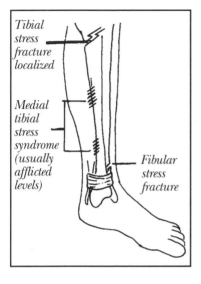

Figure 10.8: Medial tibial stress syndrome and stress fractures of the lower leg.

3. Medial Tibial (Shin) Stress Syndrome

Pain in this region is frequently referred to by the term 'shin splints'. The pain is most common along the inner border of the shin particularly in the middle and lower third (figure 10.8). This condition may involve inflammation of muscle, tendon, bone or a combination of these and occurs more frequently in those runners who pronate excessively, placing more stress on the muscles which normally support the longitudinal arch. Structural abnormalities such as tight calves, flat feet and excessively rotated shins may be obvious but in many cases are more subtle. It is important to differentiate between soft tissue inflammation (muscles and tendons) and a stress fracture of the bone. A stress fracture is usually more localized and associated with pain when pressure is applied over the tibia bone itself. Pain in this region of the leg may also be caused by chronic 'compartment syndrome', an unusual condition requiring special medical assessment. Compartment syndrome occurs when the pressure inside muscle groups rises to extremely high levels during exercise, and pain and lack of blood flow result. The muscles often feel very firm to touch and take some time to recover after the exercise is completed.

Medial tibular stress syndrome can be quite a disabling disorder and can interfere with training for a long period of time unless it is carefully evaluated when the first signs of discomfort appear. Often simple changes can be made which can prevent this condition from developing beyond a mild level.

4. Stress Fracture

Stress fractures may be sudden or gradual in onset, may produce intermittent symptoms and often only very subtle signs with examination. This often means a long delay between the onset of symptoms and a final diagnosis being made. Stress fractures may occur in virtually any of the bones of the lower limb from the hip area downwards but most

Figure 10.9: Common stress fractures

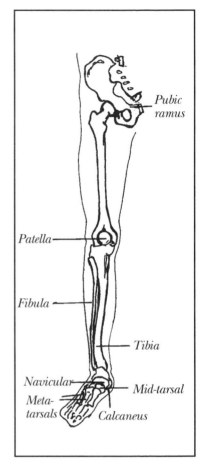

commonly occur in the shin or midfoot region. Some of the more common stress fractures are illustrated in figure 10.9.

Assessment of a stress fracture will require special medical investigation. There may be well-localized tenderness over the area of damaged bone and sometimes swelling is also present. Plain X-rays will occasionally show a stress fracture, particularly if symptoms have been present for several weeks, but usually it is necessary to use other special medical investigations, e.g. bone scan, in order to establish the diagnosis. Stress fractures often begin with very vague symptoms making it difficult to localize the exact problem area. However, over time, they tend to become more persistent often interfering with normal day-to-day activities and sometimes disturbing sleep.

5. Iliotibial Band Tendinitis

This condition is a common cause of pain along the outside border of the knee (figure 10.10) and results when the tendon of the iliotibial track becomes inflamed due to excessive friction over the prominent lower end of the the thigh bone during flexion and extension of the knee.

Pain is usually severe and once it begins during a run it can prevent any further running that day. There may be well-localized tenderness over the band and bone prominence on the outside of the knee joint. Occasionally the pain may extend both above and below the knee. A number of factors may contribute to the onset of this problem including excessively worn shoes, high arched feet, bow legs and long runs on a sloping surface. Once present the condition can then be aggravated by cycling activities.

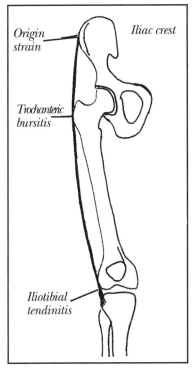

Figure 10.10: Sites of injury in iliotibial band syndromes.

6. Plantar Fasciitis (Heel Pain)

This condition most commonly causes pain on the undersurface of the heel responding to the attachment of the stronger plantar ligament which helps maintain the foot arch. However, heel pain from running can be quite diffuse and extend around the inside of the heel bone or into the midpoint of the arch. The pain is usually worse in the morning or when rising on the toe or running up hills. There is usually an area of well-localized tenderness over the inner and under surface of the heel. Occasionally an X-ray may reveal a small calcified spur but it is not proven whether this finding is relevant in all cases of heel pain.

Other important causes of heel pain include bursitis, inflammation of the cushioning fat pad and stress fracture. Calf stretching exercises together with a soft heel insert will help to settle the majority of cases of plantar fasciitis and fat pad irritation.

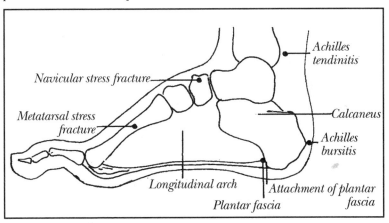

Figure 10.11: Running injuries around the foot.

7. Muscular Calf Pain

Generalized calf pain or soreness is quite a common complaint in running. This may occur in novice runners or in a runner who has suddenly changed the training program to include more speed work or hill running. There is generalized muscular soreness particularly around the middle of the calf together with some inflexibility of the calf muscles. Occasionally there might be a minor tear of the inner calf muscle group. Calf soreness can be treated (and prevented) by attention to stretching, using good footwear with adequate heel raise and ensuring adequate warm-up prior to running. Massage may also be useful. Muscle compartment syndrome may be the most severe form of this relatively common complaint.

8. Patellar Tendinitis

This condition can be differentiated from patello-femoral syndrome as the pain is generally more localized to the lower border of the kneecap. There are localized aches and pains after running or while walking on stairs. Pressure against the lower border of the kneecap produces pain as does kneeling.

Patellar tendinitis is caused by minor tearing of the patellar tendon fibres as a result of the repetitive loading and requires early intervention and appropriate advice if a chronic condition is to be prevented.

9. Adductor/Groin Pain

A runner may also develop vague groin pain or upper adductor muscle pain which is gradual in onset. Usually the symptoms are confined to one side. Occasionally there may be central pain in the region of the central pubic joint and this may cause pain to travel to the opposite side. Pain is usually due to straining tendon fibres at the attachment of the adductor muscle or inflammation of the joint itself resulting in a condition referred to medically as 'osteitis pubis'. Chronic cases may produce X-ray changes within the joint and require a significant modification to the running program before recovery is possible.

10. Trochanteric (Hip) Bursitis

Pain confined to the outer aspect of the hip region is commonly caused by tendonitis or bursitis of the muscle attachments in this area. This is a condition similar to iliotibial band tendinitis but occurs at the other end of the same muscle. The pain can be a deep ache or occasionally sharp over the outer hip area and sometimes travels down the outside of the thigh. There is usually local tenderness to pressure over the widest point of the hip and it may be painful to lie on this side.

Management includes local therapy, muscular stretching and attention to biomechanical problems such as high-arch feet or leg length differences.

Summary

Running can result in injuries to a variety of structures in the lower limb. Most of these are of the overuse variety and may be associated with problems in the running style or in the running program. For further advice regarding the management and prevention of these injuries refer to the appropriate sections in the earlier parts of the chapter.

CYCLING INJURIES

Injuries which occur in cycling are potentially the most serious in the three triathlon disciplines because of the risks associated with falls and crashes. The damage which can occur following a tire blow-out, collisions with other vehicles (stationary or moving), or from road surface damage, can all lead to significant trauma. Care must be taken when riding on wet surfaces, poorly maintained roads or surfaces with loose gravel and holes.

One of the important areas of concern with cycling injuries is the proper bike set up. Attention to correct matching of the cyclist to the frame size, seat position, frame height and seat to handlebar position are very important. In addition, the gearing of the bike may determine what types of stresses and loads occur in the lower limb, as does the number of revolutions per minute (cadence) at which the cyclist rides. Wear and tear or overuse injuries can occur if the cadence is high or the resistance of the gearing is high.

Cycling injuries can be divided into those which occur as *acute trauma* or *chronic overuse* injuries.

ACUTE TRAUMATIC INJURIES

1. Head

Injuries to the head are the most serious in cycling since they are potentially fatal. Falls onto the road or collisions with another vehicle may result in loss of consciousness, concussion or more serious brain trauma. There is clear evidence that the wearing of an appropriately fitting helmet will provide protection and it must be remembered that the commonest cause of death from cycling is due to head injury.

Triathlon: Achieving Your Personal Best

2. Face and Eye
Appropriate eye wear can protect the face and eye region from dirt and grit which can be carried in the air or thrown up from the roadway. Appropriate sunglasses will protect the rider from excessive glare and allow for better visibility on days of bright sunshine, as well as protect the eye from damage due to dirt.

3. Upper Limb
Falls can result in damage to the shoulder, arm, forearm, wrist or hand area. This damage may include soft tissue injuries, joint sprains and fractures.

4. Lower Limb
Similarly, crashes may result in injuries to the hip, leg, ankle or foot area, including soft tissue or fracture problems.

5. Skin
Injuries include abrasions, lacerations and bruising which can occur following falls onto a roadway. Most experienced cyclists will at some stage sustain a good case of 'road rash'.

6. Trunk, Abdominal and Genital
Injuries can occur in crashes and are usually associated with trauma from the seat or handlebar areas of the bicycle, sustained during collision.

CHRONIC OVERUSE INJURIES
1. Knee Pain
Cyclists commonly experience pain around the front of the knee region (patello-femoral joint) associated with the repetitive motion of cycling. This may be felt as soreness, swelling, clicking or catching during the flexion and extension movements of the knee and can be brought on following an increase in intensity or duration of the training rides. Another common cycling condition is iliotibial band friction tendonitis which is a condition causing pain and occasional swelling on the outer aspect of the knee during long rides, or when high gears or high winds are a factor.

Many knee problems occur when the seat is too low or too far forward for the proper riding set up. A low cadence with high resistance will also produce excessive knee stress. Excessive toeing in or toeing out of the foot will alter the tracking mechanism of the kneecap against the knee and this

232

abnormal rotation can result in frictional overload in the patello-femoral joint. Appropriate treatment includes adjusting the set up of the bike, reviewing the gearing and training program and occasionally, an orthotic to correct foot position. Physiotherapy and a specialized exercise program may be required for persistent problems.

2. Hip Pain

Pain may occur in the region of the outer aspect of the hip (trochanteric bursitis). This condition may arise when the seat is too high or from repetitive friction due to inappropriate training loads. Management includes local treatment to the inflamed area and adjustment of the bike set up.

3. Foot and Ankle Pain

Footwear that is too tight can produce pain across the forefoot (metatarsalgia) which is occasionally associated with numbness in the toes. Inflammation of the Achilles tendon and its surrounding sheath can also occur, particularly if the seat position is low. The condition of painful heel and arch can also occur with an inappropriately low seat position or foot position. Advice should be sought if problems persist.

4. Neck Pain

Riding for long periods of time on a racing bike with drop handlebars while attempting to see clearly in the direction of riding may result in a soft tissue strain of the neck structures. With the introduction of low profile aero handlebars of various designs there has been the advent of the condition known as 'aeroneck' which is due to hyperextension of the cervical spine on long rides resulting in excessive strain. This can also occur if the helmet is sitting too low on the face, blocking part of the vision. Management includes regular exercise to maintain mobility of the cervical spine, massage as necessary to the affected areas and frequent changing of the head position to avoid prolonged static strain.

5. Back Pain

It is not unusual to develop back ache on long training rides due to the excessively flexed lumbar spine together with extension of the upper thoracic and cervical spine to adopt a more aerodynamic riding position and to decrease strain on the musculature. Occasionally it is necessary to reduce the distance between the seat and the handlebars to avoid excessive strain while riding in the tuck position.

6. Hand Problems

A well-recognized condition in cyclists is ulnar nerve neuropathy. This condition results in pins and needles and tingling in the little and ring fingers of the hand. It may be associated with weakness of the muscles of the hand and is brought on from prolonged periods of riding with the hands/wrists in a hyperextended position. A combination of excessive dorsiflexion of the wrist and vibration from the road can produce pressure on the ulnar nerve as it travels across the wrist. Management of this condition involves frequent changing of hand position, decreasing shock on the hand and wrist, e.g. with well-padded gloves, and keeping the rides to a shorter duration while recovery occurs.

7. Seat and Saddle Problems

These most commonly occur when there is an inappropriate bike set up rather than an inappropriate seat itself! Attempts have been made to overcome these problems by increasing the seat padding but this can alter the shape of the seat and result in excessive chafing. Newer seat designs may include some incorporated lightweight padding or gel material into the seat construction. Good quality racing-style bicycle shorts may prove invaluable, especially on long rides. Care must be taken with personal hygiene and early attention given to any problems associated with in-grown hair follicles or infection in these areas. The use of talcum powder, lubricating or barrier ointments may be necessary. Occasionally one may have to resort to shaving affected areas to prevent excessive friction.

8. Heat and Sun Exposure

It should be emphasized that fluid losses during long rides can also be quite excessive and fluids should be carried both in training and during competition for rides exceeding thirty minutes. This is more important during hot weather training. Similarly, the use of hats, sunglasses and sunscreen are important to reduce stresses associated with hot weather training.

PROTECTIVE EQUIPMENT FOR CYCLING

One of the most important safety features cyclists must heed is to BE SEEN. The wearing of appropriately bright clothing in daylight with night-time reflective gear may prevent serious accidents. Appropriately fitting helmets and eyewear are important. Footwear may include riding shoes of the cleated or non-cleated variety and the choice will depend on the type of riding to be performed. Cleated shoes have a stiff midsole whereas non-cleated are more flexible but either way a properly designed riding shoe will allow for increased efficiency and force transfer through the full rotation of the pedalling motion.

Summary

It has been said that there only two types of cyclist—those that have fallen and those that are about to fall! Obviously there are a range of different injuries which can occur with crashes or collisions, but many other injuries are a result of overuse stresses associated with poor training techniques or improper bicycle set up. Care should be taken to obtain appropriate advice in these areas to avoid sustaining an unnecessary interruption to the training program. When injuries occur, prompt and expert opinion should be sought so that problems can be corrected quickly and prevented in the future.

SWIMMING INJURIES

Swimming produces the least serious injuries of the three triathlon disciplines but there are a number of conditions which can occur from swimming which will significantly affect the training program. Early attention to these problems when they occur will minimize time lost while the injury is treated and more often prevention is important if the appropriate training program is followed and assistance with technique is sought particularly for the novice swimmer.

1. Shoulder Problems

Injuries around the shoulder area are the most common trauma sustained in swimming. The classic 'swimmer's shoulder' condition is traditionally considered to be due to inflammation of the rotator tendons in the shoulder joint. The mechanism of swimming results in repetitive frictional loading through the shoulder and where the technique is inadequate or tight inflexible muscles are present, tendinitis of these important muscles (rotator cuff) can result. Further swelling can result in pressure between the tendon layer and the bony structure of the shoulder (impingement). Swimmers often develop imbalances of strength in the important muscle groups around the shoulder and often it is necessary to undertake a specific rehabilitation program to correct these faults.

2. Back Problems

Problems in the upper back or cervical spine region can occur when there is stiffness of the upper spine or neck resulting in poor mechanics of this area and compensatory movements in the shoulder. Attention must be given to appropriate stretching and flexibility work for the upper spine and neck when these are at fault. Neck strain can also occur when breathing is limited to one side only.

3. Knee Problems
Swimmers who do a lot of breast stroke kick can develop pain along the inner side of the knee due to pinching and strain of the medial ligament and sensitive lining of the inside of the knee. Occasionally the tissues along the inner side of the kneecap can become involved. Changes of technique together with reduction in general workload will often allow this condition to settle. In general, the freestyle stroke is preferred as the main swimming stroke as this is obviously the most practical to use during triathlon competitions.

4. Ear Problems
There is a well-known condition called 'swimmer's ear' which can seriously interrupt swim training. It is due to inflammation and occasionally infection in the sensitive lining of the canal between the external and middle ear. Infection may involve either bacteria or fungal agents.

The condition known as otitis externa is due to excessive moisture or retained moisture in the ear canal due to time in the water. Softening or maceration of the sensitive lining cells of this area makes a perfect environment for these infective agents to invade the lining, resulting in pain, swelling and occasional itching. The condition can be aggravated by inserting objects into the ear as these may further damage the lining tissue.

When ear problems are present they should be assessed by a medically trained person to determine which treatment is appropriate. Treatment includes keeping the ear canals clean, appropriate hygiene to maintain a dry environment and antibiotics if bacterial infection is detected. Obviously, prevention is the best means for dealing with swimmer's ear and this involves appropriate ear hygiene to keep the lining canal dry, avoiding inserting objects into the ear canal and the use of appropriately fitting ear plugs and swim caps to avoid excessive moisture retention.

5. Skin and Eye Problems
Occasionally swimmers may suffer problems due to the chemicals in freshwater pools. Any problems should be assessed to determine if treatment is required but prevention includes the use of swim goggles and seeking out pools which are well maintained by pool staff.

PART SIX
ROUND UP

Chapter Eleven

Putting It All Together

Rod Cedaro

The purpose of this chapter is to draw together much of the information contained within the preceding chapters in order to formulate an integrated approach to training and competition. Bearing this in mind, this chapter can basically be broken down into two sections. The first section will focus on constructing a progressive training routine based upon the notion of periodization, and the second will attend to race day preparation, competition and recovery.

Throughout this book a number of fundamental training principles have been introduced without a great deal of elaboration, this chapter will address this by discussing and illustrating how the notions of (i) microcycling, (ii) easy, moderate and hard training and (iii) progressive overload can be applied to the triathlete's training regimen. Rather than attempting to explain these principles in a long-winded, technical manner, the use of an example to illustrate these concepts would be of far greater benefit. Because triathlon consists of three disciplines the training regimen is broken down into four-week rotating microcyles, shown in figure 11.1.

	Swim	*Bike*	*Run*
Week 1	Hard	Moderate	Easy
Week 2	Easy	Hard	Moderate
Week 3	Moderate	Easy	Hard
Week 4	Easy	Easy	Easy
Week 5	ROTATION AS PER WEEK 1 (+ 5–10% more work).		

Figure 11.1

From the illustration (figure 11.1) it is obvious that the triathlete doesn't train in the same manner every week. Indeed the training is rotated each week to emphasize a separate discipline (a hard week), while allowing recovery in another (easy week) and maintenance (moderate week) in the third. A major point to note from the above rotation is that after a hard week in any of the disciplines the subsequent week becomes an easy week in that sport to allow recovery and regeneration prior to subsequent stressing. Additionally, week four is an easy week in all three sports. This is known as a 'consolidation week' and allows the triathlete to recover prior to applying additional stress— increased volume and/or intensity by 5–10%—in week number five, which has the same rotations as week number one, but the training load is augmented by manipulation of any of the following factors (or a combination thereof): (i) volume, (ii) duration, (iii) intensity and (iv) recovery. The microcycling concept is illustrated diagramatically in figure 11.2. The key training concepts of progressive overload, hard/ easy training and recovery are depicted in an integrated manner so that the reader is able to see how these interact to form a progressively harder training load on the triathlete to force physiological adaptation in the form of improved physical performance. A key point to remember is that the human body is an extremely adaptive mechanism and provided that the increased quantities of stress—of which physical training is but one example—are applied in a slow and progressive manner, the body will adapt and move on to a higher level of functioning. However, if any of these stressors are applied too quickly or in an ad hoc manner, maladaptation in the form of dysfunction (injuries, illness, psychological burnout) will likely occur.

Now that we have discovered how a series of microcycles go into creating a macrocycle, let us view an example of an individual training day in the three sports and see how the hard, moderate and easy concept can be applied to training on a daily basis. Let us assume that the triathlete is in week one (hard swim, moderate bike and easy run week) and has a training day which calls for the execution of all three disciplines. For example:

Morning
Swim: 400–600 metre (440–660 yard) warm up at level 1.
8–12 x 200–300 metres (220–330 yards) at level 2–3 (15–30 second recovery).
6–8 x 25–50 metres (27–55 yards) at level 4–5 (40–60 second recovery).
300–500 metre (330–550 yard) cooldown at level 1.

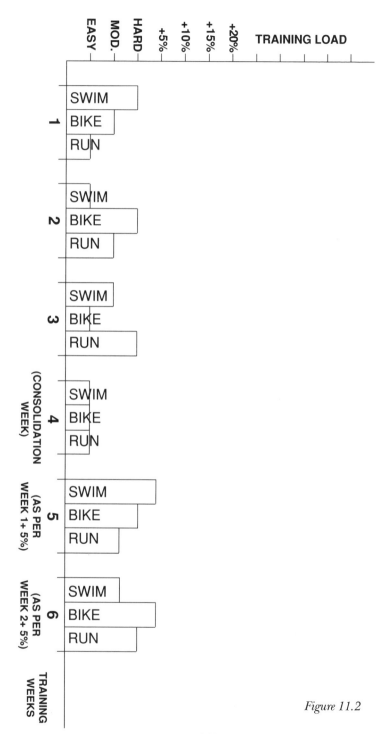

Figure 11.2

Lunchtime
Bike: Warm up at level 1–2 for 10–15 minutes.
Steady state ride at level 3–4 exercise intensity maintaining a cadence of
90–100 rpm for 40–60 minutes.
Cooldown at level 1–2 for 10–15 minutes.
Run: Off the bike 20–40 minutes at level 3–4.

You'll notice that each discipline is well structured in relation to (i)
volume of training to be completed (8–12 x 200–300 metres [220–330
yards], 40–60 minutes etc.), (ii) the exercise intensity at which the work
is to be completed (levels 3–4 etc.) and finally (iii) where appropriate,
recovery intervals are also indicated (swimming: 15–30 seconds recovery
between the 25–50 metre [27–55 yards] repeats). In this manner the
coach and/or triathlete—provided they have planned the training schedule at least four weeks in advance—can manipulate any (or a combination
of the above three factors) to emphasize or de-emphasize a sport as
appropriate. In the example cited in this instance, during a hard swim
week the triathlete would endeavor to complete:

600 metre (660 yard) warm up at level 1.
12 x 300 metres (330 yards) at level 3 with a 15 second recovery.
8 x 50 metres (55 yards) at level 5 with a 40 second recovery.
500 metre (550 yard) cooldown at level 1.

The upper limits of volume and intensity are achieved, while recovery is
decreased to minimum levels.
   Since week one is a moderate bike week the triathlete may choose the
following manipulation of the training loads to achieve the desired effect:

15 minute warm up at level 1.
50 minutes of steady state cycling at between levels 3–4 exercise intensity
and a cadence of 95 rpm.
10 minute cooldown at level 2.

Finally, because this has been cited as an easy run week the triathlete would
complete the following workout:

20 minute run off the bike at level 3 exercise intensity.

As the triathlete progresses from week one to two and three the training emphasis shifts accordingly to cycling and running. In week four, however, all three disciplines are completed at the lower levels of indicated volume and intensity combined with the longest cited rest intervals. Therefore, an example of week four training in the three sports would be as follows:

Swim: 400 metre (440 yard) warm up at level 1.

8 x 200 metres (220 yards) at level 2 with a 30 second recovery between efforts.

6 x 25 metres (27 yards) at level 4 with a 60 second recovery between efforts.

300 metre (330 yard) cooldown at level 1.

Bike: 10 minute warm up at level 1.

Steady state ride at level 3 for 40 minutes at a cadence of 100 rpm.

Cooldown for 10 minutes at level 1.

Run: Off the bike for 20 minutes at level 3 exercise intensity.

Week five rotates back to the same training schedule as week one (hard swim, moderate bike and easy run); however, by applying the progressive overload principle, training is increased by between 5–10% over and above what was completed in week one.

For example:

Instead of completing 12 x 300 metres (330 yards) at level 3 with a 15 second recovery between efforts, the triathlete would complete 13 x 300 metres (330 yards) at level 3 with a 15 second recovery. The same overload principle is applied to the cycling and running routines during this week. Therefore, the week five cycling and running routines (a moderate cycling and easy running week) would more closely resemble what was previously completed in week two. What is now considered a moderate cycling week would have previously been considered a hard one back in week two. Likewise, what is now considered an easy run week, in week two would have been viewed as a moderate run week. In this manner training is updated and increased on a monthly basis. A typical macrocycle breakdown for an Olympic distance race, considering only a limited training background, would take three months in the base phase, two in the intermediate and one in the peaking.

In figure 11.3 we shall see how a typical week's training is put together to ensure that all energy systems are addressed in the three disciplines, while still ensuring adequate recovery to avoid the possibility of overtraining.

	SWIM	BIKE	RUN
Monday	*Pyramiding Session* 400 m (440 yd) easy warm up. 100 (110) 100 (110) 200 (220) 200 (220) 300 (330) 300 (330) 400 (440) 400 (440) 500 (550) 500 (550) 10 second recovery per 100 m (110 yd) (vary intensity between level 2 for 500 m (550 yd) and level 4 for the 100 m (110 yd) efforts). 400 m (440 yd) cooldown.	*Passive Rest*	*Fartlek Session* 12–16 km (7½–10 miles) with 6–10 efforts at level 3–4 intensity for 1–2 minutes per effort. Allowing an equal amount of recovery between efforts.
Tuesday	*Passive Rest*	*Windtrainer Pyramiding* Warm up at levels 1–2 for 10–15 minutes: 53/17 (6 minutes) level 2 53/16 (5 minutes) levels 2–3 53/15 (4 minutes) level 3 53/14 (3 minutes) levels 3–4 53/13 (2 minutes) level 4 x 2–3 times Cooldown at level 1 for 10–15 minutes	*Off the Bike* 20–40 minutes at levels 2–3.

Figure 11.3 (1)

	SWIM	BIKE	RUN
Wednesday	*Threshold Set* 400 m (440 yd) pull warm up. 10–15 x 200 m (220 yds) at level 3–4 intensity with 5–10 second recovery between each effort. 400 m (440 yd) recovery at level 2. 400 m (440 yd) at level 3–4. 400 m (440 yd) cooldown at level 1.	*Long Road Ride* Warm up at level 1 for 10–15 minutes. 2–3 hours at levels 2–3 (alternate hills/flat each week). Cooldown at level 1 for 10–15 minutes.	*Passive Rest*
Thursday	*Explosive speed session* 400 m (440 yd) level 1 warm up. 6–10 x 100 m (110 yds) at level 4 with a 40–60 second recovery. 12–20 x 50 m (55 yds) at level 4–5 with a 45–60 second recovery. 10–12 x 25 m (27½yds) at level 5 with a 30–45 second recovery. 400 m (440 yd) cooldown.	*Passive Rest*	*Long Run* 18–25 km (11–15½ miles) at level 2.
Friday	*Passive Rest*	*Intervals* (morning) Warm up at level 1 for 10–15 minutes. 'ON' 'OFF' 1 2	*Intervals* (evening) Warm up at level 1–2 for 10–15 minutes. 4–6 x 400–600 m (440–660 yds) at level 3. 40–60 second level 2 recovery. 6–10 x 200–300 m (220–330 yds)

	SWIM	BIKE	RUN
		2 4 3 6 4 8 5 10 x 2–3 2:1 rest to work ratio. 'ON' heart rate levels 4–5 'OFF' heart rate levels 1–2. Cooldown for 10–15 minutes level 1.	at level 4. 60–90 second level 1–2 recovery. 8–12 x 100 m at level 5. 90—120 second level 1. Cooldown for 10 minutes level 1.
Saturday	*Long Aerobic Swim* 2000–4000 m (2200–4400 yds) at level 2 exercise intensity.	*Long Aerobic Road Ride* 2½ to 4 hours at level 2–3 exercise intensity.	*Passive Rest*
Sunday	*Passive Rest*	*Passive Rest*	*Long Aerobic Run* 1½ to 2 hours level 2–3 intensity
TOTAL NUMBER OF SESSIONS:	4	4	5
APPROXIMATE DISTANCES (KM):	11.6–15.5	228–352	65–91

Figure 11.3 (3)

Note: The example in figure 11.3 is just that—an example—and should not be used as a training routine across the board for all triathletes.

The purpose of the above example is to illustrate how a triathlete can train on a daily basis, working all three energy systems and still gain sufficient recovery time. Providing that the triathlete plans the training routine in a similar manner to the example cited above, builds up the training load slowly and progressively and ensures adequate recovery time between quality training sessions (particularly when running), minimum time will be spent on the sidelines as a consequence of injury.

THE RACE WEEK

Much has been written about the concept of 'tapering' (i.e. decreasing workloads so that the body recuperates to optimal levels to improve race day performances), the truth is that no single taper sequence will work for all triathletes. Tapering itself is dependent upon a host of factors:

(i)   Individual variations in conditioning, speed of recovery, etc.

(ii)   Duration of the event being competed in.

(iii)   The importance of the competition.

Let's look at each consideration separately:

(i)   Fitter triathletes do not need as long to recover from training bouts prior to competition as lesser-trained individuals do.

(ii)   Generally speaking, longer events require a longer taper phase to decrease training volumes than do shorter events.

(iii)   If a triathlete is preparing specifically for a particular event the taper sequence would be completely different than if that individual simply viewed the race as a 'hard training day' and decided to train through the competition.

Bearing in mind the above considerations and limitations, the following loose guidelines pertaining to tapering will be presented. First, remember that what works well for one triathlete may be absolutely disastrous for another, so experiment with your tapering programs and attempt to establish what works best for you. Generally, base/peripheral aerobic fitness will endure longer than the triathlete's central cardiovascular power. Therefore, when tapering, the volume or quantity of training that is completed can be decreased considerably, while some intense intervals should be maintained to 'spike' the central cardiovascular component and as such maintain functioning. However, considering the debilitating nature of intense quality efforts, this speedwork should also be curtailed significantly in the days prior to competition to ensure adequate recovery. For a Sunday race all quality running should be completed by no later than Thursday, cycling and swimming by Friday, and Saturday should be spent either resting completely or engaging in limited amounts of gentle (level 1 intensity) exercise.

Since the triathlete is training far less than usual there is often a tendency to gain a considerable amount of weight in the week prior to competition. While some of this weight gain is unavoidable (as muscle glycogen stores fill in combination with metabolic water) and indeed desirable in some instances (when carbohydrate loading for long course or ultradistance events), the triathlete must be careful not to indulge to the point where weight gain may be counterproductive to performance. Therefore, with tapered exercise habits the triathlete, particularly one competing in sprint and Olympic distance events, must also taper his/her eating habits.

The Night Before

Since dietary considerations have already been discussed at length, this chapter will not address nutritional concerns. Suffice to say that, regardless of what you consume prior to the event, food alone will not turn an 'also ran' into a 'world beater'. Inversely, poor food choices (heavy fatty foods, spicy meals, etc.) may have an adverse effect on performance. Err on the side of being conservative and stay with foods that are familiar and easily digested. Now is not the time to experiment.

What should be done at this time is to ensure that the preparation for the following day's competition is as uneventful as possible. It is often useful to prepare a checklist to ensure that any unforeseen contingencies can be handled with a minimum of disturbance on race day (see figure 11.4).

Swimming gear
Swimmers
Wetsuit
Swim cap
Goggles (x 2)

Vaseline
Towel
Cycling gear
Bike
Racing wheels/tires
Spare tires (x 2)
Hydration system (e.g. bike stream)
Floor pump
Frame pump
CO_2 cannisters
Bike shoes
Helmet
Sunglasses
Tools (allen keys, lubricant, chain breaker, spoke wrench, cluster tool)
Water bottles (x 2)
Toe straps
Running gear
Running socks
Racing shoes
Sun visor
Orthotics
Spare laces (x 2)
Racing singlet
Other
Carbohydrate/electrolyte beverage
Food/post-race refreshment
Tracksuit
Toiletries
Plastic bag (x 2)
Cash
First aid kit

Figure 11.4: Make a checklist of your equipment to ensure that nothing is forgotten.

Once a comprehensive list similar to the above is compiled the triathlete simply needs to run through the list and pack his/her sports bag without having to worry about forgetting some important item.

Race day

If your race is scheduled to start at 7.00 am set your alarm clock for 4.00 am, get up and eat a low-bulk, high-carbohydrate breakfast immediately upon rising. Those who suffer gastrointestinal problems may prefer to experiment with one of the liquid meal supplements. As has been discussed previously such a meal replenishes liver glycogen stores after an overnight fast and aids in maintaining blood glucose concentrations during prolonged exercise.

If the triathlete is staying at the race venue he/she may then return to bed for 1 to 1½ hours. Depending upon registration restrictions it is advisable to arrive at the race start 1 to 1½ hours prior to the commencement of the event. This will allow ample time to register, prepare your bicycle (pump up tires, etc.), prepare your transition area and undertake a thorough warm up in each discipline. As a general rule it is suggested that the triathlete warm up in reverse order to how the sports are completed during the actual competition (i.e. short run, stretch and some stride throughs, cycle—start off with a gentle spin and slowly graduate to some surging then finish off with a swim) so that the triathlete is in the water, warmed up and ready to go when the gun sounds. The reasons for warming up prior to a race are many and diverse. Some have a distinct physiological basis, while others allow the triathlete to prepare psychologically and focus on the task at hand (see figure 11.5). The analogy is similar to 'warming up' a car prior to driving it.

Physiological	Psychological	Other
To prepare the working muscles by supplying blood, nutrients, oxygen, etc. To increase muscle/body temperature. To stretch soft tissues and optimize joint range of motion.	To allow the triathlete to focus on the task at hand by helping to remove external considerations. To increase feelings of 'preparedness' prior to competition.	To ensure that equipment isn't about to malfunction (gears change smoothly, goggles aren't leaking, etc.)

Figure 11.5: Various reasons for warming up prior to competition.

THE SWIM

One of the most important considerations for the triathlete at the start of a race is to 'self-seed'. If you're not an elite swimmer it is almost suicidal to position yourself at the front of the pack. Invariably more competent, aggressive swimmers will plough over the top of you making the swim a veritable nightmare. It is far better to be conservative and get a clear passage rather than to be kicked and punched. The more accomplished swimmers should look at seeding towards the front of the pack. As the gun sounds it's a good idea, particularly over short races, to sprint out hard and early into clear water and then 'settle down' after the first couple of hundred metres; however, this should

Figure 11.6: 'Self-seed' yourself during a mass swim start.

only be attempted if a sound aerobic base has been established. Generally, drafting another competitor who is a marginally better swimmer is most advantageous as the energy expenditure required to travel through the water is diminished by up to 15–20% by swimming directly behind another swimmer. In a sport such as triathlon where efficiency is a major concern, decreased energy expenditure early in the race may translate to improved performance later on. When drafting fellow competitors don't simply rely on their navigational skills, look up at a fixed point (buoy, landmark) every 10–15 strokes to ensure that you haven't deviated from your course. The use of some type of anti-fog treatment in your goggles (e.g. common household

Figure 11.7: Drafting' or 'dragging' behind another swimmer can reduce your effort by as much as 20%.

shampoo applied to the lens and wiped out) may be useful here to ensure clarity of vision.

Towards the end of the swim, switch from a two-beat to a six-beat kick over the last couple of hundred metres as this will stimulate blood delivery to the legs in preparation for the upcoming cycle portion. Upon exiting the water, if wearing a wetsuit unzip the suit and remove it to waist level. If swimming in a long-sleeved suit the application of some vaseline to the wrists (and ankles) will make the removal of the wetsuit considerably quicker.

The actual swim-to-bike transition should be well rehearsed so that the triathlete doesn't waste time in changing from one discipline to the next. Some suggestions that can help to minimize the transition time include:

(i)   If self-selecting bike racks, choose a position at the end of the rack, close to the bike exit.

(ii)   Wear the one set of clothing for the duration of the event (e.g. bathers or tri-suit under your wetsuit).

(iii)   Have your bike set in an appropriate gear to start riding in—generally a slightly smaller gear to allow the legs to spin a little quicker and therefore aid in the redistribution of blood.

(iv)   Have your eye-wear positioned inside your bike helmet so that minimal time is lost donning this apparel.

(v)   Leave your bike shoes attached to your bicycle and ensure that the shoes have some type of velcro fastening system. Ride out of the transition with your feet on top of the shoes and slide the feet in while you are in transit. *Note:* This skill *must* be practiced in training to ensure that the triathlete doesn't lose control of his/her bicycle.

Figure 11.8: Practice your transitions in training so that they are automatic during competition. Seconds saved in the transition can make all the difference at the end of the race.

OUT ON THE ROAD

It is a common practice, particularly for 'novice' triathletes, to push too hard in the early phase of the cycle portion. This can be disastrous as the blood has to be re-directed from the muscles of the upper body to the lower limbs. Therefore, if the triathlete attempts to push too hard prior to the blood being shunted to the legs an oxygen debt will arise resulting in lactate accumulation which will ultimately force the triathlete to slow down later in the ride. It is far better to start off a little more conservatively, allow for the re-distribution of the blood to the lower limbs and then get into a comfortable rhythm. The key to time trialling is to hold a constant work output for the duration of the effort. Subjectively, the triathlete should feel a degree of 'tolerable discomfort'. Prior to competition the triathlete should have, in training, established an optimal cycling cadence. This will generally be lower than that of a road cyclist and be in the range of 80–95 rpm. Having established this optimal cadence, gear selections should be made in an attempt to keep the legs 'spinning' within this range. Therefore, if confronted with a hill that can't be taken quickly in the gear that the triathlete is already in (i.e. too long/steep—hence the importance of knowing the course prior to competiton), the first option should be to change into a smaller gear to maintain cadence, slide back in the saddle and stay seated. The last option should be to climb 'out of the saddle' by standing on the pedals. Since this requires the utilization of greater quantities of energy it should be used as a last resort (see figures 11.9 and 11.10).

Figure 11.9: When possible, climb hills in a seated position to conserve energy.
Figure 11.10: Smaller hills may be 'attacked' by standing on the pedals and surging over them.

In order to conserve energy when passing fellow competitors on the bicycle it is often useful to employ a practice termed 'slingshotting' (see figure 11.11). Here the trailing triathlete comes up directly behind the triathletes they are about to pass, entering their 'drafting zone' so as to receive some protection from the wind prior to accelerating past. If done correctly this practice helps to avoid the formation of 'bunches' as the

a

b

c

d

e

f

Figures 11.11 a,b,c,d,e,f,g: 'Slingshotting' is a useful method of conserving energy on the bike.

g

passing triathlete is obviously travelling at a greater velocity than the individuals being passed. The accelerating cyclist should be able to get sufficient break on competitors who are better swimmers but poorer cyclists, to prevent them from 'sitting on' and enjoying a free ride prior to the running portion of the race.

As stated earlier in this section the triathlete should endeavor to stay seated as much as possible throughout the ride. The chances of this happening can be improved by the use of a 'seat shifter' (see figures 11.12 a–c) which can be oriented forward and back over the bottom bracket to

Figures 11.12 a–c: The seat shifter can be adjusted forward, neutral or aft to accommodate the terrain that the triathlete is competing over.

achieve an optimal time trialling position while climbing or on the flat. This will also promote the relaxation of those upper body muscles not directly involved in the execution of the task at hand, improving energy conservation. However, towards the end of the ride it is advisable for the triathlete to change his/her position on the bike, by getting out of the saddle, to facilitate stretching of the running muscles and a re-distribution of blood to the muscles soon to be engaged for running (see figure 11.13 a, b). Additionally, choosing a slightly smaller gear to allow the legs to spin can be of benefit in preparing for the run. Prior to entering the transition area the triathlete should have already loosened his/her cycling shoes to expedite the bike-to-run transition at the completion of the bike portion.

Figures 11.13 a,b: Stretching on the bike helps to prepare for the upcoming run.

BIKE-TO-RUN TRANSITION

As was the case in the swim-to-bike transition, the bike-to-run transition should also be practiced in training so as to become almost automatic during competition. Generally speaking the changing of attire should be kept to a bare minimum. For longer races there is a need to change from cycling to running shoes. This can be speeded up with the use of stretchable/rubberized shoe laces (e.g. Sportlace) which allow the foot to be slipped straight into the shoe without the need to tie or untie the laces. For shorter races—with bike portions less than 30 kilometres, particularly those conducted on flat courses—the use of pedal adapters (see figure 11.14) allows the triathlete or duathlete to stay in running shoes after the

Figure 11.14: Pedal adapters help speed transitions significantly.

first discipline and cycle effectively without losing cycling efficiency and save considerable time by not having to change out of their cycling shoes prior to the run. This is of great importance, particularly in 'sprint'-type events, as races can be won or lost in the transition area. Theoretically speaking, all a triathlete really needs to do after the cycle leg is to dismount, change shoes (if pedal adapters haven't been used), remove the helmet and then commence the run portion of the race.

With adequate training—particularly 'brick sessions' which require the triathlete to run immediately following a cycling training session—the change of muscle groups from cycling to running muscles shouldn't be quite as arduous. Many of those triathletes who have adopted a 'forward' seat position express subjective feelings of lessened distress when changing from cycling to running. However, the key points to changing disciplines remain the same as discussed previously in relation to the swim/bike changeover. There will be some blood pooling in the working muscles which will make running a little difficult initially and if the triathletes try to push too hard immediately after getting off the bike, they will set themselves up for subsequent discomfort and decreased performance by incurring an oxygen debt—which must be eventually repaid—and associated lactate accumulation which will require subsequent dissipation. These effects can be minimized by prior training practices and preparing for the run during the cycling portion of the race (as previously discussed). Additionally, during the early phase of the run, the triathlete should 'ease' into this discipline to aid the re-distribution of blood to the appropriate running muscles prior to attempting to run at higher intensities. As the sport of triathlon has developed many triathletes have become very evenly matched as swimmers/cyclists, so many races now are often decided by the triathlete's ability to run in a fatigued state. In order to optimize this ability the triathlete should, while training, work at developing the most efficient style possible to avoid any wastage of valuable energy. An effective smooth running gait can sometimes be the difference between two evenly matched competitors.

During actual competition there are some common points that triathletes may find useful. First, as was stated in relation to cycling, endeavor to relax all those muscles not directly associated with the task of running (e.g. relax the shoulders allowing for effective arm carriage). When the run course travels uphill it is more effective for the triathlete to lean forward into the hill and take smaller steps while being up on the toes. Inversely, while running downhill, the gait can be

Figure 11.15: When running uphill shorten your strides and drive with your arms.

Figure 11.16: When running downhill 'open' your gait and stride out.

'opened' as the triathlete 'strides out' and the first point of contact with the ground should be the heel of the leading foot. During all portions of a race the triathlete may attempt to 'surge' to break away from the competition. Surging requires a decisive increase in exercise intensity beyond the anaerobic threshold, so that the rate of lactate production is greater than the clearance rate. If the triathlete's training for the event has been appropriate, i.e. some 'speed' and 'tolerance' work to allow the triathlete to lift the work intensity to a higher level despite the associated discomfort, and a sound aerobic base that will allow effective dissipation of any lactate accumulation, effective surging can be used. If the triathlete has been unable to get a degree of comprehensive training in each of the energy systems to allow for this change of pace during the race, he/she would do better to maintain a constant speed at an intensity around anaerobic threshold rather than attempting to lift the work rate which may result in what is commonly known as 'blowing up' (i.e. excessive lactate accumulation often accompanied by emptied muscle glycogen stores), a situation in which the triathlete is forced to slow down completely in order to recover sufficiently from an effort/surge. A far more effective way for a lesser-trained triathlete (who is unable to recover effectively from surging) to race is to run at a steady rate throughout the run and then try to increase the pace marginally over the final stages of the race so as to reach the finish-line prior to being forced to slow down completely.

As triathlon is largely a summer sport and conducted in conditions of intense heat, the triathlete should try to avoid overheating at all costs. As was discussed previously during the nutrition chapter, a pre-planned hydration schedule is the most effective means of offsetting the potential disasters associated with hyperthermia. Additionally, anything that is going to aid evaporative cooling (e.g. throwing water over the body) is recommended. Recent research (Gordon et al., 1990) has also shown that the wearing of 'neck cooling' devices may also have positive effects upon exercise performance under certain circumstances.

That's all!?

Figure 11.17: The 'Koolit' device is commercially available and may aid with thermoregulation.

Often, once triathletes finish a race they tend to forget about looking after their body's requirements. In actual fact this is the time at which the body should be pampered to accelerate the rate of recovery. A gentle cooldown jog or swim followed by a stretch is an effective way of helping to flush the muscles of waste products and provide fresh oxygenated blood and nutrients. This can also be effective in helping to offset stiffness and the pain often associated with racing which can adversely affect subsequent training bouts by prolonging the recovery process. As has been

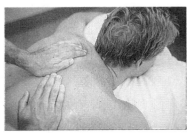

Figure 11.18: Post-race massage is an effective way to speed the removal of waste products from muscle tissue.

Figure 11.19: Scott Molina realizes carbohydrate and fluid ingestion immediately following a race will help to speed recovery.

discussed previously, post-exercise rehydration and carbohydrate ingestion (Friedman et al., 1991) are imperative to speed recovery. If the triathlete is experiencing nausea and other associated discomfort a visit to the medical tent may be appropriate. Immediate attention to minor ailments such as blisters etc., may save the triathlete from a lengthened recovery period. From a personal hygiene perspective a shower and changing out of race attire is also suggested.

References

1. Gordon, Bogdaffy & Wilkinson, 1990, 'Effect of a practical neck cooling device on core temperature during exercise'. *Medicine, Science, Sports and Exercise:* 22(2), pp 245–249.
2. Friedman, Neufer and Dohm, 1991, 'Regulation of glycogen resynthesis following exercise', *Sports Medicine:* 11 (4), pp 232–243.

Appendix A

Resistance Training

Weight/resistance training has been experimented with from time to time, only to fall into disfavor with endurance athletes because it bulks you up and as a consequence slows you down. In fact, a sensibly constructed resistance training program can be a valuable addition to your weekly training routine.

The human body can produce energy: (i) *aerobically* (in the presence of oxygen) and (ii) *anaerobically* (without oxygen), in two forms: (a) ATP–PC produces readily available explosive energy for a short period of time (up to 20 seconds) and (b) the lactic acid system in which energy production is accompanied by increased concentrations of lactic acid within the bloodstream (this is the primary energy system utilized by a 800 metre [880 yard] track runner).

The primary energy demands in triathlon are aerobic in nature. However, at certain times the emphasis shifts away from the aerobic to one or both of the anaerobic pathways (e.g. attacking on your bike at the base of a hill or sprinting for the finish-line). Therefore, triathletes need to develop all three energy systems in order to optimize their potential. Additionally, recent scientific research into muscular innervation (i.e. the pattern by which muscle fibres are recruited in order to allow for contractions to be performed) has revealed some interesting information for athletes. It would appear that there is a certain pattern by which muscle groups are innervated. Initially, slow twitch fibres are called into action, as more contractile force is required the intermediate fibres come into play. As the force requirements can no longer be met by the first two types of fibres, or these fibres simply become exhausted from prolonged exhaustive contractions, the fast twitch/white fibres are called upon.

As a consequence of this innervation pattern the athlete is struck with an interesting predicament: To optimize performance, physical tasks must be practiced in training in a similar fashion to what they will be completed in in competition so that the appropriate muscle fibres will fire at the correct time and motor patterns will become familiar. If all your training requires you to do is spin your legs around on the bike, or jog through your running program, then when race day approaches and you require your body to work at a higher level of intensity the innervation of the type two fibres will not be a familiar task and your performance will suffer. In order to optimize endurance performance a certain percentage of training time must be spent at or in excess of the individual's anaerobic threshold. We also know that performing these high intensity efforts has the potential to increase the instance of overuse injuries, etc., that may force the triathlete onto the sidelines for extended periods of time. The alternative? A blend of high intensity intervals in the pool, on the bike and track in combination with a series of carefully constructed resistance exercises designed to increase your performance by improving explosive power, speed, strength and local muscular endurance, while at the same time not placing the forces, torsions and stresses on the body's bony and soft tissues as do quality interval efforts in each of the three disciplines.

As was the case with the specific swim, bike and run training, resistance training should also follow the same four distinctive training phases discussed earlier in this book (i.e. the base phase: low intensity, long duration, non-specific efforts, the intermediate phase: increased intensity at the expense of duration and exercises of a more specific nature; the peaking phase: high intensity efforts of a highly specific nature and, finally, the restoration period during which the triathlete basically exercises at leisure). Resistance training can be tailored to fit into these criteria as well.

During the base phase of the training cycle the resistance training program should be a broad-based, general conditioning program designed to improve general muscular strength and endurance throughout the entire body. This is best served by incorporating a circuit weight-training program whereby the triathlete chooses 12–15 exercises designed to exercise all the major muscle groups of the body, and alternates between the upper and lower body in a circuit fashion repeating 30–40 repetitions of the chosen exercise before moving onto the next exercise in the routine. Here the critical factor is improving general local muscular endurance and central cardiovascular functioning by forcing the blood to be shunted from one active site to the next. In this manner, if the triathlete moves swiftly from one exercise station to the next, a degree of stress will be placed upon the heart and lungs as they endeavor to supply oxygenated blood to the working muscles. Ideally, the triathlete should endeavor to complete this type of work out three to four times per week on a day-on, day-off basis.

Once in the intermediate phase of the training cycle exercises that are completed become increasingly more specialized. Here the triathlete must look at the three disciplines of triathlon and identify movement patterns which will be employed in the course of the swim, bike and run training/racing and try to construct a weight-training program that closely duplicates these movements. For example, during the intitial base training phase the choice of seated leg extensions may have been appropriate, but during the intermediate phase a better choice of exercise may be step ups or squats. In both of these later two exercises there is dual extension of the hip and knee much the same as the triathlete would experience when cycling. Additionally, whereas in the base training phase the triathlete would choose a wide array of general exercises and complete each one 30–40 times with only a limited rest, in the intermediate phase this number of exercises should be decreased to 6–8 specific exercises, the resistance increased to the point that only 15–20 repetitions can be completed and the rest period increased slightly. Here we start to see the emergence of speed and power training within the regimen. As a consequence, the elusive type two (fast twitch) fibres will be called into play in much the same manner that they are to be employed in the triathlon. When the increased demands of competition call for their inclusion in the force generation process, the innervation patterns will have been already established. During this training phase the emphasis is shifted away from weight training as the triathletes should now be increasing the intensity of their exercise in swimming, cycling and running. As such, 2–3 weight training sessions per week should suffice.

As the triathlete enters the peaking phase much of the emphasis of the weekly training regimen should now be focused on the specifics of swimming, cycling and running intensely. However, weight training can still play an important role. The guidelines for this phase are as follows:

1. Choose a small number of core exercises (e.g. 5–6).
2. Emphasize your weaknesses—if you have a tendency to recover your arm too early in your freestyle stroke before your arm is fully extended this may be indicative of a lack of strength/endurance through the tricep region. Exercises designed to rectify this problem should be incorporated into the program (e.g. dumbell kickbacks).
3. Decrease the number of repetitions that are to be completed by increasing the resistance (i.e. 8–12 repetitions).
4. Allow a greater amount of rest between exercise sets.
5. Decrease the number of resistance sessions down to 1–2 per week, with the second one occurring no later than mid-week so as not to fatigue the triathlete prior to competing on the weekend.

The restoration phase of the training cycle should allow complete recovery for 4–5 weeks. Consequently the triathlete should cease resistance training in order to allow the body to recuperate both physiologically and psychologically from the rigors of the competitive season. The exercises that are depicted in the remainder of this appendix illustrate the type of exercises that can be performed. They are by no means an exhaustive list, but they will still serve to illustrate some basic movements.

A2

Figures A1, A2: Narrow grip, lat pull down.
Figure A3: Bench press.
Figures A4, A5: Upright rowing.

A1

A3

A4

A5

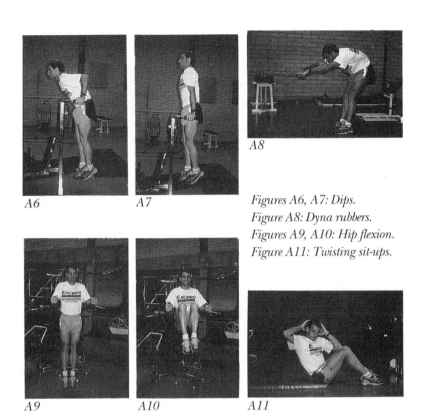

A6   A7

A8

Figures A6, A7: Dips.
Figure A8: Dyna rubbers.
Figures A9, A10: Hip flexion.
Figure A11: Twisting sit-ups.

A9   A10   A11

Figure A12: Abdominal crunches.

A12

Figures A13, A14: Leg press.

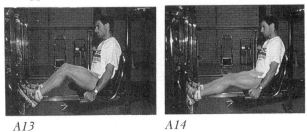

A13   A14

Figure A15: Hamstring curls.
Figure A16: Barbell step ups.

A16

Appendix B

Stretching and Flexibility for Triathlon

'Flexibility' can be defined as the range of movement around a specific joint and varies considerably from individual to individual and within an individual from joint to joint. 'Stretching' is considered to be a means of improving flexibility around these joints. Flexibility around a specific joint is limited by:

1. Joint structure—bones and the joint capsule.
2. Muscle bulk.
3. Adipose tissue.
4. Connective tissue (fascia, skin, tendons, etc.).
5. Age.
6. Sex.
7. Level of activity.
8. Blood flow.
9. Inflammation.
10. Muscle temperature.

When an athlete stretches, it is possible—over a period of time—to increase a muscle's length by as much as 50% beyond its original length. The active forces applied to the muscle (e.g. gravity, momentum, the contraction of the antagonist muscle group) also have the effect of stretching the fascia which is the substance that covers individual fibres and bundles these individual muscle fibres together. Fascia is said to incorporate certain 'visco-elastic' properties. The viscous element is similar to plastic—once stretched it remains in its new position—while the elastic component has a tendency to force the fascia to return to its original position. It is therefore imperative to work on this flexibility consistently.

Stretching is considered to have a host of beneficial effects for both athletes and the general public. These benefits include:

1. Improved range of motion around a joint.
2. An increased ability to cope with trauma and absorb shock.
3. Improved posture.
4. Decreased muscle tension and improved relaxation which helps to enhance blood flow to working muscles and aid recovery after training/racing.

Stretching can therefore be seen as a means of helping to improve athletic performance. There are basically two ways in which to stretch muscles and their respective joint capsules: (i) *Dynamically*, i.e. the joint is taken to a range of motion greater than what it can normally achieve via a forceful movement, and (ii) *Static*, slow or held stretching. Here the joint is moved to a certain point and held in this position for a period of time. Generally this second class of stretches are considered to be superior to, and safer than, the dynamic type stretches. However, there are certain instances in which dynamic stretches can be useful, e.g. for ballet dancers whose activities demand similar movements during the execution of their activities. Under the category of static stretches are those termed PNF or 'proprioceptive neuromuscular facilitation' type stretches. Here the joint is taken to the point of stretch, held in this position while the athlete contracts his/her muscle group against the direction of the stretch, relaxes and then allows the joint to be moved to a new position at a slightly greater range of motion. By contracting the muscle at the point of stretch, the sensors or proprioceptors within the muscle, which limit the degree of stretch within the muscle, are 'turned off' allowing the joint to be taken through a greater range of movement. It should be pointed out here that:

1. The joint must be taken to the point of stretch slowly.
2. Contraction at the point of stretch must be held for approximately 5–8 seconds.
3. Movement beyond the initial point of stretch must be completed in a slow and controlled fashion to avoid the possibility of incurring injury.

Stretching is both an effective way of preparing for the rigors of training/competition and a means of cooling down after such activities. But the goals of stretching at these two different times are somewhat different. In preparation for activity the goals include: Increasing muscle temperature, metabolic rate, blood flow, the lubrication of joints and the improvement of muscle contractile capacity. In the post-exercise phase the objectives of stretching are to prevent blood pooling in the extremities, dissipate waste products and develop/improve flexibility.

Regardless of the type of stretching that the triathlete decides to incorporate into their training routine the following guidelines should be adhered to:

1. Never hold your breath—breathe normally while stretching.
2. Never stretch until after having completed some gentle warm up type activity (e.g. a light jog).
3. Stretch the muscle group to the point at which you feel tension but not where the muscles start to quiver.
4. Hold the stretch at the position described above for at least 5–8 seconds.
5. Don't 'bounce' your stretches.
6. Stretch the muscles on either side of the joint capsule.
7. Complete each stretch at least twice and try to relax all other body parts while stretching a particular region.

The following stretching exercises provide some examples of the type of stretches that the triathlete may find beneficial in stretching the major muscle groups involved in the sport of triathlon. Once again the triathlete must be aware that these stretches must be done on a regular basis and in the correct manner if appropriate benefits are to be achieved. While the following examples are not an exhaustive list, they will at least provide the triathlete with a starting point. Additional exercises can be added to this list if, for example, the triathlete becomes particularly stiff through a certain region, providing that the triathlete applies the seven principles of stretching detailed above.

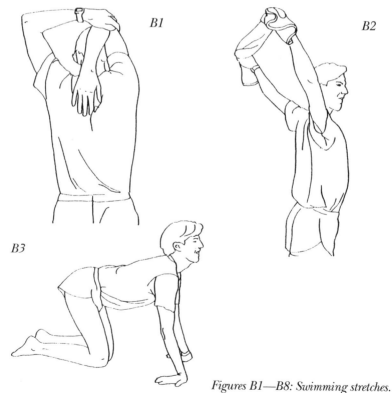

Figures B1—B8: Swimming stretches.

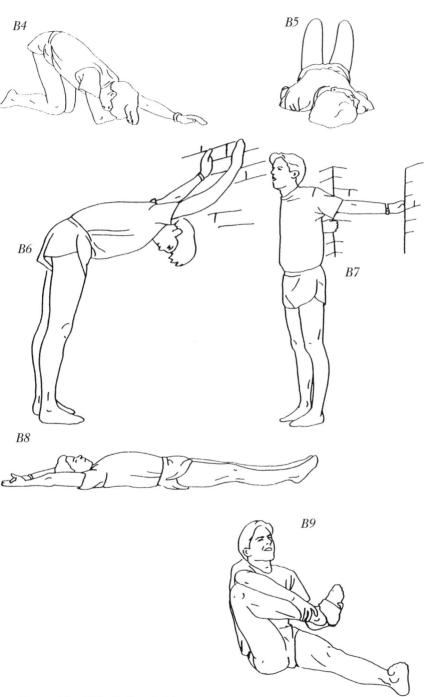

Figures B9—B13: Cycling stretches.

Figures B9—B13: Cycling stretches (continued).

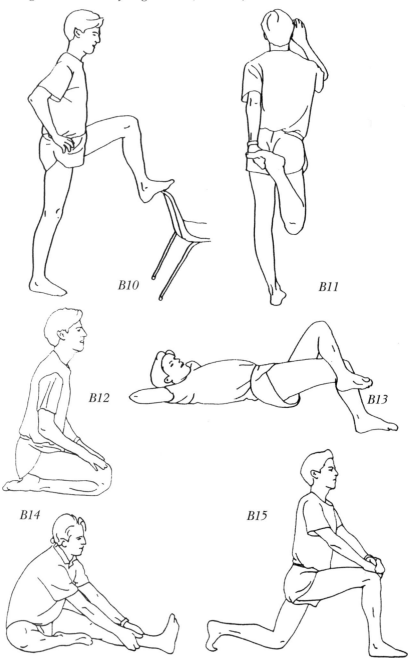

B10

B11

B12

B13

B14

B15

Figures B14—B19: Running stretches.

Figures B14—B19: Running stretches (continued).

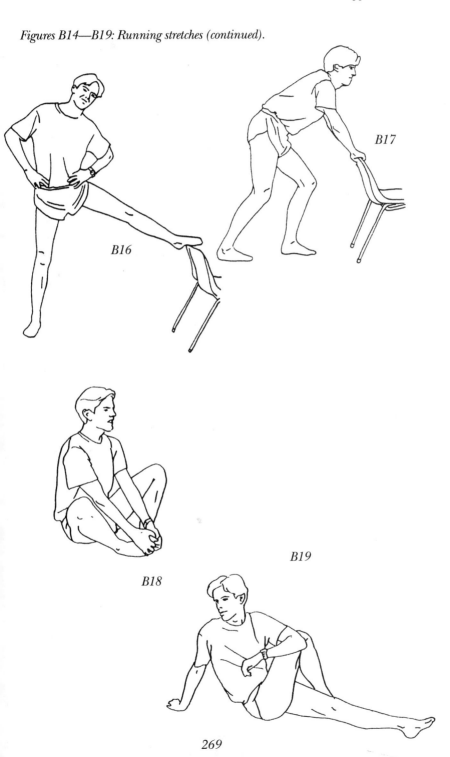

Appendix C

Heart Rate Monitoring

Heart rate monitoring can be a useful tool to provide the triathlete with valuable information as to how hard he/she has been working. It can show whether or not he/she has recovered adequately to train hard again and whether or not improvements in performance have been made. If used correctly, it is a means of providing an indication as to the intensity of exercise at which the triathlete's energy requirements cease to be met primarily via aerobic metabolism and start to rely more heavily on anaerobic energy production. The value of knowing this point (i.e. anaerobic threshold or AT) has been discussed earlier in this book. As stated, many researchers have shown the AT to be the most suitable exercise intensity to improve endurance exercise performance. With the use of a heart rate monitor triathletes will be able to make a fairly accurate approximation of their own ATs in each individual sport without having to go to the expense of visiting a sports physiology laboratory. In this manner, valuable training information can be gained and the triathlete has an accurate means of assessing the effectiveness of his/her training regimens via an objective measuring tool. The principles discussed within this section are based on the work of the Italian sports scientist Conconi, and with only minor modifications can be applied to all three disciplines of triathlon.

For simplicity, only running will be cited here as an example; however, these principles can be just as easily applied to swimming or cycling.

Example

Find a measured 400 metre (440 yard) track. Following a complete warm up and stretch, measure out 200 metres (220 yards) on the track, and place a marker at this point. Start running at an easy pace (e.g. 60–70 seconds/200 metres); every 200 metres (220 yards) accelerate so that the subsequent 200 metres (220 yards) is run at a constant pace, but two seconds faster than the previous 200 metres (220 yards). Keep following this protocol to the point that you are unable to accelerate any longer. Make sure that you have a helper available who can record your heart rate for you following each 200 metres (220 yards), as well as the time taken to complete each 200 metres (220 yards). Next you will have to estimate your running speed in kilometres per hour. The formula to achieve this is:

$$\frac{720}{TIME}$$

To use your results simply graph the data with speed along the horizontal axis and heart rate on the vertical axis (see figure C.1). Once you have done this, you will notice that up until a certain point the relationship between the heart rate and running speed is linear (i.e. as the speed of running increases, so too does the heart rate; however, at a certain point this linearity is lost). In other words, you will accelerate and run faster yet the heart rate response will be less than what you

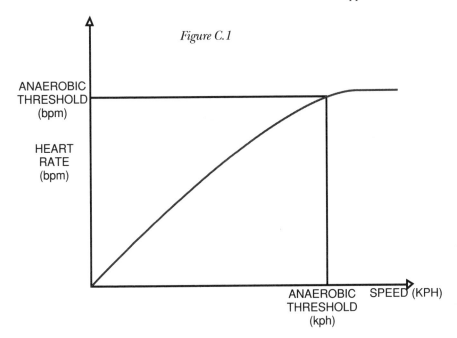

Figure C.1

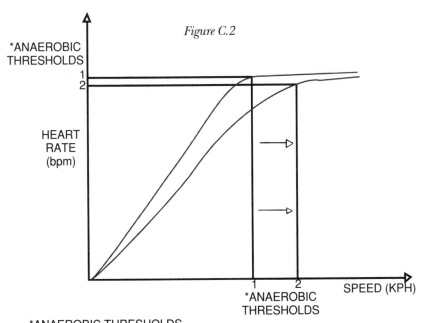

Figure C.2

*ANAEROBIC THRESHOLDS
1: PRE-APPROPRIATE TRAINING
2: POST-APPROPRIATE TRAINING

would have predicted based on the previous heart rate responses. This point coincides closely to the AT that would be normally measured under laboratory conditions). Additionally, it provides you with a tangible heart rate and running speed that you know produces your AT. Finally, and just as importantly, as long as you can duplicate similar environmental conditions under which the test was initially completed, you have a useful test by which to reassess your fitness level at a later date (see figure C.2). The information gained here will enable you to make appropriate modifications to your training regimen. With effective training you will notice that the heart rate curve will show a 'rightward' shift indicating that more work (in this case a greater running speed) can be achieved for a lower heart rate response. Conversely, if you have been unable to train due to injury, or if your training regimen has been inappropriate, the curve will shift leftwards indicating an opposite response. As far as training intensities are concerned, compensation/endurance (level 1–2) type work should be conducted at 70–90% of AT, level 3 intensity work at approximately 95–100% of AT, longer intervals or anaerobic endurance work (level 4 intensity) at 105–110% of the heart rate identified as AT, and the sprint type work (level 5 intensity), in excess of the AT. As has been stated throughout this book these higher intensity intervals are somewhat debilitating, causing an increased instance of injury and therefore should be used sparingly and at appropriate times during the training preparation.

If you feel that you would like further clarification on this topic, it is discussed in detail in an excellent publication by P. G. Janssen entitled, *Training, Lactate, Pulse-rate*. Printed by Oy Liitti, Finland, 1987.

Appendix D

Heat Acclimatization and Altitude Training

Both heat and altitude acclimatization can have far reaching effects upon the triathlete's ability to perform to optimal levels. As triathlons are largely a summer sport and competitions are generally conducted under warm to hot conditions it would be remiss of this book not to discuss ways and means of preparing for competition in hot environments. As the sport of triathlon has grown there has been a marked increase in the number of elite (as well as enthusiastic amateur) triathletes travelling to distant, exotic locations to race. This often means preparing during the cooler months at home and then travelling into hotter environments to compete. This combination can be potentially disastrous, not only from a performance perspective, but also because of the health concerns that may arise.

The purported performance benefits at sea-level from high altitude training have been reported in both the scientific and lay literature for a number of years. It is now common practice for triathletes and other elite endurance athletes to take up residence in places such as Boulder, Colorado, USA, in an attempt to improve their performances at sea-level by increasing their maximal oxygen uptake capacities via increasing the concentration of red blood cells. Red blood cells carry oxygen around the body bound to their hemoglobin component. Consequently, if any practice can increase the availability of these cells, theoretically at least, performance which is dependent upon aerobic metabolism will be improved.

It is the purpose of this section to address these two physiological phenomena and compile a short series of practical guidelines, so that the triathlete who is going away to train and race in a hot environment, or the triathlete who is contemplating racing at altitude or shifting to altitude in an attempt to improve his/her performance at sea-level is able to make an educated decision as to the potential benefits and shortcomings of such practices.

HEAT

As a result of thermoregulatory strain brought about by dehydration or inadequate acclimation, athletic performance is adversely affected. This is of particular consideration in activities requiring prolonged periods of submaximal exertion such as triathlon. Various investigations have shown reduced performance in hot, humid environments as a result of 'hypohydration' (Armstrong, 1988). As little as a 2% decrease in body weight caused by either thermal or exercise induced dehydration decreases muscular strength and endurance time (Sawka et al., 1984). With prolonged exercise, if the body experiences large fluid losses which aren't replenished, there is an inordinate increase in core temperature. This is largely due to the fact that the process of dehydration leads to a decrease in skin blood flow as a result of a decreased plasma volume. As a consequence heat dissipation via the evaporative process is reduced and core temperature rises. This rise in core temperature stimulates the sweating mechanism which magnifies the dehydration problem and creates a vicious cycle, which, if allowed to continue, eventually results in the collapse of the thermoregulatory system and resultant heat stroke.

Athletes appear to be most vulnerable to the effects of dehydration during the first four days of training in a hot environment. This is largely due to the cumulative effects of accelerated sweat losses and inadequate rehydration based upon thirst. Water restriction will not 'train' the body to cope with dehydration, rather such practices will impair performance and increase the possibility of medical complications. Sports physiologists and nutritionists have suggested that athletes weigh themselves prior to and following training/ competition and replace 1 litre (1 quart) of fluid for every kilogram (2.2 lbs) of weight loss. Thinking in relation to what constitutes an ideal fluid replacement beverage has changed somewhat in recent times tending to favor glucose/electrolyte sports drinks over plain water. Ideally triathletes should commence competition with normalized or 'hyperhydrated' fluid reserves (Lyons et al., 1990) as adequate fluid levels should be the foremost priority of triathletes exercising in a warm to hot environment. Additionally fluid should be consumed regularly throughout competition/training at a rate of approximately 100–150 ml (3⅓–5 fl oz) each 10–15 minutes of exercise (see chapter eight for a more elaborate discussion of this and related matters).

The human body is a very adaptive mechanism and provided additional stresses are applied slowly and progressively the body can generally adapt. The body reacts to heat and humidity as it would to any other stress. Attempt to exercise too hard, too soon after being introduced to a hot environment and the body will show signs of maladjustment. However, if the body is exposed to this stress in a progressive manner, a host of physiological adaptations will transpire which will make exercise under these more difficult environmental conditions more efficient with resultant decreases in metabolism and therefore heat production (Epstein, 1990).

Endurance exercise training without acclimation increases muscle blood flow and stimulates the activation of the sweating mechanism at lower skin/core temperatures so that cooling via evaporation starts sooner even in unacclimated endurance athletes. Training in the heat or in heavy sweats and windbreakers under cooler conditions (Dawson et al., 1988) produces physiological adjustments that are dependent upon the rate of heat production, duration of exposure, severity of the environmental stress and the level of conditioning of the triathlete involved—fitter triathletes generally have more effective sweating mechanisms. The process of heat acclimation generally requires a minimum of 8–10 days (Libert et al., 1988).

Bearing in mind that the various physiological changes take a period of time to transpire, triathletes should 'ease' into their normal training regimens when first confronted with a hot environment. Therefore it is not recommended that the triathlete arrive at the competition venue only two weeks prior to the event, as during this time the body is undergoing various changes to adjust to the hotter environment and the triathlete is generally in the midst of a taper phase by this time. As such the intensity/duration of exercise are reduced. Exercise intensity of 70–75% of VO_2 max is necessary to evoke full acclimation to heat stress. It is therefore suggested that triathletes commence their heat acclimation a full two weeks prior to leaving for the competition venue and arrive at the venue at least three weeks prior to the scheduled competition. In this way they allow at least one week's solid training in the environment that they are about to compete in. This 'pre-departure acclimation' can be achieved—at least in part—by (i) gaining access to an environmental chamber, (ii) exercising in a sauna or (iii) training in sweat clothing as described by Dawson et al., 1988. Provided that the triathlete eases into training under such conditions and pays particular attention to hydration status, no adverse side effects should be experienced. Acclimation doesn't provide the triathlete with complete immunity to heat stress/injury; however, provided this and other precautions are taken the instance of thermoregulatory strain is certainly lessened. Figure (D.1) provides a brief overview of the physiological adaptations that triathletes experience as a result of heat acclimation.

PHYSIOLOGICAL CHANGES	ACCLIMATION EFFECTS
Increased skin blood flow at a given core temperature	Increases heat dissipation
Increased sweat production and earlier sweat onset initially	Increases evaporative cooling
Expansion of plasma volume. Better distribution of sweat over body surface	Enhances sweat production Dissipates body heat
More dilute sweat production	Conserves body sodium
Decreased rate of glycogen utilization	Increases capacity for warm weather training

Figure D.1

IN SUMMARY

(i) The process of heat acclimation decreases the adverse effects often associated with exercising in hot and humid environments. Complete adaptation to heat stress requires approximately two weeks full training in the hot environment. Therefore triathletes should look at arriving at a race venue approximately three weeks prior to competition, particularly if they have been previously training in a cooler climate.

(ii) Try to keep the body as cool as possible when exercising in a hot environment, e.g. throw water over the body, wear hats and neck cooling devices and drink adequate amounts of cool glucose/electrolyte beverages and water.

(iii) For the first week after arriving in a hot climate take a broad range low-dosage multi-vitamin/mineral supplement, and salt meals a little more liberally.

(iv) Commence training/competition with normalized or hyperhydrated fluid stores. Consume fluid at a rate of 100–150 ml (3⅓–5 fl oz) every 10–15 minutes during training/competition. Maintain a constant check on body weight by weighing pre- and post-exercise. Replace every kilogram (2.2 lbs) of weight that has been lost during exercise with one litre (2.1 pints) of a glucose/electrolyte beverage immediately following the training bout/competition.

ALTITUDE TRAINING

As mentioned previously, elite level triathletes (and other endurance athletes) have long been attempting to gain a competitive edge in their preparation for competition by taking up residence and training at high altitude. Research has shown that by increasing the concentration of red blood cells within the body by artificial means (i.e. blood doping or the use of hormone erythropoietin), endurance exercise performance can be improved. However, apart from being illegal practices punishable by suspension from competition, both of these practices carry the possibility of severe adverse medical complications and in some cases even death due to cardiac and/or renal failure.

Endurance exercise performance can be limited by, among other things, the two following factors: (i) rate of oxygen transport from the lungs to the active musculature and (ii) the rate at which the active musculature can use the available oxygen. Therefore, in theory, if more oxygen can be made available to the working musculature aerobic performance may be improved. The key is therefore to increase the amount of the substance within the blood that transports this oxygen. This particular substance is called 'hemoglobin' and is found bound to red blood cells. Withdrawing up to 1000 ml (1½ pints) of whole blood, separating the red blood cells from the plasma and storing these 'packed cells' for up to six weeks prior to competition and then reinfusing the red blood cells—a practice known as 'blood doping'—has been shown to increase the availability of hemoglobin within the body, and it significantly improves endurance exercise performance. However, this practice, apart from being banned by the IOC, has a number of problems associated with it, e.g. the potential for infection as a result of having to draw, store, then reinfuse blood, and the increased viscosity of the blood which makes it more difficult for the heart to pump it around the body. In an attempt to remove the need to withdraw blood and lose valuable training time while the body recovers from a significant loss of its oxygen carrying capacity, some endurance athletes have taken to using erythropoietin or EPO. This is a naturally occurring hormone produced by cells located within the kidneys which stimulates red blood cell production. Once again the theory being that the increased availability of red blood cells (and hemoglobin) will increase the athlete's oxygen uptake capacity and improve performance. Apart from being banned by the IOC this practice can be fatal and in some cases deaths have been reported in athletes being injected with this hormone. After this hormone is injected into the athlete, the athlete's hematocrit (or cell population, platelets, etc.) concentration increases while the plasma component of the blood (i.e. the medium in which the cells are suspended) remains constant. When the athlete sweats during training or competition, one of the first places that water is drawn from is the plasma volume. Since the blood is already concentrated and the athlete compounds this concentration by losing more plasma, the remaining whole blood becomes extremely thick and difficult to pump, increasing the possibility of cardiac problems and even death.

Altitude training, however, has been shown to increase the RBC concentration of endurance athletes significantly even after plasma volumes have nor-

Figure D.2: Many top endurance athletes, such as Rob de Castella, use altitude training as part of their preparation.

malized following an initial brief period of suppression. In theory, therefore, all endurance athletes should be living and training at altitude!? Unfortunately the answer isn't that simple. By training at altitude the triathlete may not be able to train at the same intensity that can be achieved at sea-level; as a consequence motor patterns and muscular strength may be affected to the point that performance may be depressed. Prolonged exposure to high altitudes may be detrimental to athletic performance due in part to decreases in training intensity which will result in losses of speed and power. One possible means around this dilemma may be to have the athlete alternate between high altitude and sea-level training so as to prevent some of the detrimental effects associated with chronic altitude exposure. Other researchers (MacDougall, personal correspondence) have suggested that athletes sleep at altitude to receive the 'hypoxic' (lack of oxygen) stimulation for erythropoietin release and subsequent red blood cell production, but come down from altitude to train so that exercise intensity can be maintained.

In summary it would appear that the jury is still out as to the benefits and disadvantages associated with altitude training. While theory would dictate that oxygen carrying capacity and as such endurance performance should be improved, practical research has been unable to consistently substantiate this theory. From a practical perspective elite triathletes who have the opportunity to train at altitude should probably experiment with this practice during the base phase of the training regimen in an attempt to increase the oxidative capacity of their skeletal musculature, as well as increasing the oxygen carrying capacity of the blood. Then, closer to competition, when higher intensity training is required to force the triathlete's anaerobic threshold back further, the triathlete would probably be best served moving back to residence and training in low-lying areas.

References

1. Armstrong, 1988, 'The impact of hyperthermia and hypohydration on circulation, strength, endurance and health, *Journal of Applied Sports Science Research* 2 (4), pp. 60–65.
2. Sawka, Francesconi, Young & Pandorf, 1984, 'Influences of hydration level and body fluids on exercise performance in the heat', *JAMA* 252 (9), pp. 1165–1169.
3. Lyons, Riedesel, Meuli & Chick, 1990, 'Effects of glycerol-induced hyperhydration prior to exercise in the heat on sweating and core temperature', *Medicine, Science, Sports and Exercise* 22 (4), pp 477–483.
3. Epstein, 1990, 'Heat intolerance: predisposing factor or residual injury?', *Medicine, Science, Sports and Exercise* 22 (1), pp 29–35.
4. Dawson, Pyke & Morton, 1988, 'Effects of exercise-heat tolerance of training in cool conditions in sweat clothing', *Australia Journal of Science and Medicine in Sport* 20 (3), pp 3–10.
5. Libert, Amorous, Di Nisi, Muzet, Fukuda & Ehrart, 1988, 'Thermoregulation adjustments during continuous heat exposure', *European Journal of Applied Physiology* 57, pp. 499–506.

Appendix E

Special Consideration Groups

The mistake that many coaches and athletes make is to attempt to train all athletes involved in a particular sport in the same manner. The need to 'individualize' training regimens has been stressed throughout this book. In addition to individualizing programs based on considerations such as the triathlete's current level of conditioning, goals, aspirations, time availability and various other factors, two groups warrant specific mention. Females and young triathletes (10–16 years of age) form important subgroups within the triathlon population. They have certain physiological concerns that should be considered in order to avoid problems and optimize performance potential.

1. THE FEMALE TRIATHLETE

As has been discussed in both the nutrition and psychology sections of this book, the female triathlete's sporting experience differs from that of her male counterpart. From a physiological perspective, she also has a number of inherent differences which suggests that her training must be tempered in comparison to the male triathlete. This is particularly important for the coach who has a squad of triathletes, both male and female. It is imperative that female triathletes are not simply 'lumped' into the training schedules of male squad members. In discussing these differences, the following figure E.1 provides a comprehensive comparison of the major physiological differences between males and females. While many elite females are capable of sustaining heavy training workloads well in excess of the 'average' male, general physiological differences between the sexes suggest that athletes of similar athletic ability (i.e. elite male and female) should not necessarily be given the same absolute workloads. Female triathletes, while utilizing the same basic training principles as males (e.g. progressive overload, alternating hard/easy sessions, etc.), must guard against the potential for menstrual dysfunction and associated problems (e.g. premature osteoporosis). They must watch for telltale signs and symptoms that, if ignored, can sometimes lead to prolonged periods out of training due to various injuries (e.g. stress fractures and other overuse syndromes).

While the physiological attributes that make good athletes are similar for both sexes, the 'average' female athlete is generally smaller than her male counterpart and differs from him in three major ways: (i) Her cardiovascular system is smaller, therefore transports less oxygen to her working musculature, (ii) from a respiratory perspective the average female endurance athlete has a smaller lung mass to call upon to ventilate oxygen for her working muscles and (iii) as a percentage of total body weight, the female athlete tends to have greater ratio of fat to lean muscle mass than her male counterpart. In some

PARAMETER	EFFECT
Cardiovascular system: Female lower blood volume Fewer RBCs (approx. 6%) Females less Hb (approx. 15%)	Total oxygen carrying capacity of blood lower in females
Female has a smaller heart	Higher HR, smaller SV and lower oxygen pulse for given cardiac output and oxygen uptake
Female has a lower maximal cardiac output	Females have lower maximum aerobic capacity (20–25%)
Respiratory system: Female has a smaller thorax	Female has a lower vital capacity, lower tidal volume, lower residual volume, mean breathing capacity
Female has less lung tissue	Female has a lower maximal ventilation
Muscular system: No difference in the distribution of slow and fast twitch fibres	
Females have smaller muscle mass (fewer fibres and smaller fibres)	Females have 40–60% weaker upper body strength, 25% weaker lower body strength
	When strength expressed relative to lean body mass there are no sexual differences

Figure E.1: Major physiological differences between male and female athletes in relation to exercise performance

endurance-type events, such as channel swimming, additional adipose tissue is desirable for body temperature regulation. However, lower fat to muscle ratios are desirable in triathlons. Elite female triathletes often record total percentage body fats well below that of the average male.

Whether it is in the weight room, in the pool, on the bike or track, the workloads and recoveries must be set that are appropriate to the level of conditioning and physiology of the individual female triathlete and not simply what her male training partners are doing. For example, the occurrence of amenorrhea (the absence of monthly menstrual cycles) is often a welcomed consequence of training for female athletes, however recent reports (e.g. Drinkwater et al., 1984, Nelson et al., 1986) suggest a decreased bone mineral density in amenorrheic athletes similar to that observed in postmenopausal women. The cause of this decrease in bone mineral content is thought to be a decrease in endogenous estrogen production. When one considers that bone mass peaks around the age of thirty-five and then decreases progressively by approximately 10% per decade thereafter (White and Rosenberg, 1985), female athletes—by virtue of the fact that their menses may have ceased for a period of time during heavy training prior to the age of thirty-five—may experience lower peak bone density and therefore suffer the possibility of osteoporosis (thinning of the bones), predisposing them to ailments such as 'stress fractures' during their athletic careers and easily broken bones in later life. It is therefore imperative that female triathletes seek specialist medical attention should their menstrual cycles be affected during periods of heavy training. Medical intervention and/or subtle modifications to training regimens can have the desired effect of allowing female triathletes to pursue their athletic aspirations to the highest possible levels without running the risks of debilitating injuries.

Structurally, as indicated by figure E.2, females tend to have a greater 'Q angle' than males. Consequently, as females increase the volume and quality of their running training, there is an increased instance of lower limb injuries (particularly knee ailments) as a direct result of alignment problems stemming from their wider pelvis. Varied running sessions (e.g. water running) can form ideal training alternatives in these situations as they allow the triathlete to

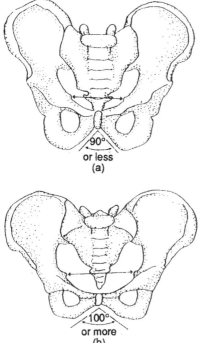

continue their specific run training (i.e. contracting the appropriate muscle groups in a similar fashion to running on dry land and working the cardiovascular system), without running the risk of suffering injury due to the contact phase of the foot on the ground. For example, while male triathletes may find it appropriate to complete two quality track sessions per week, females susceptible to injury may supplement their second 'quality' session by running intervals in the water. In this way the triathlete still gains the benefits associated with high intensity work (e.g. lactate toler-

Figure E2: Sexual differences in pelvic structure. The pelvis of a male (a) is relatively narrow, and the Q angle between the inferior rami of the pubic bones is smaller than that typical of a female pelvis (b).

ance) without suffering many of the injuries that often accompany excessive quality work. In this sense, by manipulating training sessions prior to injury, the triathlete/coach practices a type of 'preventive medicine'.

The key to all training is consistency. Providing the triathlete remains injury free—which cross-training contributes to—progression can be maintained more consistently than if the triathlete misses every second week's training due to leg pain or more debilitating injuries. Since the cardiovascular system recovers more quickly than the musculature and other soft tissue of the limbs, triathletes are tempted to complete more quality work than is appropriate, and indeed necessary, to improve performance. Less than ideal biomechanics coupled with excessive training workloads can be disastrous for any athlete, but the hip to knee angle in females at times exacerbates the problem.

While elite female triathletes are scaling the heights of human endurance and, in fact, have had a faster rate of improvement in the sport of triathlon than males, the physiological makeup of females suggests their training regimens be closely monitored to allow for their individual differences.

Allow common sense to prevail and always err on the side of being conservative when setting and training regimen for either sex, but particularly females. Remember you simply can not train a tired body because recovery is as essential to physical adaptation as the actual training stimulus. One of the hallmarks of a mature triathlete is the ability to ascertain his or her own state of being following training loads and modify subsequent training sessions accordingly. Don't become a slave to your training program; in order to achieve consistency you must enjoy your training, otherwise you will eventually allow it to lapse. Better to train consistently for slightly shorter durations at marginally lower intensities than to lose one week in four with avoidable physical and/or psychological problems stemming form excessive training loads.

2. THE CHILD/ADOLESCENT TRIATHLETE

In the early days of triathlon the sport tended to draw its participants from the legions of injured long-distance runners, bored age-group swimmers or seasoned road cyclists looking for an additional challenge—the point being that the sport attracted older single-sport athletes with 'mature' physiologies and years of cardiovascular conditioning behind them. As the sport has grown and developed over the years media attention has delivered it to the masses. Consequently, there has been a phenomenal growth in the number of young school-age participants coming into the sport. No longer are triathletes 'X-runners' or the like, rather they are 'triathletes' right from the onset of their sporting careers in high school. Due to this earlier initial involvement we are now seeing the standard of elite level performances improve at a rate that would have been beyond comprehension even a decade ago. This is exemplified by the times that are now being posted by elite male and female triathletes over the Olympic distance format. For example, in the mid-1980s if an elite male triathlete posted a finish time of 1:58 a standard Olympic distance event (i.e. 1.5 km [1 mile] swim, 40 km [25 miles] cycle and 10 km [6 miles] run), such a performance would almost place him in the top couple of competitors in that event. This is no longer the case. If that same competitor were to transpose that finish time into the 1992 World Championships that were conducted in Canada, this competitor would be more than ten minutes 'off the pace'. While no one is arguing the benefits that the sport of triathlon is enjoying from this influx of younger competitors, what must be addressed is just how these younger triathletes should be trained and conditioned for the rigors of triathlon competition.

Due to the fact that many of these young triathletes are still growing and haven't reached physical maturity as yet, it is imperative that this be reflected in their training regimens. The coach of the young triathlete must strike an appropriate balance between training volume, quality and recovery to allow optimal performance progression without burning the young triathlete out—both physically and psychologically—with the infamous 'mega mileage' syndrome or excessive amounts of high quality training and/or racing.

Triathlon Australia Inc. took an innovative step in 1992 by introducing specific guidelines and recommendations for the maximal race distances that junior triathletes will be able to compete over (see figure E.3). By limiting the race duration of these young triathletes it is hoped that many of the injuries that might have been experienced will be avoided. Additionally, by keeping the young triathlete 'fresh' and enthusiastic the instance of psychological burnout should by lessened within our junior ranks, thus allowing a greater number of highly gifted juniors to make the transition to open categories.

Age Group	Race distances (swim, bike, run)
U/15	.4, 12, 3 km (¼, 7½, 1¾ miles)
15–16	.6, 16, 4 km (⅓, 10, 2½ miles)
17–19	.75, 20, 5 km (⅜, 12, 3 miles)
Teams	.6, 16, 4 km (⅓, 10, 2½ miles)

Figure E.3: Triathlon Australia Inc., recommendations pertaining to race distances by age groups.

The objectives of junior sport in general and triathlon specifically are basically twofold. First, and primarily, junior sport should aim to promote physical and skill development, and secondly, to ensure that this development can occur, every effort should be made to minimize the risk of injury to young triathletes. A child or adolescent is not simply a miniature adult, therefore special considerations and allowances must be made. Children suffer from all the same injuries in sport that are seen in adults; however, because of the immaturity of the child's musculo-skeletal system and the small but rapidly increasing body size they also suffer a range of injuries not typically seen in the adult athletic population.

Adult bone develops from a cartilage template that is laid down in the fetus. Bone first develops in the shaft of the bone and then from the ends. By mid-childhood, the shaft and the epiphyses (i.e. ends) of 'long' bones are entirely bony, but the epiphyses remain separated from the shaft by a thin cartilaginous plate (i.e. the growth or epiphyseal plate). The time of closure of these plates varies from one area of the skeleton to another and differs from one individual to the next. However, throughout the growth period these regions remain weaknesses in the musculo-skeletal system and are subject to injury from both internal and external forces. Common injuries for junior triathletes can be summarized as follows:

(i) Articular Cartilage Injuries
In children the articular cartilage is particularly susceptible to injury. In addition to providing a smooth gliding surface for joint movement (as is the case in adults), for the child the epiphysis is a minor growth site and inner cartilage cells are replaced by compact bone as the bone end enlarges. Forceful or repetitive impact in this region (as is experienced when one runs) can sometimes dislodge part of this articular cartilage with a portion of bone attached, casting it into the joint space. These can continue to grow with nutrients supplied by the synovial fluid of the joint capsule to the extent that they can potentially inhibit joint movement in later life. If recognized early, prior to separation, this problem may be rectified by rest and/or immobilization; however, surgery will be required to remove free fragments from the joint capsule if this injury is allowed to progress.

(ii) Musculo-tendonous Injuries
In adults the application of severe forces to the muscle/tendon/joint often results in muscular tears, ligament damage or internal joint derangement, or some combination of these ailments. In younger athletes, however, the tendons and ligaments are stronger than the bones to which they attach, therefore the same forces that are applied to the adult triathlete often cause injury to the musculo-tendonous insertion in the young triathletes. As a result of a single trauma the tendon or ligament can actually separate from a bone segment, along with a portion of the bone to which it is attached.

(iii) Growth Plate Injuries
Excessive trauma to the ends of long bones can result in injury to the cartilaginous epiphyseal growth plate. Such injuries will require immediate specialist attention to avoid further implications for future growth and limb malalignment.

(iv) Overuse Injuries
These often stem from excessive repetition of movement with particular muscles, tendons and bones. These injuries arise from either prolonged high work rates or a sudden increase in training loads and lead to swelling of the affected area.

Tendonous overuse injuries result from either the inferior blood supply to the tendon (a common cause of Achilles tendon problems) or an inflammation of the tendon sheath; both lead to a restriction of free movement of the attachment.

Bone overuse injuries result in minifractures to the bone with the loss of bone mineral content due to repetitive micro-trauma. With running-based sports, this class of injury is commonly seen in the femur, tibia and fibula and causes considerable pain, which if ignored can lead to dysfunction and prolonged periods of rehabilitation.

With all of the above concerns to consider the responsibility is placed firmly on the coaches of young triathletes to minimize the risk of injury to those in their care. Where a movement is potentially stressful the number of repetitions completed should be restricted (e.g. swimming with large hand paddles, cycling in big gears, running numerous track sessions, etc.). Rather than focusing on training volume and exercise intensity coaches of junior triathletes should first work at establishing correct technique in each of the three disciplines. In this way, by executing the movement patterns of the various sports correctly, the young triathlete lessens the chance of immediate injury and starts to build a firm conditioning base to support the greater training loads that will be applied in later years.

When first introduced to the sport of triathlon, young triathletes should be involved in conditioning programs that prevent undue fatigue, as fatigue results in undesirable changes to technique which can be an important factor in injury prevention. Also the safety aspect of the sport should be emphasized right from the onset (e.g. only cycling when wearing a helmet, avoiding dehydration with appropriate fluid ingestion, avoiding hypothermia by wearing wetsuits in cold open-water swims—young triathletes are at a greater risk of developing thermoregulatory problems than adults due their higher surface area to mass ratio which gains and loses heat far quicker than larger adults; the list goes on).

Triathlon is and can be great fun. It can also be dangerous. The overriding purpose of those who supervise junior sport should be to provide an environment in which the young athlete can learn and practice new skills. This environment should be challenging, fun and safe. In order to achieve these goals the coach must consider the specific concerns of young triathletes when setting training loads.

References

1. Drinkwater, Nelson, Chesnut, Bremmer, Shainnoltz & Southworth, 1984, 'Bone mineral content of amenorrheic and eumenorrheic athletes', *New England Journal of Medicine* 311, pp. 277–281.
2. Nelson, Fisher, Catsos, Meredith, Turksov & Evans, 1986, 'Diet and bone status in ammenorrheic runners', *American Journal of Clinical Nutrition* 43, pp 910–916.
3. 'What research says about exercise and osteoporosis', *Health Education*, February 1985, pp 3–5.

About the Authors

Dr. Louise Burke PhD

Louise has been involved with the sport of triathlon for over six years at both a competitive level—having completed in excess of thirty triathlons, seven of which have been of Ironman distance—and an administrative level, where she has contributed a wealth of valuable scientific information to a host of subcommittees for Triathlon Australia. Louise completed her doctoral thesis on the dietary patterns of elite groups of Australian athletes, of which triathletes formed a subgroup, in 1989. She is a registered dietitian and is presently the consultant dietitian at the Australian Institute of Sport in Canberra.

Louise has drawn much of her technical triathlon knowledge from reading a wide array of scientific publications, as well as becoming involved directly with sports physiology research. She is a much sought after and respected public speaker in her areas of expertise, both within Australia and internationally.

Rodney Cedaro MApp Sc

Rod possesses a master's degree in applied science, with major studies in exercise physiology. He works as a consultant sports physiologist with consultancies such as the Australian Institute of Sport and the Australian Olympic Committee. He is responsible for the testing, counselling and programming of a wide variety of athletes. As well as having obtained a sound academic background in sports physiology, Rod has also competed in numerous triathlons and duathlons throughout the world at an elite level. He was the 1990 Australian Ultradistance Triathlon champion, with a personal best time for an 'ultra' of 8 hours and 46 minutes. In 1991 he placed fifth in the World Duathlon Championships in Palm Springs, USA.

He has been involved extensively with the Triathlon Australia coaching subcommittee and continues to play an integral role in the educating of certified coaches of triathlon within Australia.

Gayelene Clews BA

Gayelene has a bachelor of arts degree with majors in women's studies, psychology and anthropology. She is currently completing a master's degree in sports psychology at the University of Canberra, Australia.

Athletically, Gayelene has competed successfully in three sports: swimming, athletics and triathlon. She has competed in Australian Age Swimming Championships and represented Australia in three World Cross Country Championships. As a mother, in 1985, her victories on the United States Triathlon circuit, including wins in USTS Chicago and Denver, earned her the No. 1 female ranking for the Olympic distance triathlon that year. Acknowledging those same performances, *Ultra Sport* magazine, listed her as one of the world's top fifty athletes. Since then she has completed the Boston Marathon and continues to perform successfully in Australia, in both running and triathlons.

Gayelene is an active coach and seminar speaker on the involvement of women in sport and sports psychology. She has been a sports commentator for television, covering both World Championship and Olympic events. Her work has been published in several journals and books, including *de Castella on Running*, which she co-authored with her husband.

Dr. Peter Larkins MBBS, BMed Sc, FACSP, FASMF

Peter is the medical director of the Prahran Sports Medicine Centre in Melbourne, where his private practice specializes in the medical aspects of sport, fitness and exercise. He is a past President of the Victorian Branch of the Australian Sports Medicine Federation and National Vice-president of the Australian College of Sports Physicians. He has a special interest in the role of exercise in health, assessment of overuse injuries and health promotion. He is medical co-ordinator of the Melbourne Marathon and is responsible for medical coverage of a number of other community sports events, including, in the past, the Australian Games and World Veteran Games. Peter is also a former middle distance athlete, having represented Australia at Olympic, Commonwealth and World Cup competitions. Due to the explosion in popularity of triathlon in recent years, Peter has acquired a wealth of knowledge and experience in treating some of Australia's leading triathletes. As a consquence of his involvement in triathlon, Peter was named team doctor for the 1990 Commonwealth Games Triathlon Team that competed in Auckland, New Zealand.

Dr. Brian McLean PhD

Brian has been researching the biomechanics of cycling over many years, through master's level and doctoral studies. This research has included investigations of muscle activity patterns while riding, the relationship of the cyclist's shape and size with the position on the bicycle, as well as numerous studies on pedalling technique at different cadences, power outputs and levels of skill. He has been involved in the 'cycling subculture' for over fifteen years as a racing cyclist, mechanic and coach and has successfully coached some of Queensland's nationally ranked triathletes. Currently he works as a research scientist at the Australian Institute of Sport in Canberra.

Dr. Bruce Mason PhD

Bruce completed his doctorate in biomechanics from the University of Oregon in the late 1970s. He was appointed Head Biomechanist at the Australian Institute of Sport in late 1981 and has continued in that position until the present time. Bruce has worked extensively with the AIS swimming program to assist the AIS coaches with the stroke evaluation of the swimmers. Many applied research studies have been performed by Bruce to investigate the nature of propulsion in the sport of swimming. Papers from such research have been presented at both the Fifth and Sixth International Symposiums of Biomechanics and Medicine in Swimming held in Bielefeld, Germany, in 1986, and Liverpool, England, in 1990. At the present time Bruce and his collegues have a grant to develop a system to analyze stroke technique with a short turnaround period.

INDEX

Index

Italic page numbers indicate illustrations and captions.

appreciation *See* technical appreciation
arch (foot) 218
arm recovery 33, *33*, 34
arousal *180*, 180–182, *181*, *183*
articular cartilage injuries 283
asthma 224
AT *See* anaerobic threshold
ATP *See* adenosine triphosphate
attention *See* concentration
Australia 167, 194

B

back problems
    cycling 233
    swimming 235–236
backsweep *32*, 32–33
barbell step ups *264*
basal metabolic rate *17*
base (preparation) training phase
    18, 19–20, 50, *50–51*, *98*
    for cycling 97–102
    resistance training as part of 261
    for running 119–123
    for swimming 56–58
bathing cap 48
bee pollen 160
be-ers (personality type) 198–199
bench press *262*
Bernoulli's Principle 41, 47
Bevan, Brad 7
bicycling *See* cycling
biomechanical assessment 115–116
biomechanical faults 116, 223
biomechanics
    of cycling 71–94
    of running 114–117
    of swimming 28–48
blood doping 14, 276
"blowing up" 258

body
    awareness 178
    fat 131–134
    weight 134–135
bone development 282
Bonham, Louise 7
Boulder (Colorado) 167, 273
bow legs 218
breathing patterns 35–36
buoyancy 34–35
Burke, Louise 285
burnout 200–204, *201*
bursitis *226*, *229*, 230–231, 233

C

calcaneal bursitis *226*
calcaneus *228–229*
calcium 137, 140
calves
    injuries to *226*
    pain in 230
Canberra (Australia) 167
carbohydrates
    consuming during races 156
    in dietary supplements 160
    eating high levels of 138–139
    foods containing *141–143, 150*
    loading up on (carbo loading) 148–152, *153–154*
    replacing 25
    timing intake of 144
    training load and need for 136
carbon dioxide 14, 16
cardiovascular fitness 14, 50–51
catch (swimming) *29*, 29–30, 32
Cedaro, Rodney 7, 285
central cardiovascular fitness 14, 50
child athletes 281–284
chloride ions 14
choking (anxiety) 187